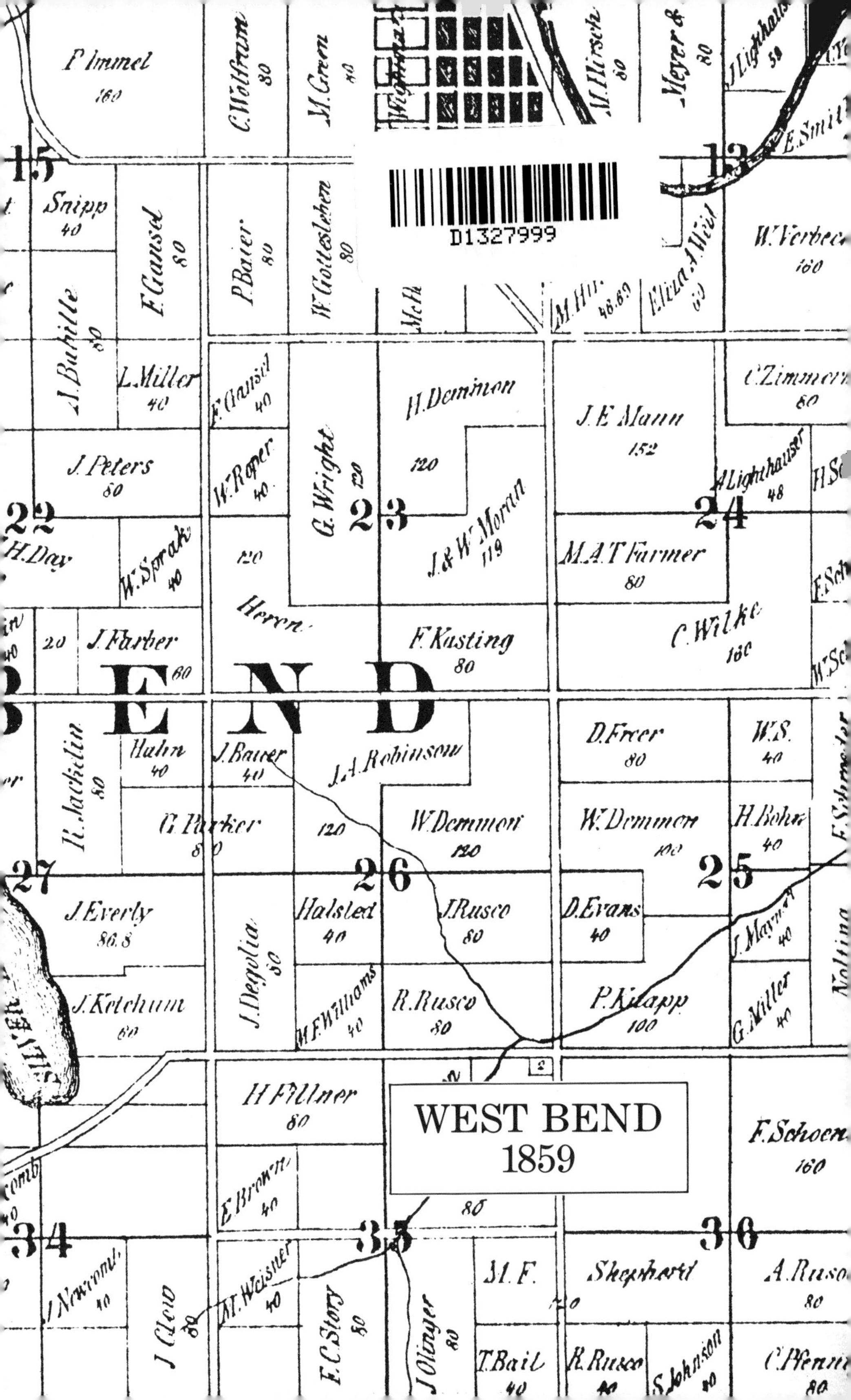

WEST BEND
1859
P. Immel
160
C. Wolfram
80
M. Green
80
M. Hirsch
80
Meyer &
80
J. Lighthause
50
E. Smith
15
13
Snipp
40
F. Gansel
80
P. Baier
80
W. Gotteslebe
80
W. Verbeck
160
J. Buhille
80
L. Miller
40
F. Gansel
40
H. Demmon
J. E. Mann
152
C. Zimmerm
80
J. Peters
80
W. Roper
40
G. Wright
120
A. Lighthauser
48
22
23
24
H. Day
W. Sprak
40
120
J. & W. Moran
119
M. A. T. Farmer
80
J. Farber
60
F. Kasting
80
C. Wilke
160
BEND
Hahn
40
J. Baier
40
J. A. Robinson
D. Freer
80
W. S.
40
R. Jackelin
80
G. Parker
80
120
W. Demmon
120
W. Demmon
100
H. Bohr
40
27
26
25
J. Everly
86.8
Halsted
40
J. Rusco
80
D. Evans
40
J. Degolia
80
J. Ketchum
60
M. F. Williams
40
R. Rusco
80
P. Knapp
100
G. Miller
40
H. Fillner
80
F. Schoen
160
E. Brown
40
80
34
35
36
J. Newcomb
40
J. Cleio
80
M. Weisner
40
F. C. Story
80
J. Olinger
80
M. F.
Shepherd
A. Rusco
80
T. Bail
40
R. Rusco
40
S. Johnson
40
C. Pfenni
80

"THE SPIRIT OF WEST BEND"

Dr. E. B. Wolcott

Known as "The Father of West Bend"

IN MEMORIAM

Norman A. Schowalter
1898-1979

Without his leadership, inspiration, and financial support, this history of his beloved city might never have been written. While he was alive, we sought steadfastly to dedicate the book to him, but he refused that recognition.

In a letter about this book, written July 21, 1971, he said . . . "In all these ethnic groups there was an urge for accomplishment, and here we think of accomplishment not in dollars and cents, but in the determination to strive for improved education, freedom of religion, and opportunities to venture forth into business of one kind or another." This, he said, was "The Spirit of West Bend".

In his life, in his service to this community, in his attitude toward his fellow man, Norman A. Schowalter epitomized "The Spirit of West Bend", which is here recorded.

Printed in the United States of America
by Straus Printing Company, Madison, Wisconsin

FOREWORD

In the Spring of 1978 a committee composed of Norman A. Schowalter, Edna Schloemer, and Don Ripple invited me to write the first history of West Bend. Previous histories had been written of Washington County, but even those were fifty years old. I was asked to try to discover what made West Bend unique, "what made it tick." Innocently, I agreed.

This *Spirit of West Bend* (entitled by Mr. Schowalter) is the result of a year and a half of research in the hours after school, on weekends, and during the two summers. The task was formidable, but exhilarating. Not being a professional, I had no idea where to start, so I decided to read each copy of every newspaper ever published in the city to try to get a feeling for the city's past. Then I branched out to nearly every written piece of evidence that exists, especially of the nineteenth century. The constraints of time did not permit much use of a third valuable resource, the memories of a lengthy list of citizens who might have provided additional valuable information. That project remains to be accomplished in another volume and it ought to be done with tape recorder in hand to provide the future citizens with a priceless oral heritage. But it awaits a future when time and a sponsor permit.

The emphasis throughout has been two-fold: first, on the origins of as many organizations and groups as could be found, and second, on the stories, anecdotes, and illustrations that have relevance today.

Someone has said that the most difficult history to write is local history, for it is read primarily by those who have lived through it, and people see through different lenses. Thus, interpretations differ. When this occurred, I chose what seemed to be the most probable. Sometimes the choice may have been unfortunate, but every date, name and place was gleaned from a written source. I make no apologies for the result.

ACKNOWLEDGEMENT

In preparing this volume I owe an incalculable debt to the financial sponsor, Mr. Norman A. Schowalter, without whom this book would never have been written. Miss Edna Schloemer served as my mentor, typed all the copy for the printer, served as the chief instrument for collecting the pictures, proof read the final copy, and contributed in countless other ways, including donating to me all the typed interviews and other material she had amassed in the past in preparation for just such a volume. There is no adequate way to thank her. Don Ripple provided much of the enthusiasm and good business sense, commuting to West Bend from his Madison home to attend innumerable committee meetings.

Aside from the committee, Miss Edith Heidner was the single most valuable resource person. Her never-failing willingness to help when I needed advice, her beautiful memory and store of written and printed materials to help me prove a point were always available.

The hours I spent in the local museum were made possible by the willingness of Mrs. Evelyn Zarling to open the doors for me on countless days so that I might research the riches stored there, and she was personally helpful in directing me to the location of much of the material. Miss Zella Loomer was also unfailingly helpful.

Mrs. Margaret Carlson and Mrs. Marilyn Grasso of the East High School library were always ready to give assistance with the obstreperous micro-film reader. Among the many others whose advice and help I cherish were: Miss Florence Stork, Miss Thecla Richter, Miss Ruth Nickle, Miss Kathleen Walter, Mrs. Marion Haebig, Register of Deeds John Steilen, Dr. Duane Ehrlich, Dean Thompson of the UWWC, Lee Flanders of Moraine Park Technical Institute, Blaine Hedburg, Dr. Huehner of the UWWC History department, Mr. and Mrs. Edward DeTuncq, Jack Weier who took many of the pictures of present-day West Bend, Jim Skrentny, and the many students of Miss Heidner whose papers reside in the Washington County Museum. The research of the latter group enabled me to branch out into areas I would never have known existed.

There were also those who chose to remain anonymous. If I have forgotten to name anyone, it is an error of the head and not the heart. It is the wish of the author that all who read this history may have a renewed interest in the past, and a desire to continue to improve the *Spirit of West Bend.*

Dorothy E. Williams

DEDICATION

With love to all my students
–those who liked history–
and those who didn't

CONTENTS

Page

SECTION I

THE BEGINNINGS

CHAPTER 1

Geological History

What an exciting history the land beneath our feet has had! Knowledge of this stage of West Bend's history will help get a feeling for, and an appreciation of, both the awesome quality of nature and our precarious existence on this part of the universe. It will also reveal the glacier's many gifts.

It is hard to realize that this climate was once tropical. Some of the paleontologists at the Milwaukee Museum feel that the land was once south of the equator, but we shall probably never know. But we do know that this land was part of a vast inland sea; for some unknown reason the earth's crust collapsed and the continent simply sank beneath the waters. Aeons ago, in something called the Pre-Cambrian era, simple one-celled animals lived in this unnamed sea, and their corpses formed minerals such as limestone that later became useful to man.

Only a few hundred feet deep, this vast inland water began to fill up as sediment washed down into it and molten lava welled up from the depths. At least three separate times this process was repeated — the sea would fill with lava and debris and rise, and at least twice it sank again, but the third time the land rose — it stayed. In one of these debris-filled oceans tribolites, brachiopods, and sea weeds appeared for the first time. So, too, did fishes, reef building corals and sea animals that formed shells. They were followed by mosses, ferns, cone-bearing trees, and the first back-boned land animals.

Last of all came the Cenozoic (recent life) age, which provided the first known land mammals and the higher order of plants. During this era the seas began to drain away, winds and rains eroded the land, the towering mountains wore down, and deep subterranean forces tilted some of the gigantic rocks.

And then came the ice. What causes great climatic changes is debatable, but at least four times during the Pleistocene Epoch huge ice sheets, up to two miles thick, advanced slowly southward from their Canadian home. These glaciers had been formed when centuries of snow piled up, could not melt, and moved down at the rate of a few feet a year. When the sun melted the ice the glaciers retreated northward again.

During at least one of these receding periods huge creatures known as mastodons and mammoths roamed the land, while Indians from the southern part of the United States moved north to hunt them. All that is left of that era here are a few bones and some teeth, for the glaciers pushed most of the evidence southward into Illinois, and either ground up the other evidence or buried it beneath tons of rock and soil. Enough remains, however, to convince historians that all this was true.

The Wisconsin Glacier

The last of these glaciers, probably about 25,000 years ago, was called the Wisconsin glacier because it left its mark on Wisconsin more impressively than elsewhere. When it moved into the area that is now Door County, it split into two lobes, and the one called the Green Bay lobe moved over West Bend. This lobe left West Bend 930 feet above sea level, and brought down a rich debris, completely covering the older rocks which lie buried deep, deep beneath us and form the bedrock of the land on which we live. This rubble formed an amazing variety of soils: sandy loams, brown loams, clay, peat, and sand. If there is need of evidence of the rich variety of soil, the land under radio station WBKV, for instance, is beach sand, scooped up from an earlier lake bed which once extended east to Newburg and a mile north of Lizard Mound State Park. Writing in the 1923 Blue Book, a geologist called these glaciers the "greatest real estate improvement ever undertaken in the United States." How infinitesimal, by contrast, are man's puny efforts at draining and grading! Thus the first useful gift of the glaciers to West Bend was its rich and varied soil.

As the two lobes of the glacier continued southward, they pushed against each other and formed mounds of special gravel in the Kettle Moraine area. This good grade of gravel, which is always rounded, enabled West Bend to have better roads more cheaply than in many parts of the country. So the gravel is the second gift of the glacier to West Bend.

When some of the huge ice blocks melted, they formed the lakes that adorn our landscape, five of which are within a four mile radius of West Bend: Smith Lake, Big Cedar Lake, Little Cedar Lake, Wallace, and Silver Lake. Hence the third gift of the glaciers — a fine nearby recreational area.

Then, too, kettles or pots which often had steep sides up to one hundred feet thick formed in some of the land. Sometimes these holes filled in and became marshes; at other times they formed kames or eskers, kames being the neatly rounded hills, and eskers the elongated ones. So the glacier left us, in addition, an interesting landscape much like parts of Central Europe, which helped to attract the Europeans who settled here.

When experts were testing the earth beneath West Bend in 1905 to find the most suitable place for a city well, they drilled through 150 feet of Niagara Limestone, 240 feet of Cincinnati shale, 200 feet of Trenton and Galena limestone, 125 feet of St. Peter sandstone, 190 feet of lower magnesium limestone, and 180 feet of Potsdam sandstone before reaching that Pre-Cambrian rock spoken of at the beginning of this chapter. A total of 1100 feet down to that good water. All in all, then, the glacier was extremely kind to West Bend, creating the proper land surface for a future prosperous city.

CHAPTER 2

The Founding

It was 1845. James K. Polk sat in the President's chair, elected on a platform of expansion. People in the East had "western" fever, and rejoiced over the annexation of Texas and the addition of Oregon. An obscure editor wrote that it was America's Manifest Destiny to occupy the entire continent "allotted to us by God."

And in the fall of that same year three men prepared to leave the then tiny hamlet of Milwaukee for their own small version of Manifest Destiny. The Wisconsin Territorial Legislature had authorized the building of a road between Fond du Lac and

Milwaukee, and a point half way between the two towns was needed to accommodate travellers. So three Commissioners were appointed to lay out the road and seek that half way point.

Byron Kilbourn, one of the three Commissioners, together with surveyor Jasper Vliet, left Milwaukee on a Monday morning, November 15, 1845, on two Indian ponies to seek that midway place. A second Commissioner, James Kneeland, using a crude section map and scratches on trees as his guide, followed on horseback the next day. He blazed trees along the way for a future road, later called Wolcott's road, named after the third Commissioner, E. B. Wolcott, and paralleling part of the route of the present Highway 45.

On Wednesday the three men met at the westward bend of the Milwaukee River and decided that would be the ideal spot for a village. Already occupying some of the land was a squatter, E. N. Higgins, who in either late 1844 or early 1845 had thrown together a shanty of split basswood logs on what later became the residence of Herman Wagner. Squatters were common in those days and were preferred to land speculators, so the law gave them the first opportunity to buy the land they had selected. Kilbourn and Kneeland agreed to make Higgins an equal partner.

James Vliet platted the land into lots 40 feet wide and 120 feet long and laid out the streets in 80 foot widths with 20 foot alleys. An area designated as a park was set aside along the west bank of the river, never to be used for any purpose whatever except as an open park or public promenade. The men also agreed to allot one full block to the county for a future court house, to save two lots for a jail, and to set aside two others for a schoolhouse.

Hurrying back to the Milwaukee land office, Kilbourn, Kneeland, and Higgins purchased 720 acres of land, paying the government price of $1.25 per acre for a total of $900. The Third Commissioner, E. B. Wolcott, who had not accompanied them, was also interested, so he was admitted to full partnership when he agreed to build a gristmill and a sawmill, the first two necessities of a frontier community. The document, signed on November 28, 1845, bears the signatures of Byron Kilbourn, E. B. Wolcott, Charles (E. N.) Higgins, James Kneeland, and Land Commissioner James G. Southwell. They were advised to do their building west of the river to avoid construction of costly bridges.

Now the area had to have a name. Before Kilbourn and

Kneeland returned to Milwaukee they discussed many possible names. In an interview with Mrs. P. W. Harns in 1902 Kneeland recalled how one suggestion had been Pikatomaea, but Kilbourn* preferred a simple name, and suggested that inasmuch as there already were a South Bend and a North Bend, there ought to be a West Bend, too. Besides, it would be easy to spell. So West Bend it became, and the future city's written history had begun.

*Byron Kilbourn was an interesting man, and a rival of Solomon Juneau for control of Milwaukee. He owned the land west of the Milwaukee River in an area that bore his name, Kilbourntown; east of the river, Juneau owned Juneautown. Originally an engineer in Ohio, Kilbourn had been sent to the future Milwaukee to survey the area, had seen the great future possibilities, and had purchased a large number of acres there. He and Juneau and a third man, George Walker, owned most of Milwaukee. Who is not to say that Kilbourn's practiced eye did not foresee a great profit for himself when he bought a fourth of the future West Bend, as it is known that he was responsible in the first place for urging the passage of legislation to authorize the road to Fond du Lac! Later many thought of him as an under-handed schemer when he was involved in bribing legislators at the time of the railroad scandals.

Kneeland owned a store in Milwaukee and also made a fortune in real estate. As the half-brother of one of the early residents, he had been influential in bringing the Wightmans to West Bend. Wolcott was often called "The Father of West Bend" for he built the mills that made the town possible.

CHAPTER 3

The Land

Today as one looks down Main Street it is difficult to imagine West Bend as it was in 1845. Instead of the concrete and neon there was an abundant forest. Here grew the hornbeam hickory and the red oak, the hard maple and the black cherry that would please early furniture makers. Here, too, towered the shagbark hickory and the cedar, the green ash and the quaking aspen, and the lordly elm. Down by the river flourished soft maples, the willows and the reeds. So many trees that early housewives anxiously awaited the autumn, when the leaves would fall so that they could see the sky! It was twilight all day and one barely ever felt a storm.

The trees were the home of the bobwhite, several species of owls, hawks, and woodpeckers. Flickers, warblers, tree sparrows, robins and blackbirds caroled their joy. The bald eagle nested here, and there were butterflies without number.

All manner of other loveliness abounded. There was the hepatica in blue, lavender, and pink to greet the spring. The white Solomon's seal, violets of white, yellow and blue, lilacs, honey suckles and marsh marigolds brightened the woods. Wild roses provided petals for lovely jars of scented beauty. Pasque flowers and milk-white bloodroot, the waxy white trilliums, yellow lady slippers, Jacob's ladders, Dutchmen's breeches, maidenhair ferns and anemones nestled among the prairie grasses. Every fall there was sumac, bittersweet, goldenrod and purple asters.

The clearings were full of more of nature's largess: wild plums, raspberries, grapes, strawberries, gooseberries, currants, ground cherries, crabapples and chokecherries. Then, too, there were butternut and hickory nut trees, hazel nut bushes, mushrooms in season and watercress in spring. Cattails furnished filling for pillows.

Hunters discovered Canada geese, Mallard ducks, sharp tailed grouse and teal. Wood ducks, canvas backs, woodcocks, and prairie chickens, together with partridge, woodhens and wild turkeys kept the tables of the earliest settlers well supplied. Imagine a bevy of partridge alighting on a tree in such numbers that it would break a limb! Or more impressively, imagine a flock of passenger pigeons so numerous that the sky was darkened when it flew over. Alas, they are all extinct now.

In addition, there were deer, muskrats, wolves, a few martens, some mink, foxes, raccoons, rabbits and squirrel. No beaver were left in the area, for the fur traders of the earlier age had bought them all from the Indians. A few deer showed occasionally. Wildcats and panthers ("painters") prowled the wilderness, adding an element of danger.

Bullfrogs and tree frogs sang and harmless garter snakes slithered through the grasses. Snapping turtles waited in the river to catch the unwary: rock bass, perch, sunfish, bullheads, bass, crappies and brook trout filled the river, while the nearby lakes sported pickerel.

All this for the asking. West Bend was truly blessed.

CHAPTER 4

The Indians

No one has any more than an educated guess as to what manner of pre-historic man lived in this area. It is known that the mammoth, an animal similar to, but larger than, the elephant known today roamed here, as did its relative, the mastodon. Early in this century excavators found a long pole buried vertically 15 feet deep in the northwest section of the city of West Bend. The six foot pole was encirled by an iron ring; the assumption is that the spear was used to kill the mastodon, as similar implements have been found in other parts of the country near mastodon bones; perhaps the first Indians in southeastern Wisconsin were in pursuit of the gigantic beast.

Estimates vary widely as to the date of the first Indians in the area. A conservative guess would be 7000 years ago. If only they had possessed the gift of writing! Probably several Indian tribes lived here at one time or other; one supposes they were exterminated by warfare or disease. Because they possessed no knowledge of sanitation, all manner of pestilence kept their numbers low, for epidemics were common. Some of them were mound builders, as evidenced by the graves at Lizard Mound State Park, just five miles northeast of the city. When the first settlers arrived and questioned nearby Indians, however, they had no knowledge of the mound builders, for theirs had been an earlier era in history.

The first written evidence of Indians in the West Bend area occurs in the struggle between the French and the English in 1763. Unlike most of the Indians in Wisconsin, those in the area cast their lot with the British, because the goods they traded were cheaper. The second mention of Indians occurs in the various treaties which the United States government made with the Indians over the years. The white man considered the various tribes as nations, treated them as such, and made treaties with them. Among the treaties affecting West Bend was the one in 1833 by which the Winnebagoes ceded their land south and east of the Wisconsin and Fox rivers and south of Lake Winnebago. The United States government then purchased land from the Menominee and the Winnebago to build a road from Lake Michigan to Dekorra, Iowa, for the purpose of swiftly moving

Emma Big Bear
Direct Descendant of
Chief Decorah

the United States Army to put down Indian uprisings. Part of the road roughly parallels Highway 33; part of it bears the name "Decorah Road" today. After the road was surveyed, the army felled trees and dragged the trunks onto the swampier parts, while horses and wagons trampled them down. Often they plowed two furrows 20 feet apart and scraped the loosened dirt into the space between.

Chief De Korra

There is an interesting story behind the Indian name Decorah. In 1729 a French army officer named Sebrevoir de Corrie (there are other variant spellings) resigned his commission to become an Indian trader with the Winnebagoes. He married WA HO PO E KAW (Glory of the Morning), the Chief's daughter, and had three children. One day de Corrie left his wife and two sons and took the daughter to Montreal, never to return.

Of the two sons who remained with the mother, the older became the tribal chieftain, and the other, the one-eyed De Korra (various spellings, also) cast his lot with Black Hawk and was captured with the great chief. Decorah Road was originally named after him, and both a street and a subdivision in the southern part of West Bend bear his name.

Later Indian Dealings

To return to the story of the treaties affecting West Bend,

another treaty was concluded with the Potawatomi in 1835. They were given three years after that date to vacate the land, so the land north of the Milwaukee River was open to settlement years before the land south of the river. Between 1825 and 1848 eleven separate treaties were made with the Indians, after which they owned no more land in Wisconsin.

But the Indians did not like the prairie land west of the Mississippi, for they were forest people. As a young man Fred Stork talked to a Kansas Indian who longed to return "home." Often they drifted back, singly, in families, or small tribes, and lived peacefully among the white settlers. The nearest such village of returnees was south of West Bend in the Silver Lake area, although some families also lived in West Bend.

Those who remained were farmers. They grew beans, tobacco, pumpkins and corn in fenced community gardens which were more easily guarded from predators — both man and beast. Evidence of these old Indian cornfields and gardens has been uncovered. The earth in the city has yielded flint arrowheads, stone tools, knives, shreds of pottery, copper and shells from distant shores; the Washington County Museum contains a collection of many of these artifacts. We know that they created clay pots, and used copper for tools. They used reeds for mats, made birch bark canoes and bows, tapped maple trees for syrup, and collected honey from the honey bees. Naturally they hunted the then plentiful animals, and ate of the fruits, nuts and fish. Most of them possessed neither the wheel nor the horse although some of them did have Indian ponies. Nearly all had given up their migratory habits and left home only to hunt and fish, or when driven out by another tribe on the warpath.

True to their heritage, they did not store up food for the winter, for they lived for the day only and let tomorrow take care of itself. So in the summer they fattened; in the winter they were often reduced to eating acorns and tree bark, and sometimes begged from the white man after his arrival. Nothing indicates that the local Indians ever stole; rather they were of the type to give something in return for a favor. Sometimes they begged milk for their babies. Many an early settler was often startled to look up and see an Indian who had slipped noiselessly into the house to ask for something. They particularly coveted metal tools, metal pots and pans, cloth, warm blankets, guns, liquor, or a piece of beef. In the proper season, they traded corn or a deer for the white man's goods.

Indian-White Amity

From the very first, local settlers and the Indians lived together peaceably. One lively account tells of two white children aged five and three who wandered away from their home in 1847 in the nearby Poor Farm area and no one could find them. A neighbor dashed into West Bend to one of the Indian groups to ask the men to help find the children. Without any hesitation the Indians jumped on their ponies and joined in the search, and it was they who found the youngsters unharmed after being lost in the woods for 2½ days. The grateful family offered the Indians a $20 gold piece, a goodly sum in 1847.

No evidence of any animosity on the part of local Indians toward the white man exists. Everyone spoke of the red man's kindness. Such sadly mistreated people!

When the first settlers arrived in West Bend there were no Indians living in the village itself, but shortly thereafter some returned. Many early settlers recalled the Indians and the gratitude they felt for the Indian trails, all that the white man had to use for roads at first. It was common for white and Indian children to play together, especially along the river. Adam Held remembered that Indians would walk through the village in single file, the Chief first, followed by the young men, the women with papooses on their backs and the rest of the children, while bringing up the rear would be the old ones, who could not walk as rapidly. Sometimes they would march through on their way south to trade furs; occasionally a family would walk through on its way to a new location. As late as 1865 an editor of the *West Bend Democrat* mentioned casually that a family of Indians including the squaw had "honored his establishment with a visit last week." Later, too, they marched through on their way to Milwaukee to pick up their pension money.

Once there was a near tragedy. Someone spread the rumor on August 26, 1861, that the Horicon Lake Indians were on the warpath and the cry spread to West Bend, "The Indians are coming!" The message arrived at ten o'clock at night, and those who received the news drummed on drums and shot off guns to waken the populace. Someone made a speech, urging the men to defend their homes, and the local gunsmith was busy all night mending muskets.

Nearby farmers and townspeople gathered to plot their strategy. Men were assigned definite stations to guard. Some hid in barns to await the "savages." Hours passed. Tension grew. When no attack materialized, the people took their clubs, pitchforks and guns and went sheepishly home. The sole casualty was a man who wounded himself with his own gun!

The only negative murmur about even one Indian concerns Bad John, who whooped and scared Abigail and Huldah, daughters of Mr. Farmer, who were returning at night to their home after staying with a neighbor while their father went to look after some land. The next day about 40 local men went to the Indian's camping ground — the land that became Hamlyn's farm. Pointing their guns, they told the Indians to move on. Now, Bad John was the Chief's son and he felt genuinely contrite and promised to be good. The Indians begged to stay. The peace pipe was smoked in honor of the agreement and all was well thereafter. Surely this has to be a record of amity between two races, as this is the only difficulty ever experienced locally.

One by one, through death or removal, the Indians left the area. By the first decade of 1900 the only Indian left in West Bend was a skull dug up from the Kruse farm and exhibited in the Gerlach-Haas store as a curio.

CHAPTER 5

The Early Settlers

How does a community begin? What manner of people brave a wilderness to make a new start in life? Even before the road to the future village had been commissioned and the village platted, word of a fertile area to the north along the Milwaukee River reached the few pioneers in southeastern Wisconsin. One of those who listened to such talk was Isaac Verbeck, who had come to Wisconsin from Pennsylvania and had put down temporary roots in Waukesha County. One summer day in 1846 he left his family and set out to find the new paradise. His long walk along the route of the future Highway 45 eventually brought him to an Indian village just south of what would become West Bend, where he spent the night.

Legend repeats that in the morning an Indian told him "White man walk on," so he left to continue his search. Liking what he saw in the wilderness near the west bend of the river, he hurried back to his family and enticed his brother-in-law, M. A. T. Farmer, to join him. Verbeck, his wife Mary and their five children and Farmer with his wife and four children waited until the crops were harvested that fall to set out for their new home. The Farmers put up the first shanty, about a mile south of the village on land that would later become Decorah Lawns. Verbeck erected his crude hut on the land on which Badger School now stands, next to the creek that once ran through that land.

Verbeck and Farmer and two other families had brought 2,000 pounds of goods from their home in Pennsylvania, some of it in an old chest, the four sides of which were the four doors of their eastern homes. When the chest was dismantled each family then had a ready-made door for its wilderness home, something that would have been impossible in an area that as yet had no mill. Huldah Farmer reminisced at an Old Settlers' meeting that their first hut could not use the door, but instead they hung a blanket over the opening and she often had to spend her time fending off both wild animals and friendly but curious Indians.

An unmarried Verbeck brother, Joseph, was in no immediate need of a home, so he merely chopped down brush and some trees and piled them in a heap near the river to indicate that he had a claim on the land. This method of establishing ownership was a common practice in the western areas of the United States. All three of these men, the two Verbecks and Farmer, were known as "preemptors," men who intended to buy the land eventually, but who wanted to beat the land speculators to the unclaimed areas. Later that same year, Verbeck's parents, Amos and Abigail, and ten more of their children (Nelson, Amos, Philip, William, Anson, Charles, Sidney, Abigail, Mary and Sarah) settled in West Bend also.

More Settlers Arrive

Other families began to arrive. Accounts differ as to the order in which they arrived, but it is known that most of them were single men, as it was hazardous to bring a family into the wilderness. Among the early names are those of Jehiel Baker, who came from Michigan in 1846 to become the first storekeeper, the Young brothers (Jacob and Christian), Walter Demmon, Elder Babcock, Sinn "the blacksmith," the Rusco brothers, and

Hannah McDonald
First Bride in West Bend

Edward Helm. Other early names on the 1846 fall election list include Joseph and Herman Mann, James and Patrick Costello, Peter Beck, John Vaneps, Dan Cotton, Sylvester Rowe, and William Morehouse. Little of substance is known of any of them.

Among the more distinguished early names was that of Moses Weil, the first European Jew to settle in West Bend. He came from Alsace and used to vividly describe the return of Napoleon from the Battle of Waterloo, which he had witnessed personally. He brought his two sons with him, built the first frame house in the new settlement, operated a general store from his home and tended a flourishing vineyard. In fact, one sight that is long vanished from the area is that of the vineyards that prospered here; some were in an area approximately across from the brewery and just to the south of it. Because the sawmill was not yet completed, Weil had to haul the lumber from Milwaukee with his pair of oxen; all the goods for his store were brought in in like manner also.

George N. Irish came early in 1846 and built a log house named The American House which served as hotel and tavern to accommodate the growing number of workmen pouring into the area to build the mills. Irish also ran the sawmill which he had rented from Dr. Wolcott, who had fulfilled his prior agreement to build the mill in exchange for a quarter of the land. Wolcott hired workmen to cut down trees and brush to create a temporary dam on the river before he could build the mill. When the grist mill was finally completed in 1848 there was general rejoicing, for now the settlers would not have to carry the grain on their backs to Milwaukee, the site of the nearest grist mill, and then trudge back with the flour. Most often this task fell to an adolescent son in the family.

The story of early settler Jacob Young has a moment of interest. When he went to the land commissioner in Milwaukee to pay for his land, he absentmindedly left the remainder of his assets, nearly $1,000 of precious gold, at the land agent's office. Fortunately the agent, Mr. Helfenstein, was an honest man, so he followed Young and returned the money with the legendary admonition, "You ought to have a guardian." Young built a frame house on what became Sharp Corner, later known as the Smoke House, and approximately where the Marth building is located now.

Young looked forward to the privacy of his own house for himself and his family, after living in one of the crowded "hotels," but the demand for housing was so great as mechanics begged for a place to stay, that he, too, opened his home as a hotel. He became the first Justice of the Peace. His brother Christian and his wife followed, but he became homesick and longed for civilization, although he remained and later became the first Deputy Sheriff.

The record mentions that Walter Demmon built the first "large" log cabin, its dimensions being 18 x 24 feet. One wonders how small the others must have been, but fortunately privacy was not so important as it seems today. For several to crowd into the same bed was commonplace.

Wightman's Leave a Printed Record

One of the few written records of the early settlers is that by the daughter of William Wightman, who with his wife and four daughters, Kate, Fannie, Martha, and Hattie, arrived from Michigan in 1846. Wightman was born in 1798 and used to tell of hearing the noise of the battle of Plattsburg during the war of 1812, for which he trained, but the war ended before he could serve. The Wightman's came in a "comfortable" wagon to the land that his half-brother James Kneeland, one of the aforementioned Commissioners, had purchased for him. After visiting relatives in the comparative security of Milwaukee, they came north along the route where farmers had crudely lettered signs which read: "Entertainment for man and beast," which was one of the ways for the people to earn a bit of the almost non-existent money, as well as a way to learn the news and alleviate the deadly loneliness.

When they arrived just south of West Bend at the shanty of M. A. T. Farmer, they purchased a loaf of bread from Huldah Farmer and drove on into the settlement where they spent the first night with the Jehiel Bakers. Mrs. Wightman refused to leave the security of the covered wagon for a night in the overcrowded cabin, but in time she conquered her fear of the wilderness and became an important and beloved social leader in the community.

The Wightmans elected to live in their covered wagon until their house was completed, the first home, incidentally, that was built with lumber from the new sawmill. They immediately also converted their home to a hotel and named it the West Bend House, and so used it for about ten years.

When Herman Zimmerman came in 1847 he found 30 people in the area, with three buildings on the east side of the main road constituting the "town." He built on the site of the former First State Bank. There were but two buildings (homes) south of Hickory and Main Streets at that time.

Other early settlers included Ira Spencer, the first Postmaster, Walter Dennison, James Bailey, John Wagner, Ben Thompson and his wife (perhaps the first woman to live "down town"), Daniel Freer, Lewis Bates, Mr. Bullin, Mrs. Betsy Visgar, William Ramsay, and Leander Frisby. What a pity that the names of the earliest are all gone now; not one of them remains to trace their history in West Bend.

The First Village

All the dwellings were clustered on the west side of the river. People worshipped in their own homes, if at all, at first, and then joined others for joint services until they built churches. Mail came once a week from Milwaukee by ox cart, and the moment was one of great rejoicing as it provided the chief touch with the outside world. Women were in short supply and any wedding was a cause for elaborate celebration. Anson Verbeck and Hannah McDonald, one year after the founding of the village, had the first recorded wedding, performed by Justice of the Peace Jacob Young.

Life was crude in the early years and the settlers suffered countless privations, but progress was rapid. It became evident from the beginning that Kilbourn and his friends had chosen the site wisely, for all the traffic and trade in the entire western part of the county, which then included Ozaukee County, soon centered on West Bend. By 1850 people were complaining about the heavy traffic and the crowded streets! One settler wrote that settlers were arriving in "platoons" and the three hotel-taverns could no longer accommodate the "hordes" of people who wished to move here, so private homes took in roomers, too. West Bend was on its way.

And what happened to those early buildings? Typical is the fate of the first cabin of Isaac Verbeck, which became an embarrassing eyesore in 1919, a blot on the landscape. A poet spoke of the fact that it had survived its time in the moving world and now it was time to go. He spoke of the brave hearts that had dared the silence and solitude to begin to build a community, and concluded:

"And now it stands by the wayside, close onto the busy street,
And the alien over its threshold may wander with careless feet.
Nor window nor latch to the broken door to bar the curious way,
And the storms have swept and the snows have crept through the walls this many day."

And so it was demolished to make room for progress, as have all the other buildings of that earliest era except a log shed in the alley between Fourth and Fifth Avenue at Chestnut, and we are the poorer for the demolition, but the spirit of the community the early residents established rests on the strength of their character.

CHAPTER 6

Wisconsin Becomes Wisconsin

The land on which West Bend is located has been under the flags of four countries and six different states. Technically, Spain claimed the area from 1512-1634, but no Spaniards ever lived here. There was a brief interlude and then France owned it from 1671-1763, at which time the British decisively defeated her in North America. Consequently, the British flag flew over the soil until the intrepid Americans routed their mother country in the Revolutionary War, and the area then became part of the fledgling United States of America.

Defeat did not diminish the rule of Britain here, however, for the British retained the lucrative fur trade for years because the new Americans were too weak militarily to oust them. It was not until the second war with Britain in 1812 that the territory became American in fact as well as in name. Neither the French nor the British left any mark here, unless it was in the extinction of most of the fur-bearing animals, such as the beaver. The few forts that both countries had built in Wisconsin were too far from West Bend to affect it.

Based on their original charters from England, several states claimed the future Wisconsin, among them Virginia and Massa-

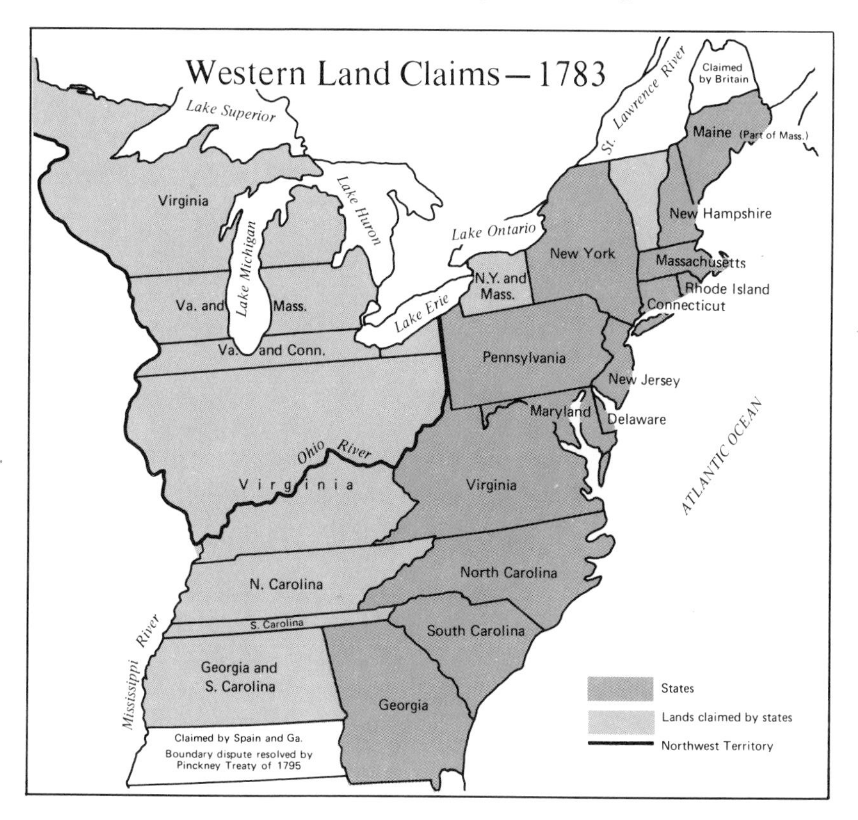

chusetts. Had either of them maintained their claim, our address might have been West Bend, Virginia, or West Bend, Massachusetts. But in 1786 all of the original states ceded their western claims to the United States government, and the following year Congress passed one of the most far-reaching documents in all world history — the Northwest Ordinance.

This ordinance created a territory from which not less than three nor more than five states were to be created, and from which slavery was to be forever barred. There was generous provision for schools, a plan for eventual statehood, and a resultant full equality with the original states. One of the more remarkable provisions of the 1785 Land Ordinance was the one which divided all the land into six mile square townships. This stipulation was largely the work of Thomas Jefferson who chaired the Committee of Western Land in the Congress under the old Articles of Confederation, and would forever prevent the troubles that Eastern residents were having with their boun-

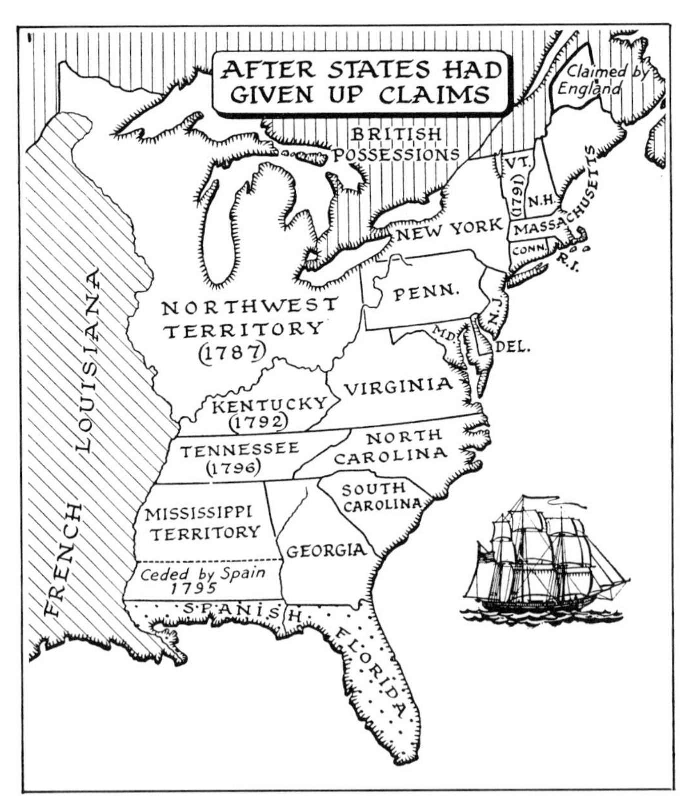

daries. Imagine the difficulties that could accrue if the boundaries of property in Wisconsin had been a river, which could change course, or a large boulder which could be moved, or a clump of trees which could be hewn down. One has only to look at a plat of the eastern states to realize the blessing the old Northwest Territory states have in that respect.

One by one new states were created from the Northwest Territory. First there was Ohio, the area nearest to eastern civilization. Then in 1800 Indiana was granted statehood and Wisconsin was officially made a part of Indiana with Vincennes its capital. So our address might have been West Bend, Indiana. Soon Illinois achieved statehood and Wisconsin was transferred to it, with its capital at Kankaskia, and we might have been West Bend, Illinois.

Next it became Michigan's turn to attain statehood in 1818, and once more Wisconsin was transferred to the newest state, but those were unhappy years for the territory, as Michigan laws were crude by comparison to those of other states. An offender might spend six months in jail for a minor offense, for example, and public whippings were numerous.

Wisconsin Becomes a Territory

July 3, 1836, was a happy day for the last territory in the old Northwest; at long last Wisconsin became a territory in its own right, and for the first time the name "Wisconsin" appears on public documents. The newly created legislature divided the entire territory into only two counties at first, Brown for the northern half, and Milwaukee for the southern half, but on December 7, 1836, Washington County was carved out of Milwaukee County, the land to extend from Lake Michigan to the present county's western boundary.

There were too few settlers to administer a government here, so Milwaukee continued to administer the county's business until 1840, but even then there was too scant a population to warrant a separate court system; hence it took another five years for courts to materialize in the county.

But a territory does not have full equality with other states, and one of the most annoying difficulties for the territory of Wisconsin was the way in which neighboring states kept stealing land along the borders. Illinois started the depredations by moving its northern boundary so it could have Chicago and an outlet on Lake Michigan. Wisconsin protested vociferously, but the cries were unheeded in the nation's capital. When Ohio coveted land from southern Michigan, that state was mollified by taking all of the area of northern Wisconsin that eventually became the northern peninsula of Michigan. Wisconsin had thus lost valuable property to her two neighboring states; where would the larceny stop?

There was only one recourse—full statehood—so in 1846 the legislators drafted a Constitution and offered it to the voters for approval, but it was rejected in the general referendum as "too liberal." However, the voters of Washington County approved it overwhelmingly, possibly because of the generous voting privileges for those who were not yet full citizens.

Two years later a second Constitution was written and this time it was accepted. Again there was the proviso that foreign born males who were at least 21 and who had declared their intention of becoming a citizen could vote, a highly important stipulation for settlers of Washington County, as German immigrants were literally pouring into the county.

It is most interesting to note how the people of Washington County voted on that 1848 Constitution. Instead of ONE question on the ballot, as was done throughout the state, this county had TWO. The first one asked if the Constitution should be adopted and the voters were in agreement, 1476-353. But for the second question, they extracted a clause from the Constitution that asked if Negroes should be allowed to vote, and 1328 voters marked NO while a mere 84 checked YES.

In summary, the land on which West Bend stands has technically been under the rule of five Spanish kings, three French kings, 25 French governors, one English king and six territorial governors, including William Henry Harrison of Indiana, who later became the 9th United States President, and Edward Ninian of Illinois, so often associated with Lincoln lore. All this before West Bend might finally claim West Bend, Wisconsin, as its address.

CHAPTER 7

West Bend Becomes the County Seat

The first court house was built in 1854 on Court House Square facing Fifth Avenue and later moved. The office building was built in 1857 and alleged to be fireproof to retain the county records.

The manner in which West Bend became the county seat of Washington County is a unique story; nothing like it exists in Wisconsin's annals for sheer confusion and bitterness. The trouble began back in April of 1846, when the county held an election to determine the county seat. Every village competed for the honor except Hartford, which had visions of becoming the county seat of a new county they hoped would be created out of western Washington County and the eastern part of Dodge County.

There were 861 votes cast in the election of which West Bend received the grand total of — 12! But the law required that the winning village have a majority, and there was none for any other place either, so they voted again but not until almost two and a half years later — in September of 1848. This time the results were: Cedarburg 570; Port Washington 697; Newark (Barton) 149; Saukville 82; County Farm 180; Newburg 11 and West Bend 336. But again there was no majority. It was becoming increasingly awkward to try to conduct county business without a county seat so there was another election on November 7. By this time, four places had dropped out of the running and West Bend now received a whopping 1117, while Cedarburg garnered 944 and Port Washington 640 — but, again, there was no majority.

This was becoming burdensome, so two months later in January of 1849 they ballotted once more. This time there were but two villages in the running, Cedarburg which received 1643 and West Bend 1111, but this time there was a new twist: 986 voters marked their ballot: NEITHER. All the latter ballots were declared illegal and arguments reached a fever pitch as to WHO had stuffed the ballot box.

Little county business could be conducted, so various pressure groups, with their own welfare in mind, began to trek to Madison. Petitions were circulated and taken to the state legislators. The County Board sent an interesting petition, too, begging the state legislators to solve the awkward dilemma.

Such a furor! Unfortunately the divisions of the citizens now took a religious turn, for the southern part of the county was largely German Lutheran, while the northern part was primarily Roman Catholic. A new idea formed; why not split the county by an east west line, separating the two religious groups?

This concept angered the good citizens of Port Washington, so they circulated among the few Lutherans in the northern part of the county, telling them that the proposed division was only a nasty plot to give the Roman Catholics a ruling majority there. This riled up the Lutherans. Then the same plotters roamed among the southern half of the county and roused the feelings of the few Roman Catholics there by telling them that if the German Lutherans were in control, they would establish parochial schools and all the Irish would have to learn German. Perish that thought!

So the delegations to Madison continued, with religion the new hot issue. It seemed to call for a Solomon to solve the predicament and to quell the hatred and mistrust that had arisen in a heretofore relatively compatible community.

Wisdom finally prevailed. A solution appeared. The county would be split on an east-west line, thus creating two counties, Washington, with Port Washington as the county seat, and Tuskola, with Cedarburg as its county seat. All that remained was for the citizens to approve of it in formal balloting.

April 5, 1851, was the big day. Can you guess the outcome? There were 275 ballots FOR the proposal and 1716 AGAINST. Hartford, which by now had given up its dream of a new county for which it would be the center, was particularly incensed, for they claimed the vote was only a choice between two evils.

State Legislature Acts

Now what? Five years had passed since the first election to determine a county seat, and Port Washington had been serving temporarily as the place from which business was conducted. *Everybody* was unhappy. On February 13 the state legislature chose Grafton as the new temporary seat and ordered a new election to consider making West Bend the official county seat. April, 1852. Another ballot. 1789 voters liked the idea, but 2496 say — NAY.

Immediately afterward, charges of gross cheating were leveled. Belgium had about 300 legal voters and yet turned in 763 ballots. Several voters throughout the county were patently well under the legal voting age of 21. Several voted twice. New York City had nothing on Washington County for corruption. And again — EVERYBODY was unhappy. Port Washington was jubilant because its archrival, West Bend had lost, but then, it did not have the honor anymore, either.

State legislators could not get the business of the state accomplished for they were deep in trying to sort out the innuendos, the disagreements, the petitions, and in meeting with the numberless delegations from the county.

Now West Bend and Port Washington conspired together. Divide the county on a new north-south line and let each of the old rivals be the county seat of the newly divided areas. This seemed to the weary legislators to be the most logical solution, so they quickly passed the bill before protestors could organize. FINALLY, then, in 1853, the question seemed solved. Only one stumbling block remained.

The state had a law which set the legal acreage for each county and the newly created Ozaukee County did not meet the requirement. NOW what to do. The answer was simple. Just declare that the eastern boundary of Ozaukee County was in the middle of Lake Michigan! Success at last. West Bend was now a county seat.

What really caused the imbroglio? No one can say with certainty. It was not political, for the County was heavily Democratic and remained so for almost another 50 years. It was not, in the last analysis, religious, for if they had voted on church lines, the problem would have been settled years earlier. Perhaps that sage of county history, Carl Quickert, is right — that the county was full of new immigrants who had it in their power for the first time to make a big political decision and they made the most of it. While they were caught up in the ecstacy of being able to express themselves politically at long last, they were too inexperienced to handle the issue wisely.

Several enterprising local men were responsible for instituting the county division so that this village could become a county seat. State Senator Baruch Schlesinger Weil was probably the most influential. One of the aims, of course, was to boost the price of real estate, and the larger land owners would profit handsomely. Be that as it may, it was another milestone in the history of West Bend, and this one would help to make it the prosperous city it would become.

One Problem Remains — The Records

But wait a minute. Did we think the issue was settled? Not quite. At the time the counties were divided, all but one of the officers were unfortunately from Port Washington and that is where the records were, of course. Their homes and businesses were there and they emphatically refused to move to West Bend. In those days of difficult travel it was essential that the officers live in or near the county seat.

How to get the records to the right location became a problem. West Bend obtained a court order to have the records moved here, but the only judge in the vast judicial circuit was holding court way up in Marquette. Yet two determined local citizens,

Paul Weil and L. Frisby, set out to find him. It took a week, but they triumphantly brought back the official paper.

But having a proper court order and having the records became two different things, for the Port Washington people absolutely refused to surrender the documents. So, one dark night, on the fourth of March, four representatives from West Bend drove stealthily to Port Washington with plenty of gunny sacks to "steal" the records that were rightfully theirs. As they were loading the documents from the office of the Register of Deeds, an alert Port Washington official saw a suspicious light in the room, suspected skullduggery, and rang the riot bell. Well, this woke up the town, and they grabbed the West Benders and ignominiously hustled them out of the building — without the records.

It was a sad trip back to West Bend for the unlucky four. But worse, by next morning, all trace of the records had disappeared, and the county STILL could not conduct its business properly.

In June an honest Port Washington editor, R. A. Bird, wrote to Leander Frisby, telling him where the records might be found, and advised him to come unobserved and retrieve them. So about one o'clock on a very dark night the men chosen for the "theft" arrived in Port Washington, heard the editor tell them exactly where the books were, and triumphantly retrieved them. Such a homeward procession! As they neared West Bend, they stopped to cut some branches from the brush by the road, fastened their handkerchiefs to them, and entered the village with flying banners.

At last the purloined material was in its proper village home. But nothing is ever easy, and when the records were sorted, it was discovered that Volume "M" was missing! This is a long story, also, but one day in 1878 the missing book was discovered intact in a wall where it had apparently been hastily thrust on the night of the first attempted rescue. West Bend really WAS the county seat at last.

County Buildings

Now that West Bend was truly the county seat of Washington County, it was necessary to erect buildings as rapidly as possible. To hasten the process, William Wightman donated four lots of land in 1853 to add to an area named "The Park," with the provision that county buildings be erected upon it, and that it

Court House, 1890's.

be enclosed with a board fence. Until the buildings were completed, the newly elected county officers met in the schoolhouse and lived in private homes in the village. In 1855 the county built a courthouse and a jail with jailor's living quarters, as well as a "fireproof" building for the records. The Courthouse and jail were frame buildings and served the purpose until they were outgrown and outmoded. In 1889 the county received its handsome new Courthouse and jail and the old courthouse was moved down to Main Street where it served as a hardware store for many years.

The only recorded instance of malfeasance in the 19th Century courthouse was that involving County Treasurer Albert Semmler in 1876. He had gambled or otherwise wasted over $14,000 worth of county money, after which he fled the area. Apprehended in Nebraska, he was tried, found guilty, and sentenced to Waupun. After he fulfilled his term he returned to West Bend, but his misdeeds stayed with him in people's minds, so he left town. Otherwise, the spirit of West Bend remained high.

SECTION II

THE 1850'S AND 1860'S

CHAPTER 1

Why the Settlers Came to West Bend

As immigation increased, it is well to ask why so many were willing to leave their homes to come to an absolute wilderness. First of all, it was the eastern Yankees (native Americans of British descent) who came in search of better land. Unlike the conservative Germans, the Yankees did not practice soil conservation, and the constant planting of the same crops each year depleted the soil. It was at this juncture in history, also, that farming in the East changed from subsistence farming to dairying, which required more land. But it was almost impossible for farmers to expand their holdings because the land bore too high a price tag, so if they wanted cheaper land they had to move westward.

Then, too, strange as it seems to our ears, the East was becoming crowded. Too many skilled mechanics and workers could not find employment, so if they wanted to work at their trade they had to leave home. This was particularly true of the young, most of whom, like youth everywhere, longed to be independent. Others left because of personal or family tragedies or simply to escape. Basically, though, the reasons for the Easterners coming were largely economic ones.

Wisconsin was the easiest of the western states to reach by water, the cheapest mode of transportation, which was a major factor in bringing settlers to this state. They could buy a relatively large tract of land for less than two dollars an acre and in a few years could sell it at a handsome profit. The Yankees knew that the first ones in a new area stood to gain financially, especially if the site was near water power. Those early Yankees were most often the sons and grandsons of those who had fought in the Revolutionary War and they brought their old swords and

Charles H. Miller
Early Resident — Born 1826 — Died 1897

Tom Farmer, son of first resident M.A.T. farmer.

muskets with them, knowing at first hand what freedom meant.

On the other hand, the Germans had other reasons for leaving home and coming to West Bend. Germany (not yet a unified country bearing that name) was an area where a man was likely to remain forever in the economic strata into which he was born. Those who were ambitious to "rise" had no such opportunity. They also had a real hunger to own land, but land was scarce and the taxes on their meager holdings were oppressive. Different German states provided other reasons. The Prussians, for instance, were involved in continual wars or threats of war, and the young were victims of compulsory military training. In Pomerania there was religious intolerance, for the ruling princes wanted everybody to join the Evangelical church to which they themselves belonged, while the majority of the population was staunch Lutheran. Then, too, the massive resistance to the politics of the German states, especially during the Revolution of 1848, left those on the losing side fearing persecution. In addition, there was wanderlust, the love of adventure, or simply that sometimes whole communities left together, so that even though one might not be particularly interested in migration, it was common to leave with family and friends.

Other nationalities came, too. There were French, Swiss, Welsh, Scots, Norwegians, and Dutch. The Irish came to escape burdensome taxation and the dread potato famine of 1848. Some Irishmen came because the Orangemen forced the Irish Catholics to pay taxes to support the hated Anglican church. Miss Agnes Beck recalls one Irish ancestor who, when he saw the orange day lilies growing wild in West Bend, tore them out by their roots because their color offended him. She reports that the plants were hardy and are still blooming.

Why They Chose West Bend

Next, let us examine why they chose West Bend. For the Germans, the big factor was the land agent. Wisconsin's State Board of Immigration asked three Germans from each county to give them the names of three friends back home, and then they sent a German speaking agent there to recruit. Other active recruiters were the Wisconsin Roman Catholic clergy, who sent priests back to Europe to encourage more of their faith to emigrate. Then, too, there were the glowing letters from settlers already here, praising the ease of obtaining land, and the glorious bounties of nature here. Probably the most forceful argument was money. A single worker could save enough in one year here to purchase 80 acres of land and become independent; this was more than he could ever hope to inherit at home. An added inducement was the nature of the land itself, for it looked like home to the Central European. The glacier had done its work well.

Farmers were attracted to the good soil, and the varied types of soil near the large Lake Michigan proved ideal for growing fruits and vegetables, something every European wanted in his new home. Being conservative, they wanted to be near a market, and West Bend was relatively close to both the lake and to Milwaukee. The water was pure, too, and wonder of wonders for Germans, there was no need for most of them to drill wells then. All one needed to do was dig. There was also a great quantity of wood for houses and outbuildings, as well as for furniture; all that it took was muscle, which they were willing to supply. So it was the land that brought them and when the flour and saw mills were completed, West Bend became a magnet.

In addition, the more liberal minded were attracted because

they could vote shortly after their arrival, and the thought of being able to participate in government and run for office once they were citizens intrigued them, for this was denied them in Europe. Women liked the liberal atmosphere, for here they could inherit property, as Wisconsin was one of the relatively few states to permit this.

And so they came from Bavaria and Budapest, from Pomerania and Prussia, from Brandenburg and Bohemia, Helsingfors and Holland, Hesse and Hanover. They trickled in from Finland and Frankfurt and France, from Dachau and Duesseldorf and Damstadt, Choburg and Coblenz, Leipzig, Luxemburg and Lorraine. They arrived from Montreal and Munich, from County Cork and Canada, from Saxony and Scotland and Sweden, as well as Wales, Thuringia, Alsace, and the Isle of Riga.

They carried their own food on the long journey to America — oatmeal and flour, ham, potatoes, sugar and spices, butter and brandy. Tinware utensils did not stand the trip, so theirs were of iron. They brought their traps and their axes. Some stopped in Milwaukee to buy a cow or a plow or perhaps even a team of oxen.

In addition, they brought their linens, usually handwoven from their own flax, dishes, quilts, silver or tin cutlery, shawls and other clothing, the family Bible and family pictures, a pistol often, and if skilled, the tools of their trade. But regardless of their place of origin, they possessed a firm belief in the wonderful idea of freedom, as well as a willingness to work to succeed. If success did not come immediately for them, they were determined that their children would have a better life.

Life was not necessarily what they expected, at least for the very earliest settlers. Most of them had spent up to 52 weary days at sea, and then up to another 18 days to reach West Bend. Tricksters were at every port to relieve the green newcomers of their precious hoard, and all too often they succeeded. There were no churches. No banks. Crude shanties at first. Mattresses of straw or worse. Dirt floors. Most owned a cow and acquired a few chickens and the inevitable pig or two and, if German, some geese. Sometimes they had a sheep to provide their own wool. There was little time for pleasure, for the work of clearing land was exhausting. But they had all types of "bees," from barn raising to quilting bees, and other joint activities for fun. There was little or no surplus wealth. Holidays were happily celebrated, even by the poorest among them.

Differences Arise Between Settlers

Almost at once the differences between the "natives" and the newcomers surfaced in West Bend. By 1868 the newcomers were primarily German and they now controlled the village politics, whereas the first officers had been primarily Yankee. One of the most ticklish problems was over the subject of temperance. Local Yankee women were among those who spearheaded the temperance drive in the state, and largely due to their influence Wisconsin passed a law in 1849 which stated that any liquor dealer had to post a $1000 bond and could be sued for damages to a community or an individual resulting from the sale of liquor. Think how a law like that would please the beer drinking Germans! The law, it might be added, was honored more often in the breach than in its enforcement. Yankees tended to be teetotalers, while a brewery to quench the thirst of the Germans was one of the first industries in West Bend. In countless other ways the two cultures differed and often clashed. Sometimes the difference was as inconsequential as the use of quilts by the Germans, who had brought their own, versus the feather beds of the Yankees.

Socially the two groups tended to remain separate for many years. This was even true of the regiments in the Civil War. Each formed its own clubs and societies. When it came to dances, the chief form of recreation at times, the two cultures had such different styles that they were not comfortable with the other's music at first.

One incident points up the attitude; in 1864 there was a public dance at Vieth's Hall and the editor of the *Democrat* reported that it was attended by "mostly Americans. Our German friends did not turn out. Possibly they think we do not want them but that is not the case." Actually, he went on, Americans are happier when the mixture is 50-50 and besides, "we prefer the German music to the American music; they can have a gay time with the German-type music."

In a letter written in 1860 in the *Milwaukee News,* an anonymous correspondent noted that the Germans live for today, while the Americans live for tomorrow, but he envied the ability of the Germans to enjoy themselves. He had attended a rally for Stephen A. Douglas in West Bend in a grove across the river and lamented, "I never realized one tenth of the enjoyment that the Germans do."

Those who came first were apt to think of themselves as the "Americans" and the Europeans as outsiders. Stereotypes formed quickly, with the Germans pictured as beer loving pluggers of emotional make-up with fine musical talent. The Yankees, on the other hand, were thought to be emotionally cold, narrow-minded, hardworking, and intelligent. During the Civil War the Germans were portrayed as evaders while the Yankees were the supporters. Germans retained close ties with their homeland and when news of the German victory over the French in 1871 reached West Bend there were wonderful celebrations in honor of the event.

Other differences were obvious, among them speech patterns. Germans went "by" someone's house instead of "to" it. "Ainah't" or "ainna" was used instead of "isn't it?" When something was gone it was "all," and they had to "go the hill up." If they meant to turn the corner they might "bend over" instead. They asked "Is this from before already?" When the Germans kept the sentence word order of their native tongue, a translation might read, "Throw me over the fence the horse some hay once." One student reported to his teacher that his sister "married herself yesterday." They "made the lamp out," and the Yankees had all sorts of sport with this misuse of English.

When James Finnegan, County Superintendent of Schools, deplored Germanic speech patterns, he used this example as an excuse given by a pupil to his teacher. "It was first nine o'clock when John spit me full, then he made we whole wet, pushed me to the sidewalk off, and then laughed me out."

Superstitions Abound

Another source of difference was the superstitions. While many of them were also common in much of German Wisconsin, others were peculiarly local. Many of the early ones dealt with death. If a corpse was kept over a Sunday before burial, there would be another death in the family within a year. If a bird flew against a window of a house, it presaged death, as did a smile on the face of a corpse. Other omens of death included a white dove on the roof of a house, a howling dog at exactly midnight, or rain on an open grave. It was bad luck to dream of a wedding, for someone close would die; there were reports of vases cracking at the same hour that a loved one far away actually died. The large number of deaths in early West Bend possibly fueled the superstitions.

Weddings were another source of superstitions. If a girl placed a piece of wedding cake under her pillow she would dream of her future husband. Happy omens included rain on the wedding day, a bride crying behind her veil, and the husband carrying the bride over the threshold.

One must never kill a fly at Christmas time, for a fly denoted prosperity for the coming year, nor open an umbrella in the house as it would bring bad luck. Spilled salt signified a quarrel and dropping scissors meant a sure disappointment. People wished on a star while others thought the animals actually talked to each other on Christmas eve, a notion brought directly from Europe. Stepping on a crack in the sidewalk presaged bad luck and one must never cut his hair in the month of March or he would have a headache.

There were also frequent Ben Franklin-type quotations. "The world is your cow but you'll have to do the milking" or "God sends every bird its food, but doesn't throw it into the nest." Thoughts such as these help to explain local attitudes toward welfare.

Germans Begin to Dominate

Hard working and hard playing, the Germans soon dominated the village by their sheer numbers. Most of the business transactions were in German, as were the church services. As their children began to master English, the older generation feared that the beauty of the German language would be lost along with the "priceless pearls of its songs and poetry, and the wealth of the German literature," so German was taught in the schools. Periodically the teaching of German was questioned, but it persisted and is still taught as a foreign language today. There was only one interruption, that during World War I.

When strangers came to West Bend in 1909 they noted that the city was clean and gave credit to the German extraction of the inhabitants. They were known as lovers of cleanliness and neatness. People trusted each other, also, and locks on doors were practically unknown.

After the first difficult year the immigrants ate well, and the different peoples learned to like each other's native dishes. There was meat, often three times a day, something unheard of in Europe, and white bread, a symbol of wealth which only the gentry could eat in the "old country." What would they think as the present generation turns to putting the darker flours and fiber back into bread today!

There was no typical menu, but it might include pork, the most common meat (usually fried), some type of potatoes, pickles, homemade bread (with the flour milled in the local mill), homemade cheese, a pie, possibly of fruit, and always tea or coffee. Usually there was freshly churned butter and fresh vegetables in season, or taken up from the cellar in the wintertime. They felt rich if they had a cellar full of beets, carrots, onions, potatoes, a jar filled with sauerkraut, together with a cow, some chickens and a pig. What more could they want, for they could survive on that very well.

And thus, for varying reasons, they came to West Bend, some for a short stay and others to make it their home, laying the foundations with their spirit for the future city as they resolved their differences.

CHAPTER 2

The Lynching

Probably nothing illustrates the bad feeling between the early Yankees and the immigrant Germans as well as an 1856 lynching, the second such in Wisconsin's history. Northerners tend to believe that all lynchings occurred in the South, but that was not the case.

Almost from the beginning there was friction between the two peoples. The early arrivals, the Yankees, felt superior to the "Dutchy" Germans who "talked funny," and hurled names at the slightest provocation, two of the more printable being "hideous monsters" and "religious fanatics."

Now for the lynching story. George DeBar was a nineteen year old Yankee (either physically or mentally incompetent or shiftless, depending upon whose version one wants to believe) who worked for the German immigrant John Muehr. DeBar always wore a white hat, the symbol of the hated Know Nothing Party, which was anti-foreigner. The two often clashed over politics and were known to have argued mightily.

One night DeBar left West Bend for the Muehr farm to collect some back wages due him. His former boss invited him in, and apparently started for the cellar to get something to drink when DeBar drew a knife, attacked his former employer, knifed Mrs. Muehr, who had come to her husband's assistance, and then killed the hired man ("slit his throat from ear to ear"). He set fire to the home to hide his crime and fled. Neither Muehr nor his wife were mortally wounded, however, and were able to escape the burning building and summon help. DeBar was hotly pursued, finally caught in Milwaukee, and brought back to the county jail in West Bend to await trial.

As the trial date approached, all bedlam began to break out. Germans "by the hundreds" congregated in the village. No "Yankee" could mistreat one of their own and get away with it! Trial Judge C. H. Larabee did not like the atmosphere and feared more bloodshed, so he called for the militia, the Ozaukee Rifles from Port Washington and the Milwaukee-Washington Artillery from Milwaukee. Both were composed primarily of Germans, and were soon commingling happily with local Germans in the hotels and saloons.

A Mob in Action

When the trial opened, DeBar pleaded "Not Guilty." While being transferred from the courthouse back to jail, surrounded by at least 50 of the militiamen, a local mob broke through the line effortlessly and grabbed the accused murderer while the supposed guards watched uselessly. Exactly what happened next is a matter of some dispute, but he apparently was first mercilessly stoned. Then the mob took turns stepping on him. Attaching a rope to his legs, he was dragged about a half mile toward the river and then hung head down from a maple tree by the grist mill. Not yet satisfied (mobs rarely are), they cut him down and began the torture all over again; they clubbed him and dragged him around by a rope. Several witnesses claimed he was thrown into the Milwaukee River. At any rate, he was retrieved and strung up again — this time by the neck.

When the furor died down, nineteen of the mob* were brought to trial for the hanging of DeBar. Among the lengthy number of witnesses against the men were those who swore DeBar was still breathing when he was finally hung. Nathan Emery described the agony he displayed when he was hung the second time. George Parker swore he was breathing and that his hands moved. People accused George Meyer of putting the rope around his neck. A physician, Dr. Wendell, testified that he was alive when finally strung up. Yet after all the witnesses had spoken, the predominantly German jury returned the verdict: NOT GUILTY! The indictment against them had read that they had "strangled him by the neck until dead," and the jury concluded that he was *dead before* the final hanging, so the accused 19 could not have been guilty as charged. The verdict was locally popular.

The anti-German feeling was a long time dying. As more German youngsters began to attend school and master the English language, as German and Yankee women shared each other's joys and sorrows and assisted each other at births and funerals, as the two groups of men began to help each other in a neighborly way, the feeling waned, and in time, disappeared. But the story of the hideous action of the early Germans remains as an example of early intolerance.

*The names of the accused were: Mathias Weiss, Joseph Immel, William Frick, Jacob Muehr, Frederick Knouth, George Weldt, Hubert Rack, Mathias Wilger, Ferdinand Born, Joseph Heckel, Peter Immel, George Mayer, John Burckhardt, John Muehr, Henry Herrin, Henry Bingenheimer, William Zimmerman, John Thoade, Anthony Rosekupf.

CHAPTER 3

The Fair

While West Bend may have been a tiny community, it possessed far-sighted people. One such group joined others in the county in 1858 to form the Agricultural Society whose purpose was to "promote and improve the condition of agriculture, horticulture and the mechanical, manufacturing, and household arts in Washington County," and it served to help unite the different nationalities. They organized a fair on Courthouse Square and what a spectacle it was! Farmers for miles around brought in their best cattle, driving them over the frozen ground, for the first fairs were held in December after all the fall work was com-

Cattle Parade — County Fair.

pleted. On the opening day of the fair the chief attraction was the livestock parade through the downtown region, and everyone who could possibly get to town watched and marvelled.

While most of the settlers used oxen, there was a growing interest in horses, so one of the most interesting events was the annual plowing contest. Horses had to plow a quarter acre at least four inches deep in under one and a half hours. Oxen were allowed two hours, for of course they were slower. During the first several years all the judges were local people and the losers often uttered loud cries of "prejudice." It was not until the 1880's that "experts" were imported to do the judging for all the events.

Early Exhibits

The prize record shows that the early exhibits included fat oxen, native cows, native bucks and Merino ewes, heifer calves, stallions, Black Hawk colts, Morgan colts, breeding mares, matched teams, mules and Duroc hogs. There were prizes for nearly every category of fruit and vegetable; women brought in their best knitting, art work, jelly and baked goods. Proud winners divided $81 in prize money that first year and the Agricultural Society reported a profit of $24.58.

Washington County Fair Grandstand — Horse racing in the early 1900's.

As the fair grew, the original site proved too small, but H. J. Weil came to the rescue by donating over twenty acres of land on the northeast side of the village, bounded on the west by North Street, on the east by Fair Street, a bit beyond Po Street on the north and by the alley behind Wilson Street on the south, the area approximately due west of where Fair Park School now stands. A half mile track was laid out for the popular horse races, sheds for cattle and horses and a hog and sheep building were erected, as well as an agriculture and horticulture building, a large display area for farm machinery, and stalls and booths. One of the most popular areas was the baseball diamond, for interest in that sport was growing. A large dining hall served the hungry and was both popular and profitable.

By 1911 farmers were arriving at the fair in the first automobiles and the city was filled with excitement. Observer Carl Quickert wrote in his weekly paper that he had witnessed "farmers, homely farm women, pretty country girls in the latest Parisian fashions, and young gentlemen in faultless dress suits." Early writers were not ones to mince words! He further noted all manner of poultry from pigeons to Toulouse geese. He exclaimed over the bronze and white turkeys, the African geese and the Chinese geese, and wondered if the latter had slanting eyes, but an inspection proved that NO! the eyes were as straight as those of the African geese. His practiced eye noted every detail and his words were often purple prose. For example, he spoke of the "glossy leaves of a mangle-wurtzel — the prototype of a Gothic cathedral."

The event that brought the people to the fairs in droves in 1911 was a balloon ascension. A year later the feature attraction was a "cross country flying machine flight" — from Cedarburg to West Bend in a 34 foot French biplane. The plane had room for one passenger and someone from the county was asked to take the first ride. H. P. Schmidt volunteered in advance, but letters of protest poured in from friends and relatives and he was "released" from his bargain for the sake of peace and safety. Truly the fairs were memorable events to be planned for days and talked about for weeks afterwards. It was the first event to bring the people of the county together on a social basis, and was held every year except 1860 and 1862, when interest in the Civil War overshadowed the fair.

But by 1920 the Fair began to have financial troubles. It managed to endure until 1937, when the creditors foreclosed after the fair and everything had to be sold to pay the debts. Rather than disband completely, Guido Schroeder, Chairman of the County Board, helped persuade the county to bail out the fair. After the sale, a small profit was turned over to the Washington County Board and the Agricultural Society was disbanded. The new plan was to concentrate on youth, and in 1938 the fair was reborn in Slinger, with a carnival-like atmosphere to draw the crowds and insure financial success. It continues to be successful as a Youth Fair to this day.

CHAPTER 4

The Civil War

As the Civil War approached, a great deal had happened in the United States since the founding of West Bend. There had been a successful war with Mexico; gold had been discovered in California and some fortune-seeking youths from West Bend, among them Tom Farmer, had gone west, only to return disillusioned. Edwin's discovery of an oil well in Pennsylvania promised to revolutionize American heating and lighting, and the local wives were discussing the possibility of acquiring one of the new-fangled kerosene lamps. Men spoke in awe of the Winchester repeating rifle, while farmers talked excitedly of a new machine called a binder that could save hours of toil. New music appeared and people were humming and singing the tunes of Stephen Foster ("My Darling Nellie Gray," "My Old Kentucky Home" etc.) and were about to make "The Battle Hymn of the Republic" and "Jingle Bells" their favorites.

But there was a disturbing cloud on the horizon, for Kansas had its civil war, a man named John Brown had been hung, and the southern states had seceded when word of the election of Abraham Lincoln reached the south.

A meteorite shower deposited the largest meteorites ever discovered in Wisconsin in an uninhabited spot near the village, and in 1858 a comet frightened many who felt the end of the world was at hand. It was seen for all of four minutes in West Bend.

West Bend was growing, though, and most of the news seemed remote from their mid-west isolation. By 1860, fifteen years after its founding, the village had 28 city blocks; Cedar Street was the main east-west street, and River Road (the current Main Street) was heavily travelled. The farmers were beginning to prosper and much of their money was spent in West Bend.

The most difficult of all nineteenth century subjects to discuss is that of the Civil War, for the West Bend history of that era is full of ambiguities. On the one hand are the patriotic meetings, beginning shortly after war was declared. Amid general enthusiasm for flag and country the local citizens resolved on April 23, 1861, in a meeting in the Court House: "Whereas our government has been attacked by rebels and traitors, and the Union thereby endangered, therefore let it be resolved that our sentiments are: "The Union forever, and if necessary our blood and treasure to sustain the conflict." G. H. Kleffler, B. S. Potter, W. Horton, W. P. Barnes and L. F. Frisby signed the resolution. After the unanimous agreement they gave the flag a tiger and a three times three and the old wooden walled Court House rang with their enthusiasm.

But the reality was that they were ready to give neither their blood nor their treasure. Washington County paid the highest bounties, $625 average, of any county in Wisconsin to keep their blood at home. West Bend contributed the least amount of money of any of the "major" cities in the county, so they were not willing to part with their treasure either. Hartford collected $41,000, Germantown $31,000, Kewaskum $21,000 and West Bend but $13,600 of which taxes paid $10,000 and the rest was raised privately.

West Bend simply did not like the war. This was, primarily, a German community and among the major reasons for coming to America was the desire to escape the continental wars and the mandatory every-man draft. Many of them were trying to make a living on marginal land, most were clearing land for the first time, and they said they needed every boy home to help. Never mind that other counties had the same problem and they had no trouble finding volunteers. That was a reason given in West Bend, at any rate. The parents were not about to send their boys to a shooting war in their adoptive country.

Then, too, most people were anti-Republican. In Wisconsin this brand new political party was composed largely of Whigs, who were noted for their anti-Catholic and anti-foreigner feelings, especially if the latter did not speak the English language. Lincoln was a Republican. A third reason was that West Bend simply was not interested in freeing the slaves. They could have cared less about that, most of them. (On the other hand, Barton was alleged to be one of the stations on the underground RR to help the escaped slaves flee to Canada.) When the report of thousands of free Negroes coming to the north reached West Bend an editor wrote: "We look upon this extensive immigration of these free blacks to mix with and compete with free white labor of the north as a most outrageous policy. The equality will be formed by reducing the whites to a level with the blacks. It must be stopped soon, if ever. The only way to stop these sons of Ham from over-running our state and disgracing our race is left with the Democrats. See that you vote for men who will free our state from the curse."

The issue for those who did support the war was preservation of the Union. They knew it had to be saved. But the anti-Negro feeling ran deep. Newspapers, letters, and memoirs are replete with expressions of that sentiment: "We believe in guaranteeing the protection of life and property, but why assist them? They are of an inferior and weak race."

West Bend and the Army

It is time to look at the record and see what West Bend actually *did* do. Shortly after the war was declared, Governor Randall appointed George H. Kleffler, a West Bend resident, Colonel of the 23rd Regiment of the Wisconsin State Militia. He had served previously, but had been removed for an unstated cause and was now recalled to duty.

At first, of course, there was no draft, for the army relied on volunteers. Because there is no breakdown by town as to the residence of the men, it would be difficult to know how many of the first group of Union Guards came from West Bend, but some number between 57 and 112 (figures differ) began training on the Court House Square. Mary Goetter, a pupil at the private German school in the Court House, recalled the men drilling on the grounds and sleeping in the tents pitched on the lawn. As they left for service, the boys were each given a warm blue flannel shirt and the women gave the entire group a handsome flag, valued at the time at over $40. The men took an oath to support the flag and bring it back unsullied or die in its defense. In truth, the flag was returned in fine condition after the war and it now rests in Madison. The incentive for enlistment for that first group had been $100 in gold and 160 acres of land, and the soldiers were promised that their land could not be sold for unpaid taxes nor would they owe any mortgage payments during their enlistment period. A volunteer's family would receive five dollars a month while he was gone.

On the day that they departed for Camp Randall in Madison, 45 wagons took them and their family and friends to Schlesingerville for a rousing sendoff. They entrained for Milwaukee, stayed there overnight, and then left for Madison the next day. After training for two months they enjoyed a brief furlough at home and left for the front, still not having been issued any rifles, indicative of the frightful unpreparedness of the north for the conflict.

The second group of young men to leave the area was the Corcoran Guards, composed of 75 "mostly Irishmen" who left for Madison in January of 1862. The third group was the 95 "mostly German" Washington County Rifles, whose leader was Captain Jacob E. McMann, editor of the West Bend *Post*. In his absence his wife managed the newspaper. One must remember that anyone who could find enough recruits to serve under him could be an officer. Jacob Heipp served as First Lieutenant and Charles Ottile Second Lieutenant and formed Company G of the 26th Wisconsin Regiment. Hartford, which had raised a considerable number of men, asked to join the group, but West Bend declined their offer, unless they all wanted to be privates, an offer that Hartford in turn declined.

Six months later Captain McCann wrote: "Six months ago we raised a company of brave and sturdy men and joined the 26th Regiment bound to fight, bleed and die in defense of that glorious Constitution bequested to us by our forefathers. But alas! How soon was our youthful ardor dampened under the influence of a Southern clime, hard crackers, and Mother Earth for a pillow. All our ambition . . . all our eagerness and anticipation of a glorious death on the battlefield soon vanished and after a protracted illness we turned our faces homeward." Enlistment periods were short then, usually for a period of three months, and it was true that many of that first group served out their brief terms and returned home.

West Bend Resists the Draft

It was possible to legally pay a substitute $300 and local boys were urged in the pages of the newspaper to bring the money with them when they came to register "for there would be no opportunity to go after it." West Bend helped to raise money to keep the local boys at home. One notice in the local paper read: "Wanted! five able bodied men for substitutes. Forward your name to the West Bend Draft Agency and state your terms. The amount agreed upon to be paid in gold." A typical 1862 newspaper item read: "Lyman Root, a drafted man, procured a substitute. Price $150." Inasmuch as men were credited in the draft from the place of enlistment and not from their place of residence young fortune seekers drifted around to find the place with the highest bounty. West Bend proved to be that place; therefore West Bend was the only town in the county to fill its quotas. At first, too, the immigrants claimed that they were not yet citizens, but inasmuch as Wisconsin permitted them to vote if they had started their citizenship proceedings, this reason did not hold. So the immigrants simply failed to begin their citizenship requirements. After 1864, they were supposed to prove they were really conscientious objectors, a more difficult task, but it was still legal to pay a substitute. Many were desperate and paid $1000 to escape and those who were paid the most usually served the least. Mary Goetter told of one young man who was paid $2000 to serve for another, but by the time he reached Milwaukee to start his enlistment the war was over.

It was the draft that was so unpopular in West Bend, but this was equally true of the whole county, for Washington County had the lowest proportion of volunteers of any county in the state. Therefore it received the highest quota in the 1862 draft, and it was highly unpopular. One of the first troubles with the draft was the problem of obtaining a proper draft list. Men who were over 25 claimed they were over 35 so they would not have to go, and many who were under 21 claimed they were 19 and thus exempt. Sons of widowed or aged parents were legally exempt.

Whether or not any West Bend people were responsible, there was even a riot in the town. On November 16, 1862, the second day of the drafting process, a mob alleged to be "primarily German," and inflamed by an angry man from Trenton, threatened E. Gilson, the Draft Commissioner. He picked up his precious papers and fled down the hill from the Court House with the mob in pursuit. When he dashed into the comparative safety of the law office of Frisby and Weil, Frisby, who had himself been drafted, came out to soothe the mob, giving Gilson enough time to flee out the back door and make his way to Milwaukee where he spread the alarm of a riot. Inasmuch as Port Washington* had a dandy riot just previously, the state government took no chances and dispatched six companies of soldiers to the village so the draft then proceeded in orderly fashion. A total of 758 names were drawn, "mostly Germans," and it was they who were so incensed. That night an angry mob, possibly the same people, marched down the main street to the store of H. Trakot, who had made known his belief in the abolition of the slaves, and demanded drinks. When they were not forthcoming, the mob broke his store windows with rocks. "Just as California has seen the inherent danger in the German immigrant and excluded them from the voting process, so should Wisconsin" (exclude the

*(If it is any consolation, the draft riots were worse in neighboring and rival Port Washington. There they wrecked homes, threw people down the Court House steps, loaded the cannon and declared they were ready for the army! Then followed a day of imbibing and when the army came they were so inebriated that they could do nothing but allow themselves to be peacefully arrested, 120 of them.)

black). "Iowa voted to put blacks on an equal basis, so let's send them the blacks from Wisconsin." Those were the local sentiments. Many of these protestors were Copperheads who urged that the war end by compromise to save the Union, stop the fighting and bring the boys home. "Slavery was a necessary evil, not a crime. The crime was that Africans were in the country in the first place!"

When it comes to the names of the boys who either volunteered or were drafted, there is no complete record. In various places one finds a name here or a list there and from those oddments we learn that Thomas Farmer, W. Dennison, Isaiah Culver, Oscar Rusco, Wm. Ducher, W. Aiken and Wm. Lowe were "early enlistees." A list of commissioned officers includes Isaiah Culver and Thomas Farmer as 1st Lieutenants; Andrew Fullerton, Captain; Jacob McMann, Captain; Jacob Heipp, 1st Lieutenant (out in '62 with McMann); John Jones and Charles Lemke, 2nd Lieutenants; Wm. Norton, 2nd Lieutenant (dismissed); and Charles Ottille, 1st Assistant Surgeon.

Another list gives the following names from the Union Guards as killed in battle or dead of wounds: Corporal Emery Smith and Privates Edwin Frisby, Wm. Hockman, Mathias Lampert, Wellington Stannard, Chris Schmidt, Nicholas Harris, Terry Goldman and John Holt. Two boys died in the infamous Andersonville prison camp: David Waller and Moses Whalen. All may not have been from the village.

From the Washington County Rifles Jacob Dixheimer, George Rusco, John Schmidt, Ermerson Smith, Peter Stoffel and Richard Daily were killed; Christian Frenz and Peter Ruplinger were listed as wounded. A complete accounting awaits a historian with unlimited time to put it all together.

Village Life During the War

In the meantime the village of 800 population suffered comparatively little. Farmers prospered and brought their business to town. Merchants shared in that prosperity and those who repaired machinery made a small fortune. Labor's wages rose but slowly, out of keeping with the prosperity, but as the number of job openings increased, it became more difficult to recruit soldiers. The ladies were faithful to their knitting of sox and mittens; they rolled bandages, and made necessity bags. Mary Goetter's account is one of the few extant, and she recalls that coffee reached a dollar a pound which nobody could afford, so they roasted barley and called it "Lincoln's coffee." Women also collected clothing and food for the families of the soldiers; the winter of '63-64 was a terrible one when "it was dreadful to be poor."

The worst burden was borne by the families of the soldiers, for it was not common for the women to leave the home to work, and the federal allotment of five dollars a month was insufficient. Some suffered; others were helped by family, friends or charity.

In addition, there were deserters. One day a Mr. McDonald was visited by three men who had come to capture his workman, Henry Allen, an alleged deserter. McDonald took his pitchfork to the agents and they fled.

For those who did serve, being from Wisconsin was a bit of advantage at first, for the state sent men with the various regiments to look after their health, and to provide such amenities as fruit and tobacco. But, of course, the medical trials were grievous, and the boys wrote home about the rampant diarrhea which could become a killer. Maggots infected their wounds; infection was rife. Influenza killed men, too, and amputations were carried out wholesale in lieu of other treatment, often without benefit of any anesthesia, so the shocks were great. One local resident, Matthew Regner, received a gun shot wound in the leg at the battle of Hatcher's Run in January, 1865. The surgeons amputated his left leg so maladroitly that a second operation was necessary, nearly costing him his life.

When news of the medical troubles reached West Bend the paper began to advertise patent medicines to take to the front. "Don't trust the army surgeon. Take along Holloway's pills and ointment." Other advertised cures were for fatal fevers, sores, dysentery, etc. Possibly the worst disaster of all was to be a prisoner in a southern camp, for which there was no cure available.

Several soldiers brought back souvenirs. Adolph Lemke, for instance, was the proud possessor of an order signed by General Lee himself. He was there at the surrender and when the Union army entered Petersburg they took everything they could get their hands on as souvenirs.

At war's end (1865) West Bend had a population of 941, and soon it was impossible to rent a house, for there were none vacant. Picket fences now enclosed most residences. Lots were only forty feet wide but many owned more than one, and huge gardens were everywhere. Most families now owned a horse in addition to their cow, pig or sheep, and chickens, so there were outbuildings on each piece of property. People felt that civilization had indeed arrived, for the last bear on the streets of the city had been reported in 1862. The biggest need was for a train to move supplies, and agitation to persuade one to build tracks to the village had already begun.

Later Celebrations

When the first Memorial Day was celebrated in West Bend in 1880 the Andrew Fullerton Post #193, the first Veteran's organization in the county, gathered in the Court House Square under their Captain, George W. Jones, and Orderly Andrew Schmidt. From there they were led by the Geier band and accompanied by three young ladies (Tenie Everly, Hattie Miller and Ada Farmer) carrying wreaths, marched to the cemetery to lay the wreaths on the "graves of the six heroes." That seems to be the only record of the number who lost their lives in the conflict from West Bend. (When the Soldiers' Memorial at the Court House was prepared, no one could find an accurate Civil War list.) After the appropriate ceremonies the veterans were treated to a big dinner in Schlitz Park.

And those who did serve and lived to return were proud of their service record in defense of their country. Mrs. Ethel Weiss Gill wrote of the pride of her grandfather when he marched in later Memorial Day parades, flag held high — the flag they had fought so hard to retain.

By 1885 the paper reported that 25 veterans lived in West Bend. Their biggest concern was with the indigent veterans among them, and by 1888 they were instrumental in securing awards of from four to eight dollars a month pensions for their comrades, which of course was immediately insufficient. That was the same year that the locally hated war taxes were removed.

In 1911 the Jubilee Celebration was memorable, for Billy Mitchell, who would gain fame in the next war, played drums in the city band under Commander Heipp. Mrs. C. C. Henry sang patriotic songs from the Civil War, "Tenting Tonight on the Old Camp Ground" and "Tramp, Tramp, Tramp the Boys Are Marching"

So ends the Civil War Story. Men from West Bend served in every major campaign from Bull Run through Gettysburg and the infamous march of Sherman from Atlanta to the sea. They fought in Kansas and Kentucky and Tennessee. And six graves in the Union Cemetery are the sole remaining testimony in West Bend of man's inability to solve his problems peaceably — the country's one rebellion — the Civil War.

West Bend High School Light Brigade —1871.

SECTION III

GOVERNMENT AND POLITICS

CHAPTER 1

West Bend City Government

Little of substance is known of the government of the earliest years of West Bend. Carl Quickert stated it well when he wrote: "Few of the old settlers who made local history were inclined to write it down. This is the general rule for all who make history and the historian of the later generation is puzzled how to fill the many gaps and not use his fancy. This is why county histories appear so incoherent, not to say anything of the errors which are naturally inherent in history."

Yet there are remnants that tell us a bit about this wee settlement clustered along River Road and a side street or two to the west. The first official record shows that a town meeting was held on April 7, 1846, very soon after the first houses were built, in the home of Isaac Verbeck (on the present Badger School grounds). Because the political units as we know them were not yet established, the town embraced not only West Bend but also Barton, Farmington, Kewaskum, and Trenton.

Barton Salisbury of Barton was elected Chairman, Verbeck, Secretary, and M. A. T. Farmer, Treasurer. The reader will remember Verbeck and Farmer as the two earliest residents of West Bend. Although no poll lists remain, at least 30 voters were present, most of whom could neither read nor write. Nor do any minutes remain of that first meeting; only the memory of one who had been there was recorded for posterity years after the meeting. The recollection was that "some kitchen utensil" from Verbeck's kitchen, probably a coffee pot or candle box, was used to collect the ballots.

George Treveranus
First Village Clerk, 1868.

Before the village was incorporated one civic event aroused the citizenry. When the County Board in 1853 voted to change the name of West Bend to the fancier one of Lamartine City to honor the first great French poet and historian, the citizens were in an uproar. They quickly circulated a petition against the change and within 18 hours the name reverted to the people's choice — West Bend.

When the village was incorporated 22 years later, at a morning meeting held in the village school on April 7, 1868, the male citizens elected Schoolmaster Frederick Regenfuss as clerk of the election. The first Village Board was composed of President Simon Hornstein and board members John Shelley, B. S. Potter and Ernst Lemke. In addition Clerk H. G. Treviranus, Marshall Charles F. Haas and Justices of the Peace H. J. Weil and F. H. Haas served on that first Board. In just three weeks the officials began to enact needed legislation, and the very first ordinance dealt with — pigs! NO swine were to be permitted to run at large in the streets and alleys. The second ordinance prohibited citizens from leaving manure, barrels, casks or boxes on 5th and 6th Streets.

Because the first ordinance regarding the pigs had little effect, the Marshall was then empowered to restrain any hogs at large and sell them for the costs and charges. It would be nice

Potter and Miller Store, west side of Main Street between Hickory and Elm — 1870. Washington House at extreme right. Note the wooden sidewalks.

to know if this were actually done, but at least people were beginning to take an elementary interest in sanitation. Bathing habits were different then, too, and many people preferred to use the river in the summertime. Complaints arose as to the impropriety of this, so the Milwaukee River and the Mill Race were declared off limits for bathing between 6 A.M. and 8 P.M. Presumably the "sight seers" were at home early in the morning and later in the evening. Thus we see that the first concerns of the village fathers relate to conditions that no longer exist.

Sewage was a perpetual problem. At first people just pitched everything into the streets, the river, or the unused lots. To remedy matters in the central part of town a wooden sewer was constructed to carry sewage down Mill Street to the River. One day in 1878 the wooden contraption collapsed in front of the Washington House and the stench nearly drove everyone away from the entire area. When it was pointed out that disease might follow, the primitive sanitary system was eventually repaired.

Incidentally, the aforementioned Mill Street, the shortest street in town, has been the site of countless businesses. Running from Main Street to Mill Race it has been the site of a roller mill (flour), the American Hotel, a pumping station, powerhouse for village lights, a sawmill, and a big barn where farmers left their horses when doing business in town overnight.

One of the positions in town that was a source of personal pride was that of town marshall, the forerunner of a police force. In 1879 the Council authorized the tailoring of a suit to fit Marshall Kuester with "brass buttons all buttoned down before." The gentleman was so excited when it arrived that he couldn't sleep and paraded all over town showing it off.

In 1880 the town was becoming concerned over its property taxes, which had risen to a bit over $5000; simultaneously they were becoming conscious of the need for education, and $2200 of that sum was for education. John Reiss was now the President and F. H. Haase, John Thielges, George Leisgang and Matt Regner were trustees. Adolph Arzbacher served as clerk, Jacob Herdt as Treasurer, John Knippel as Assessor, John Eckstein and L. Neuberg as Justices of the Peace, John Kuester as Marshall, and John Burckhardt and Jacob Heipp as Constables. One is struck by the large number (proportionately) of peace-keeping officers.

West Bend Becomes a City

The next big step forward for West Bend was to become incorporated as a city on March 19, 1885, but the affair was treated with little fanfare and according to the newspapers there was almost a "so what?" attitude. John Potter was the first Mayor; George Treviranus, Clerk; John Knippel, Assessor; George Leisgang, Treasurer; John Stein, Marshall; Lyle Emery, Constable; A. Fuge, Justice of the Peace; S. S. Barney, First Ward Supervisor; Joseph Ott, Second Ward Supervisor; and Matt Regner, August Bastian, Jacob Fink and Henry Lemke, Aldermen.

In 1882 the city had 238 families with 1409 people, of which 195 families were German and the rest English, American, Irish, French and Bohemian; half were over 15 and 209 belonged to no church. One fifth of the families had six or more children and one had 18.

The Issue of Sidewalks

The lack of sidewalks posed a problem for the town. The mud was so deep that it could pull a man's boots off when the snow melted in the spring. Ladies were afraid to walk "down" town, and the local editor railed at the officials' lack of action. Some of the early storekeepers erected crude wooden sidewalks in front of their stores to attract customers, but they were rare. Finally the council authorized the goodly sum of $92.50 for 4000 feet of wooden walkway. When it was completed it became a fine place on which to drive horses so an ordinance had to prohibit that, as well as to forbid anyone to tie horses to the structure. The council further decreed that no one was to permit horses or mules to run loose in the streets as it was "dangerous to life and limb." Those sidewalks were three feet higher on the west side of Main Street than on the east, a situation not remedied until city gas mains were installed.

Sidewalks were a perpetual topic for years. By 1886 a new one had been erected down town that was wide enough for "two couples to pass without compelling the gentlemen escorts to step behind the ladies." By 1900, too, the city had a new dam to replace the early inadequate stone and brush one.

At the turn of the century sidewalks were still an issue. The old three foot wide ones had "every other nail gone" and "other nails popped up to catch the unwary." But the question was not whether to have new ones built — the issue now was which material to use — cement or planks. The *NEWS* editorialized that at the risk of making the lumber companies angry, there could be no more plank ones built, for cement would outlast a "dozen plank walks." There was also the burning question of whether the city or property owner should bear the expense. "The time will come when property owners will be compelled to build walks and keep others in repair at their own expense."

The controversy seemed endless. As soon as cement was selected for the material, people began to complain that sidewalks would interfere with their terraces and front steps. And where should the line be established? The Council decided that if the sidewalks already installed were straight, then their center line should become the center line for all future constructions.

The sidewalk isssue never really died, for in 1926 the *WEST BEND NEWS* editor asked "Is there anything between heaven and earth capable of moving the powers that be to build a sidewalk between the city and Barton?" They were now "farther apart" than 40 years ago; Barton had built its share to the island, and this had prodded West Bend to put down some gravel to meet it, but a new highway had destroyed that. "The merchants want more trade, yet they won't facilitate it" moaned the editor. On that issue at least, history has a way of repeating itself. On the sidewalk issue, again, more recently the City Council and Mayor clashed with the homeowners over the issue of extending sidewalks to every street in the newer subdivisions; this time the citizens lost the round.

The Issue of a City Hall

It is a wonder that as many early records are left to us as we have, for there was no special building to house the city records or to provide a meeting place for the Council. Someone always had to keep the records in his home. In the 1870's Lawyer Frisby let the officers use his building, at times they rented space elsewhere and on several occasions they held meetings in Peter Boden's tavern. Then after the need for a city building was clearly established, there was no action by the City Council.

Finally in 1893 the village fathers responded to local pressure and paid $600 for two city lots for a future building and allotted a like sum for the building itself. But nothing further happened. Another six years passed while many citizens became incensed and when it was evident that nothing further would be done, the aroused citizenry circulated a petition requesting a special election to vote on a city hall. Two months later alderman Mayer read into the minutes an ordinance authorizing a contract

The West Bend City Hall as it appears today.

for up to $10,000, with the issuance of city bonds at 5%. It was to be decided by a referendum.

Another two months passed while the pros and cons organized forces for the special election. On the night of the voting, the progressive forces in town claimed victory, 131-122. Almost at once there was official action. The bond issue passed, the low bidder received the contract for $10,420, and work began in early 1900. Local concerns received most of the contracts; A. C. Fuge installed the cast iron furnace, A. Althaus supplied the paint. In the late winter of 1901 the electricity was installed and by March the Council was ready for its first meeting in its new home. In the cornerstone of the building were placed the original petition for the city hall with its 101 signatures, all the proceedings of the City Council in reference to the building, a list of the current city officials, a copy of the local newspaper, and the last pamphlet of the proceedings of the County Board of Supervisors.

But in one respect the conservatives had the last word, for Mayor Franckenberg was defeated by Joseph Ott, and Aldermen Warnkey, Wendleborn, and Storck all lost the spring election because they had favored the building. Only Aldermen Meyer and Kaempfer weathered the storm in their wards, but the city government did have a home at last.

City Growth

In the 1890's West Bend was struggling for an identity. By 1893 it had finally outdistanced Barton in population; this had been a particularly sore spot with many. When the city fathers ballyhooed the town they told of the well chosen site on both sides of the river so that people could dump their garbage and the river would carry it away, while the air from the river helped purify the city! Industry boomed and Silberzahn employed 20 men making farm equipment, Schmidt had 40 workers on their wagons, H. Krieger used 40 men to make harnesses and other leather goods, P. W. Harns was becoming noted for his marble and granite works and hired between 12 and 20 men, while 21 people made bottle covers of straw, and the brewery employed 40. Why didn't the city grow faster, though, many wondered.

Reading the old city minutes and/or the newspaper accounts of them, one is struck forcibly by the eternal dispute between those who wish to keep things as they are and those who wish to progress. At one time Henry Rolfs, for instance, was accused by his political opponents of favoring the following "frivolous" items: paving Main Street, constructing a city water works instead of the continued use of private wells, and of wanting electric cars on Main Street. All of his proposals were rejected, but eventually progressive forces seem to win, after months or years of demonstrated need.

City Water System

When it came to the issue of the city water system, the script reads much like that for the city hall. The need for a public water works had been evident for years. The State Board of Health urged that one be installed; the local Board of Health had tried for years to convince the Council that the private wells and privies were a continual health hazard. As early as 1887 the issue became devisive, and Mayor Potter resigned because he felt that the Council was not meeting the needs of the community, a city water system. An eyewitness reported that the night the mayor resigned he put on his overshoes and vanished. Several councilmen did likewise. One of them tried to move to adjourn, but by then there was no one left to second it! The marshall put out the lights and "calm settled over the place where a few minutes before there had been strife. The wind swept around the corner of the building moaning 'water power, water power, water power'." It must have been a grand row.

The issue simmered for twenty more years before it came to a public vote in 1907. Then the First Ward approved the system by 143-71, while the Second Ward's approval barely squeaked by, 116-112. But again — nothing happened. By September the disappointed citizens resorted to another petition to promote action. So ANOTHER vote was authorized to be sure that that was what the people wanted. The vote in the First Ward was now 141 to 7 and the Second Ward approved 111 to 35, which was clearly a mandate. Success at last, but only after the people took the initiative. The waterworks and sewerage treatment plants were built in 1908 while Mayor Gray served the city. Mr. W. G. Kirschoffer superintended the construction.

When the water system was completed each resident desiring the service was asked to send in $10 and state the purposes for which he intended to use the water. This was to prevent "unnecessary waste," for if one wanted the city water for the sole purpose of fire protection, there would be no further charge other than the charge for installation. So people kept their private wells and back door privies for years. Because the city did not know how much water would be used, residents were requested to stop any sprinkling if there were a fire, and someone was empowered to shut off the public drinking fountains, such measures to take place immediately and for two hours after the fire to allow the water supply to replenish itself. When the drivers of horses took to hitching their horses to the convenient hydrants, they were ordered to desist or risk a fine of up to ten dollars.

The first two wells were located near the City Hall and the old high school respectively. When sand entered the pipes at the one near the City Hall, it was abandoned. F. Nehrbass was the first local water superintendent, following a Mr. Kohl from Chicago. A state water inspector declared the water in West Bend as pure as any in the state, but the use by private citizens was slow. By 1913 there were only 65 domestic users, as most people clung to their private wells to save money.

While the city water was now pure enough, the sewage system was old fashioned and raw sewage was still running into the river. The odors were disagreeable, especially in the summer; people complained and some threatened to move out. To alleviate the problem, but not solve it, some septic tanks were installed to take the sewage before it drained into the river. This went on for years until by the 1930's the State Board of Health became alarmed. Thirty-six interceptor mains were therefore laid, beginning in 1935, which separated the liquid from the solid waste; a plant was built to add chlorine, heat the material to a temperature of 112 degrees, screen the solid material, and then send the waste into the river. An earlier health ordinance (1906) attempted to further improve the city's health by passing an anti-spitting ordinance. Would that it were enforced today!

Other Legislation

As always with governmental bodies, the question of the morals of its young arose. The city fathers were appalled in 1898 at the number of young boys smoking openly. The number of young drinkers increased yearly, too, so the saloon keepers were made liable for prosecution if they sold liquor to minors or let them play billiards, pool, or cards in their establishment. As is true of all such laws, the effect was minimal. Boys were accused of wantonly destroying, maiming, or killing insect destroying birds, or their nests or eggs, and if found guilty could be fined up to $15.00.

Other interesting legislation in the first years of the twentieth century involved a public testing of Standard Oil products against those of a competing Pennsylvania product and Standard Oil won. In 1910 the Council reminded couples that if they chose to marry out of the state they had to report it within ten days or face a 30 to 60 day jail sentence and a $20 to $300 fine, according to state law, and the city intended to enforce it to the letter. Even love was not immune from an ordinance.

Streets and Roads

Streets and roads continued to plague the officials. Since before the Civil War people had had the option of either paying a road tax or working on the road in front of their property for two days a year. Most chose the latter and it does not take too much imagination to envision driving on a road where some people kept the road in as good repair as the dirt would permit, while others worked so minimally that there were deep ruts at best, or impassible roads, at worst. The move to have the public maintain the roads in West Bend was strong, for "half the money spent on public roads was thrown away. No business enterprises could last a year with such fearful waste."

The first such road that involved the city (other than the

Oiling the West Bend Streets. Left to right, Fritz Heipp, unknown, Mr. Schachelmeir, John Lohr.

Street Maintenance, 1901. Gust Burckhardt, Sr., and Louis Duernberger.

city streets, that is) was the road from the County Asylum to the Woolen Mills on what is now Highway 33 east of town. The need was so great that farmers and businessmen donated money in 1913 for the project, hills were lowered, stone was crushed, and the road was graded. It took John Geib, N. N. Emery and P. Gutschenritter to start the proceedings for which the state government paid more than $500 out of the $2685.

Yearly the issue of paving the city streets arose. A new state law in 1913 permitted state aid for cities under 5,000 population, so the topic was hotter than ever. Tempers flew. It cost $1,000 a year to sprinkle the streets in the summer to try to keep some of the dust down some of the time, and to constantly repair the ruts and holes. The state would ante $3,000 and the county a like sum if the City Council would part with the third share. The street was paved. However, an unexpected problem arose when the horses, who were unused to smooth surfaces, kept slipping.

Another situation involving city government was the physical state of the public schools. The City Clerk, F. W. Bucklin, appeared before the City Council to urge the correction of the deplorable conditions, for students were freezing in the winter and there was as yet no sanitary plumbing. With the facts before them, the Council voted "Aye."

Along with the street issue, mention ought to be made of

street cleaner Bill (William) May and his father Adam May. The senior May pushed an old fashioned wagon cart for 33 years, cleaning the city's streets, while the son worked for 24 years at the same trade, calling his cart a trolley car. He would start at 3 A.M. and finish about 1 P.M.

River Restoration

Because of the current interest in restoring the river area and renovating the downtown area, it is rather intriguing to learn that in the 1920's big plans were made for just such action. Plans were printed in the papers to show how the natural resource should be renovated. Manure was still being dumped along and into the river, and a junk dealer was located there amid the debris, the "ideal spot for such a business," all to the shame of the city. The Commercial Club also tried to persuade the city to remove all the ugly lights and other poles from the downtown area, build a sidewalk to Barton, and install city lighting in every block, along with a retaining wall along the river, and the planting of wild flowers along the sides to beautify the area. Those flowers have yet to be planted more than a half century later. The mills of the gods grind exceedingly slowly.

In 1920 the citizens made elaborate plans for a memorial encompassing an entire city block which included the site of the City Hall, but the idea was lost along the way, for a reason that the author cannot fully deduce. Snow removal remained a burning issue over the years. When the snow melted the city was found to be full of debris and smelled terrible and looked worse. Eventually both snow removal and garbage collections were approved after interested local groups such as the Woman's Club pressed the issue.

Over the years the Council authorized cleanup and paint up campaigns to beautify the city. As late as 1916 the city had to enact a law to fine people for letting the chickens run loose. "We have outgrown the village stage long ago and cannot allow chickens to promenade through the streets" agreed the editor.

Housing was scarce, for the burgeoning industries needed more and more workers and there was no place for them to live. But many of the citizens liked the city just the way it was and had no desire to see it grow. When 28 houses were built in 1919 it was referred to as but a "drop in the bucket" by the industrialists, but referred to as a step in the wrong direction of growth by some.

But growth is inevitable and cannot be denied, so periodically there have been new subdivisions. In 1920 Highland (from Fourth Avenue to Oak Street to Sycamore) had 107 lots to sell to become the "finest residential section of the city." Three years later Walomar subdivision (on land previously owned by Walter Ottmer) from Chestnut to Oak had 25 lots to sell along Eighth Avenue, a 100 foot wide street with a park in the middle. In 1945 ground was broken for Decorah Lawns on what had been Franz Eder's 147 acres to absorb the returning veterans and newcomers to work in the rapidly growing industries. The city has continued to add others until it now encompasses 5670 acres, or about eight times the original plat, and the government has grown proportionately.

The following is a list of the mayors who have served the city of West Bend:

John Potter, Jr. 1885-1886
Henry Lemke 1886-1887
Barnabas S. Potter 1887
Patrick O'Meara 1887-1888 1894-1896
Charles E. Miller 1888-1894
Joseph Ott 1896-1899 1901-1906
Ernest Franckenberg 1899-1901
Albert Gray 1906-1908
Andrew Pick 1908-1910
William G. Bratz 1910-1916
Joseph F. Huber 1916-1920
Frank Schoenbeck 1920-1926
Henry O. Regner 1926-1930
Joseph M. Knippel 1930-1940
Clyde J. Schloemer 1940-1948
Michael Gehl 1948-1954
Walter Schmidt 1954-1960
Paul Henke 1960-1966
Ralph Schoenhaar 1966-1978
Jack Pick 1978-

CHAPTER 2

West Bend Politics

Closely coupled with the subject of city government is that of politics, and that of West Bend has undergone a metamorphosis. It was a solidly Democratic community at the outset, and West Bend's very first votes in a national election went to Lewis Cass in 1848 as opposed to the winner, Zachary Taylor. The reason for the preference may have been Cass's belief in squatter sovereignty. Interestingly, the village never did have Free Soilers, as did its Yankee neighbor, Hartford, for the communities developed in vastly different ways after the Yankees left West Bend to be replaced by the Germans, while Hartford remained predominately Yankee. This was also the period of very unsavory Wisconsin state politics, with fraud and bribery being the order of the day, but no evidence is visible that those twin evils existed here except for the flap over the county seat.

West Bend remained firmly in the Democratic camp for 50 years, and someone should do a complete political analysis of the preference. West Benders never favored the politics of Abraham Lincoln and the paper had almost vitriolic language about him. Why? He favored Negro sufferage, and the locals voted by a whopping 60% against the extension of the vote to blacks. This is reminiscent of their earlier stand on the same issue at the time of the adoption of the Wisconsin Constitution, although the percentage against the basic right was considerably less in 1860 than it had been earlier.

Grant drew their ire in 1868 (they never liked military men, probably a holdover from their German antipathies), and by a 3-1 majority opted for Tilden over Hayes in the infamous disputed election of 1876. When the eventual winner, Hayes, came to Milwaukee to speak, the local paper warned that the readers might "better give money to the Yellow Fever fund" than to spend it on going to hear that "fraud." The people preferred Tilden because he promised to "sound the death knoll for military rule in the South," a sore point in West Bend. Researchers must be careful, though, for editors speak their own mind and do not necessarily reflect the feelings of many of their readers, although the vote totals bear out the editor's feelings at this time.

Young people were actively involved in politics in the nineteenth century, probably reflecting their parents' feelings. In 1881, for example, about 100 of them carried pumpkin heads lettered BLAINE in a parade down Main Street, stopping every few minutes to cheer for Cleveland. Political parades and celebrations were common occurences at that time.

When Garfield was assassinated in 1881, the village observed his funeral with the firing of a cannon every half hour from 6 A.M. until the procession to Schlitz Hall in the mid-afternoon. Luchnow's band played a dirge, and such notables as S. S. Barney, Mr. Frisby, P. O'Meara, Professor Regenfuss, etc. orated on the virtues of the slain man. When Grant died in 1885, all the business places closed and the GAR conducted a memorial ritual.

Ferdinand Kuechenmeister, father of G. A. Kuechenmeister, wearing Harrison Campaign Hat — 1888.

When it appeared imminent that the voters might switch parties, the editor of the *Democrat* threatened to print the names of the defectors if they could be made known to him. At the time the voters of the city finally backed a winner, Grover Cleveland, they celebrated his March 1885 inauguration with a torchlight parade and a huge bonfire, at which Mayor Miller spoke in German and P. O'Meara addressed the crowd in English. It had been a long wait to get a candidate of their choice in the President's chair.

1890 local Democrats had their headquarters in Lemke's

Hall and on the twelfth of November they led a procession down Main Street. Participating were the West Bend City Band, Fire Marshall Peter Boden, 150 citizens with torches and another 150 with brooms, a carriage containing the oldest Democrats, Math Regner, Math Haas, George Ott and John Knippel, and that grand old lady, one of the earliest founders of the village, Grandma Wightman, now infirm but still politically active. A cannon was fired, bonfires were lit, and every time the name of Grover Cleveland was mentioned in a speech the citizens cheered, making "considerable racket."

Politics could always raise an argument and stories of wild disputes were rife. In 1895, for example, an argument in Ziegler's saloon sent stones, knives and bottles flying. Several were arrested and jailed but all agreed it was a grand row!

West Bend Becomes Republican

By 1900 the town began to change its political affections, and the *Democrat* supported the Republican William McKinley, crowing, "Where are the Democrats now?" Then they listed the advantages of voting for McKinley, all of them being financial: first, there was a government surplus (how one's thoughts on the propriety of a surplus changed!); both farm and business incomes were up, as were wages; the number of savings banks deposits had increased in the years of McKinley's first term. The election, however, was a close one, for the first time in the city, with Bryan receiving 203 ballots to McKinley's 182. When the winner McKinley was assassinated, the entire populace mourned, regardless of their political affiliation. A civic memorial service was held in Moser's Hall at which Professor Keeley called the deceased a "wise and just man"; Reverend A. C. Keyser of the German Methodist church used the occasion to show how the absence of fear of the Lord led to the assassination; P. O'Meara, who always orated on momentous occasions, spoke primarily to the youth, urging them to visit other countries so that they would then come to appreciate their own more. The main address (people still were addicted to long services and many speakers) was delivered by Congressman Barney who counted McKinley a personal friend, and felt that his death had brought the people closer together. Not all the people of West Bend were together, though, for both Holy Angels and St. John's Lutheran church held their own private memorial services.

A genuine favorite of the city voters was always Robert LaFollette, and when he came to town in the fall of 1900 an immense crowd gathered at the depot to welcome him, and followed on to Moser's Hall to cheer his every pronouncement wildly. The memory of his visit was discussed for years, with an "I was there when" feeling lingering. That fall was a great one for West Bend anyway, as the football team trounced Hartford 21-0, a cause for wholesale rejoicing then.

In 1912 a third party made its appearance in West Bend, Local #1 of the Socialist Party. They campaigned vigorously locally on the platform that the Republicans never kept their promises and the Democrats stood for both free trade and free silver, neither of which had worked in either Mexico or England, so the only logical choice, therefore, was Socialism. They did not do well at the polls. All the county officers except sheriff were Democratic, however.

West Bend favored the Progressive Party several times, and in 1902 the West Bend editor believed that the Republicans were tired of trying to beat a Progressive at the state level, and stayed away from the polls. By the 1920's the switch from the Democrats was such that it was 5 to 2 for Coolidge, and the city celebrated his victory with a torchlight parade led by Marshall Rix and his squad on horseback, the city band, a large galvanized iron full dinner pail, citizens, wagons, and fireworks, after which there was a celebration in food and drink.

But the Democrat Al Smith won their hearts over Herbert Hoover in 1928 concerning the temperance issue. During the depression Franklin D. Roosevelt was the local favorite, again tipping the scales to the Democrats, but he was generally despised by most local businessmen and city leaders.

By 1938 West Bend disillusionment with Democrats was expressed in the county elections, when deep tall black headlines proclaimed Republican victory in every county office except that of Sheriff Leo Burg and Register of Deeds Edwin Pick.

Since the days of FDR the political balance wheel has shifted back to the Republican party at all levels, although the number of Democrats is slowly increasing. The county has been under Republican control so long that only one lone Democrat now serves in a county office. Perhaps, as has recently happened in the South, two party county government will come some day, a luxury that this county has never had.

S. S. Barney

Hy P. Schmidt

Local Politicians

Some local politicians have made it to state and national levels. Probably the most famous was Judge S. S. Barney, who was the first white child born in Hartford (1846) and was an 8th generation American, a rarity in Washington County in the 19th century. Admitted to the bar in 1872, he served with various law partners in West Bend for several years, as well as being County Superintendent of Schools. Elected to Congress in 1876, he was re-elected four times from the old Wisconsin 5th District, but when redistricting occurred, he accused the politicians of gerrymandering and refused to run again in 1905. Theodore Roosevelt appointed him to the United States Court of Claims in Washington, D.C. in 1905 where he served for 4 years. He was labeled the county's most able speaker.

Leander Frisby was one of the delegates to the Republican National Convention that nominated Abraham Lincoln in 1860. Born in Ohio in 1825, he had two grandparents who had fought in the Revolutionary War. A wheelright, he studied in his spare time, came to Wisconsin in 1846 and taught school in Walworth County. After studying law in Port Washington he arrived in West Bend in 1850, but had such a small law practice at first that

Judge Edward Gehl

Judge Bucklin

he resorted to teaching school, too. Because he was an anti-slavery man, he was not elected to public office at first, but when his many talents were eventually realized he had a distinguished political career thereafter. He went from District Attorney to County Superintendent of Schools. Then he was a Washington County Judge in 1856 and was elected to the state legislature four years later. In 1868 the voters sent him to Congress from the Fourth Congressional District and in 1881 he became the Attorney General of Wisconsin.

On another note entirely, there was Justice Charles Hayden, who in 1955 was still serving as Justice of the Peace on his 100th birthday, the oldest office-holder in Wisconsin, and probably in the nation.

"Hy" Schmidt, a West Bend attorney, was elected Assistant Secretary of State in 1901. He always claimed that he was Governor for a day, when the Governor, Lieutenant Governor, and Secretary of State were all absent from the state at one time (either in 1902 or 1903) and he assumed he was the chief executive officer. Schmidt was the one sent from Milwaukee to revive West Bend's Republican party.

Judge Edward Gehl served on the Wisconsin Supreme Court

from 1949 to 1955, after having been United States Attorney General for the Eastern Wisconsin District. He was a World War I veteran who had won the Purple Heart, among other awards.

Another distinguished West Bend High School alumna is Mary Lou Berg, who served at the top echelon of the Democratic Party as Deputy Vice Chairman of the Democratic National Committee. She had formerly managed a local radio station.

Meeting President Roosevelt's train in West Bend — 1934.

Famous Visitors

In addition to the aforementioned political visit of LaFollette, there have been visits by other prominent politicians. William Jennings Bryan brought his famous "silver tongue" to town and people flocked to hear him; the crowd was so vast that plans had to change so that he could speak in the open air to accommodate the throngs. In 1911 William Taft made a surprise stop in the city. Woodrow Wilson appeared briefly on March 23, 1916, at Strube's Hall. "Veep" Alben Barkley visited the city while Vice-President, and in 1934 over 3000 perspiring citizens gathered at the depot where it was 96° in the shade to see FDR. Horns blew, whistles tooted, the Civic Concert Band played, the Legion paraded — and — FDR stopped for three minutes. Wendell Wilkie came to town in 1943 and 1200 people crowded into McLane School to hear the gifted speaker, who, incidentally brought about his own death with his superhuman effort to unseat FDR. He lost, of course, and died shortly thereafter.

Wendell Wilke and Clyde Schloemer.

Both Earl Warren and Harold Stassen arrived in 1952 to speak to interested groups.

In 1958 it was not possible to have Richard Nixon appear, so a sizeable group organized to go to Oshkosh to hear him at the airport. The *News* reported that he seemed like a member of the Lion's Club, and spoke of his warmth of personality and his obvious sincerity. "I think they are a genuine part of him."

Perhaps the biggest political event in the history of West Bend was the coming of President Gerald Ford in 1976, when 5000 people crowded into the Field House at the twin high schools to see and hear him.

CHAPTER 3

West Bend Welfare

The subject of welfare is so closely allied with politics and government that it is well to consider it now. It might seem that with so many opportunities in a frontier area that there would be no need for welfare, but misfortune is ever with mankind, and the Bible reminds us the poor, indeed, are always with us. Terrible tragedies befell people in West Bend's early history: the death of a wage earner when there were young children to care for; an accident rendering the father helpless; inability to save for old age; crippling diseases; fires; all took their toll.

But the idea was rampant that this was America where everyone SHOULD succeed, and it was considered a sin to be in want. Because of this, pride kept many deserving individuals from letting anyone know of their dire straits and an occasional local obituary read: "died of starvation." As a preliminary attack on the problem, Washington County established a 160 acre poor farm northeast of Jackson, later enlarged to 200 acres, and the poor were sent there after 1850. A house was erected on the premises to hold the inmates, at a cost of less than $300. The first overseer was Mr. M. Schaefer, who was paid $293 a year; when he struck later for $300 he was peremptorily fired! Harvey Strong of Newark replaced him. The overseer received $29.65 per pauper inmate per year, averaging 57 cents per week. In a few years this rose to 70 cents and in 1877 a boast in the area was that Washington County "keeps its poor as cheap as any in the country" at $1.04 a week.

Because the poor farm was able to grow good crops — primarily barley and winter wheat — the farm quickly became profitable, for inmates were expected to work on the farm. In 1861 George Keefer submitted the following report on the poor farm (recorded in the April 8, 1861, issue of the *Democrat*):

> "I ask him (the pauper) what him git for his supper? He say he git sum tee and some brodt (bread). I ask him pauper he git sum sugar in him tee. He say no. I see in de bill many hundert pounds sugar and de pauper say he not git any." Etc.

The implied question: what became of the money or the sugar?

In 1863 local ladies held a festival on the Court House lawn for 70 to 80 destitute families, with Mrs. J. Potter as treasurer. Many a housewife carried food to unfortunate neighbors. Local churches often took care of their own members, also.

Two stories illustrate public welfare in West Bend in its formative years. In early November of 1871, according to Village Board proceedings, a committee was sent to visit Mrs. Morrice to ascertain conditions of destitution, as had been reported. On November 29 the committee reported that there was indeed destitution: "The children want the necessities." For their pains the committee was discharged! The Board then sent the Village Marshall to tell Mrs. Morrice that she and her children were to go to the poor house.

That same year a Miss Lisette Dickop was reported as destitute. Another committee of two was appointed on January 28, 1872, to see if she did indeed require supporting. On February 4 the committee reported her lack of food; on March 28 there is this terse financial statement: "$3 for flour for L. Dickop; $2.00 for a cord of wood; $4.11 for provisions; and $10.00 to make coffin for Lisette Dickop." So much for early welfare.

In 1888 the County Board of Supervisors paid its annual visit to the Poor Farm. One wrote: "The inmates present a strange sight. One has been a college professor; another was a great military man in the old country; here we find a once-successful farmer who in his declining years deeded his property to his ungrateful children; . . . etc." America was not the land of promise for everyone.

Paupers and Tramps

Later the Village Board enacted a law requiring that paupers who came to West Bend could be cared for for one day and no more. Then they were shoved on to become a charge in the next town. This was commonplace as there was as yet no concept of state or national welfare. The spirit of materialism ran high, and there was little time, effort or money expended upon the needy. Sometimes minors were bound out to anyone who wanted cheap help, either in the household, on a farm, or in the early days of industrialization, into a factory.

Another aspect of life in the nineteenth century was the tramp. What to do with him? Some were just passing through and merely asked for a handout from a kind housewife. Some were willing to chop wood or do other chores in exchange for a meal. Residents always claimed that hoboes had a secret way to mark the households that would be most apt to give them food. In 1886 the local newspaper complained that the city was almost daily invaded by tramps, but "they are promptly seized by the marshal and lodged in the jail until the next day when they are presented with a walking pass." Today's generation has no conception of opening a door to a needy character, usually hat in hand, to beg for a handout. Because tramps are no longer part of the landscape it is easy to forget that the poor still exist, for they are surely less visible.

From a financial standpoint, Ernest Lemke was the lowest bidder to care for city tramps in the 1880's with a bid of 75 cents a day for lodging, supper and breakfast, and he was directed to accept none unless they bore an official order from the city council.

The other people requiring early welfare were the chronically insane, of which there was an astounding number. Because there was no other place for them they were often jailed, but in 1889 a County Home was built for them east of West Bend. Peter Lochen, born in Prussia, was the first superintendent, while his wife served as matron. They hired two women to cook and clean and launder, the hours of employment being 4 A.M. to 11 P.M. The load was so heavy that inmates were expected to help; in fact they were enticed to do so by being promised an extra meal. Breakfast was served at 5:30 and as the next meal did not appear until noon, the extra food was welcomed. There was punishment for the insane, too, but few means of restraint brought as many complaints as the common practice of chaining a patient to the floor.

In 1901 one of the inmates felt abused and went on a hunger strike. For 20 days he refused to eat, and sat in the road, vowing that he would never again eat another meal in the asylum. So someone carried a meal out to the middle of the road in front of the asylum and he promptly ate it. The fast was broken. For entertainment there was a dance held every three months or so, with the orchestra made up of inmates. How the women patients would primp for the occasion!

There was as general a suspicion among the rest of the citizenry as there was among the Village Board members as to the validity of a claim for assistance. Among the exceptions was druggist Matt Regner who took in a Miss Cecelia Gramse as a "poor person" when she became ill with typhoid fever. Later when he asked the Village Board for financial help, the request was "laid on the table." Typhoid was rampant in some years and one day in 1923 16 year old Thomas Keller, an orphan who had come to the United States at the age of 14, became ill and no one paid any attention to his complaints. One cold January day he was found lying in the street, too ill to move, and so some kind-hearted citizens hired a nurse and doctor to care for him. He was one of the "lucky" ones.

Organized Assistance

Over the early years of the twentieth century the American Red Cross Home Service section tried valiantly to cope with the ever-increasing number of needy, but in 1925 it was largely replaced by the local Welfare League of which Mrs. Henry Gerlach was President, Mrs. Alma Wagner, Vice President, and Mrs. Robert Wentorf, Secretary-Treasurer. The City Council gave them a working budget of $1200.00. Inasmuch as this was insufficient, the heads of all the women's organizations in the city put on a concerted drive for another $1000.00. A description of their help is in the *West Bend News*: "The nature of the work is such that it would not be proper to detail it in the newspaper."

By 1929 the Red Cross reported that West Bend had served 120 civilian cases and 190 ex-soldiers during the decade, although they were now primarily a family clinic for neglected children and related needs.

In spite of brave words that there was no depression in the area, the Red Cross issued a desperate plea for help for the destitute in 1932, and placed barrels in the three leading grocery stores to collect food and clothing. In truth, it is hard to reconcile the reputed prosperity with the facts extant about poverty.

Today, of course, most welfare is handled by the impersonal government, and the role of the individual in caring for the needy is minimal. Needs still exist but they are so well hidden, according to those who work with the unfortunate, that the average citizen is unaware of them until he thinks of his taxes. Washington County built a new County Home in 1966 east of the city on Highway 33 to care for many of the unfortunate, but people have forgotten the role in the past of the home, school, church, and the individual in caring for those in need.

SECTION IV

FIRE AND POLICE DEPARTMENTS

CHAPTER 1

Fire Department

Fire was a daily threat in the 19th Century. As yet there were no lightning rods on houses or barns and every time there was a severe thunder storm some buildings suffered. Because everything was constructed of wood at first, and the only heating methods involved live coals, fires were frequent in stores and houses.

Two different accounts of the first fire department exist, but it was organized on May 1, 1869, by Albert Semler, George Duerr, Henry Lemke, F. Duetsch, and Peter W. Westenberger, as the organization team, with Henry Voss, John Stein, George Bastian, Charles Troedel, and Wenzel Wachtel as the active members. All the latter were German, and, therefore, the minutes were kept in the German language, but unfortunately all the records are lost up to July, 1883. For equipment, the village purchased a hand pumper that had been used for years by both the Racine and Milwaukee fire departments. It was housed in a downtown barn.

Only a year later the Village Council heard the fire department members declare the long-used pumper unusable — absolutely. But the Council hemmed and hawed and told the firemen to take the pumper to Lucas's shop — that man could fix anything — and report back in four days if there was to be a major repair bill. Money was not to be spent foolishly. The men returned promptly — the old machine was indeed totally unusable. Meanwhile the fires roared on.

One of the duties of early firemen was to raise money for equipment, so they sold beer and other refreshments at picnics.

In fact, 95% of the money they had came from such picnics. They also paraded in neighboring towns which had celebrations, in return for the promise that that town's department would appear at West Bend's parades. To keep firemen in line, there was a fine system; every unexcused absence at a parade cost the absentee 50 cents, often a whole day's wages. For drinking on duty the fine was a quarter. Parades were obviously important; when the city celebrated the Centennial in 1876 the firemen WERE the parade.

First Major Fires

The first major fire in West Bend occurred in 1864 when the Washington House burned. 1879 was a year of bad fires. One local resident, Mr. Ruplinger, had a fire in his kitchen which spread to the stave factory. Because the hose could not reach the river, the firemen filled a big kettle with water and used a bucket brigade to try to control the fire, but it was impossible. However, they did rescue 10,000 staves. That same year the worst fire of all occurred in the middle of the night when 11 buildings burned in the block in which the Sears store is now located. The business places of Peter DeTuncq, John Althaus, Theo. Thielege, John Findorff, Nic Immel, John Jung, John Goetz and A. C. Fuge burned. People sometimes do strange things during a moment of emergency. At the Theo. Thielege home one "helper" threw a French clock out the window and carried the blankets downstairs.

By 1883 there were some improvements. A volunteer hook and ladder company was organized with Peter Boden as the first fire chief. The company was authorized to buy a hook* and ladder outfit (the author could not determine what happened between the time of the "unusable" machine of 1871 and 1883, but presumably something was purchased), and the fire marshall was authorized to compel citizens to assist at a fire to work the fire engine or for "any other purpose." But this improvement did not satisfy the downtown businessmen, who had watched one after another of their businesses burn to the ground, so they organized a private company in 1893 to serve north West Bend (between Beech and Elm Streets), with hose carts and hose

---

*Fire companies carried a big hook attached to a long pole to pull down walls of burning buildings to try to contain the fire. Hence the name "hook" and ladder.

driven by water power from the Milwaukee River. There were then two fire companies in reality, the private Neptune which had 15 men, and the Active Hook and Ladder Company with another 15 men. Eventually (in 1908) the city bought out the Neptune's equipment and added it to its own.

In 1886 the *West Bend Democrat* editor wrote that the "tiresome work of getting the aparatus to the fire" meant that the men were completely played out and hardly able to work the pumper." The least they could do was to get new wheels so the machine would not sway "like a ship in a storm." This was before horses were used to pull the engines; it was the firemen who suplied the horsepower.

A City Block Burns

It is difficult for one today, having seen the efficient modern system in West Bend, to realize all the difficulties of an earlier day. In 1893 another city block burned to the ground on east Main Street. John Goetz saw the flames at night and told the night watchman to sound the alarm and wake up the citizens, who rushed out of their homes crying the dread word, "Fire!" There was as yet no fire alarm system for the village. When the firemen arrived, the heat was so intense that they had to push the machinery way around and across the river, resulting in a dangerous delay. By this time the livery barn and slaughter house behind Main Street had caught fire too, and burned. Men were stationed on nearby roofs to watch for further trouble. It looked for a time as though the whole town might go up in flames, so Postmaster Fairbanks was authorized to send to Fond du Lac and Milwaukee for assistance, as the local machinery was again inadequate. All the arguments over the past years concerning the purchase of an "expensive" steam engine now bore fruit. Fire was king.

Hose Company #1 was organized in 1894 by 11 members of the Hook and Ladder Company, and the two were not reunited until 1917. That same year, 1894, the fire department celebrated its 25th anniversary with several bands, 300 visiting firemen and much merriment. At that time A. Semler was the foreman; M. Mueller, the first assistant; M. Hartman, the 2nd assistant; E. Franckenberg, the treasurer; J. Goetz, the hose captain; H. Dean, the steward, and 31 other members include the names of Babille, Lampert, Jaeger, Saxe, Zimmerman, Miller, Hildebrand,

Warner, Hartman, Fick, Eckstein, Kuester, Reisse, Huber, Reynolds, Regenfuss, Kaempfer, Lemke, Westenberger, Burckhardt, Arnemann, Heberlein, Duetsch and George.

There were other difficulties, too. The editor of the *Democrat* took the fire chief to task in 1895 for failure to call out the men for regular practice. Because he never seemed to have the treasury report ready, the editor thought that if he were that busy he ought to resign. That was the year when the first steam engine finally arrived, two years after the disastrous downtown fire.

West Bend Fire Department—early 1900's.

By 1900 the department had split into four rival factions, so busy, according to one observer, fighting each other over who would put out the fire, that a building would burn to the ground in the meantime. The next year the division was healed, and there was one department again, with the men working in harmony.

Another trouble that is hard to believe today was the social structure that existed in the fire department until the middle of this century. If anyone who volunteered to join the firefighters did not meet with the approval of the other members, he might be blackballed. The fine system also continued — until 1966 — and valuable members often left the organization.

The first steamer had cost $2200 and in the intervening years over $1000 had been spent on it for repairs; everytime it was used there were more repairs necessary. The south end of

West Bend Fire Department personnel — early 1900's.

town was listed as "practically without fire protection," so the city bought a new $5000 engine from Cincinnati — the best on the market. It could pump 625 gallons a minute; one of the provisions of the purchase was that the engine had to be able to throw two one inch streams of water over the steeple of the Catholic church.

1911 was another notable year for the fires. The Wagon Works burned one night and the inadequate alarm system had not awakened half the town, even though by now the fire department members who did turn out were becoming efficient. Gehl's had its second fire in that year also. The city team of horses that was to pull the fire engine was on duty at the time operating the street sprinkler, so there was a delay. While Ferdinand Nehrbass was driving the hose cart to the fire, one of those "newfangled" autos blocked the access, and he had to drive beyond the fire and backtrack. The law about vehicles granting the right of way to emergency vehicles had yet to be enacted.

The fire engines had all been kept in the City Hall building after it was built. At first, all the equipment there was horse drawn, of course, but by 1917 the first motorized truck was added to the equipment. It took until 1926 to get rid of all the horses and the horse drawn equipment. All this is a far cry from the

West Bend Malt House.

Hangartner Building — early home of Amity Leather Company.

19th century machines which had to be pushed to the fires by manpower.

By 1922 their first motorized fire equipment had 1200 feet of hose and from then on most fires were controllable. The last major fire occurred in 1947 when the Woolen Mill burned to the

Gehl Brothers Fire.

First Motorized Ladder Truck, 1926.

ground. On one of the coldest nights of the year with dense snowdrifts and howling winds, the firemen were hampered in getting to the fire. First they had to shovel a path for the engine, and when they arrived they had to clean the snow off the river and then chip through the ice to get at the frigid water. By this time, of course, the fire was out of control, and the brave firemen resembled cakes of ice.

Famous Firemen

Two of the most noted firemen were George Kuelthau and Ackerman Schultz. Kuelthau served for 58 years in the department, retiring in 1958. He recalled the time it took 20 men to work the pumper, and if the fire happened to be a big one, the men would fall from sheer exhaustion. He became fire chief in 1915 when George Boden retired. One of the first innovations he introduced occurred after he and Engineer Seth Meyer saw a mechanized truck in Chicago. Meyer fitted one on a Model T chassis and it served until 1935. One of the saddest days for Kuelthau was the time three boys tried to steal some gasoline from the O'Neil bulk station. One boy lit a match to see how much they had in the can and it burst into flames, igniting the ramp which held the five huge bulk tanks. The tragedy cost one boy his life, and the brave firemen, knowing that if the gasoline tanks caught fire there would be a real disaster, waded in and put out the flames. As a consequence, the bulk tanks had to be moved outside the city limits.

Schultz served in the department from 1909 to 1960 and was noted for his ability to enter a smoke-filled building and find the source of the fire. He was the type of leader for whom the men had the greatest respect, for he never sent them where he would not go himself, and men trusted him. Two firemen were killed while on duty in the city — Rudolph Schloemer and Edward F. Groth.

At one time West Bend had its own factory to make fire engines. In 1949 T. R. Kittelsen, an engineer and fire engine repairman, operated the Wisconsin Fire Apparatus Company in town. He would buy a bare chassis locally and then frame it and fit it out with everything from siren to hoses. Employing six men and working on two engines at a time, he had a steady and profitable business, selling more fire trucks in Wisconsin than any other such company, but he did not stay long and left for northern Wisconsin.

Over the years the fire department grew in both size and efficiency. By 1958 there were 60 good volunteers under Chief Carl Peters, who had spent the years from 1925-1949 as treasurer, at which time he was appointed the chief. Altogether Peters spent 45 years in the fire department, 18 of them as chief.

There were only two paid employees at the time, Peters and Henry Warner, the engineer. The department was responding to about eighty calls a year and had added a rescue squad. In

Left to right, George Kuelthau, Mike Kratzer, Clyde Schloemer.

Fred "Ackerman" Schultz.

1961 the Barton Fire Department added its resources to those of West Bend. Today the recently built fire house on the corner of 7th Avenue and Washington Street has a full-time crew who responds promptly to calls for help and has become noted for their efficiency. Anyone want to go back to the "good old days"?

Ferdinand Nehrbass, first policeman.

CHAPTER 2

Police Department

Early Crime

It is intriguing to read of the crimes that were practiced in early West Bend and to compare them with the crimes of today. In addition to the prohibitions already mentioned in the early ordinances, one might go to jail for abusing a horse; terrible stories abound of animal abuse, one of the worst being of the man who became so angry when his horse balked that he tied a rope around the animal's tongue and pulled it out, a crime for which he paid time in the local jail. It was also necessary to make it illegal to poison livestock, and jail was the lot of those who were caught.

There were horse thieves, arsonists, burglars (who took such things as revolvers from a hardware store), and ordinary thieves who stole buggy cushions, clothes off the clotheslines, and poultry. Some one drove a buggy over the graves in Wightman's cemetery, and tramps would sometimes break a downtown window to earn a meal and a night in jail.

In 1882 the jail was declared unfit and a local editor said "inasmuch as it had not amounted to much when it was built 30 years ago it had not improved with age and now the green lumber had sprung so that it would not hold a healthy criminal two hours!" Many times there was no heat, and meals were often meager, so a sojourn there was not necessarily a pleasant experience.

Juvenile Crime

Youths made the front page then, too. They were found guilty of playing in the street and "harassing businessmen." B. Goetter told the boys outside his establishment to stop it or he'd get them acquainted with the law! Some "crimes" don't change over the years. More physically dangerous, though, was their play around the railroad cars, especially at night, so a new ordinance was enacted; the editor felt the new law unnecessary if the "parents would take matters in hand and apply the latter more freely." Children committed other crimes, too. In 1895 they broke into the fire house, spilled gas on the floor and scattered the tools, losing the valve to the fire engine. Then the fire house had to have a lock on it for the first time and all the firemen were issued a key; the alarm bell rope was then moved to the outside of the building so everyone would have access to it. Once someone, possibly a juvenile, threw a rock through the *West Bend News* office window, and a "mean, contemptible person ripped off a part of the awning at the *Pilot* office and ought to be thrashed to a standstill."

When juvenile crime increased, an irate editor asked parents: "What have you for boys and girls to do? What responsibilities have they in your home or business office? Do you expect a little school book education and a great deal of irresponsible idleness will make them successful men? . . . Do you expect to fit them for business by letting them run the streets nights, and furnishing them good clothes and pocket money? If you do, prepare at once to put the blame of their failure on poor schools, skating rinks, saloons and inefficient police." The same issue is strong today, and schools and other public institutions still bear the onus for parental irresponsibility.

By 1907 there was so much juvenile theft that the *West Bend News* began to print the names of the youthful thieves. The young offenders refused to go to school and "were in all kinds of devilment." "Had there been a little more vigilance and a prosecution or two before, it is doubtful whether these crimes would have been committed." There are many today who would echo these sentiments. Halloween pranksters were trouble for the law, too. So many Halloween stories abound that everyone has surely heard of what yesterday's youngsters used to do. In 1908 they took to tearing up the wooden sidewalks in addition to the usual deviltry.

Other crime stories make interesting reading. One time a tramp stole a man's horse out of his barn, tied it to a post outside H. Krieger's leather shop, and went inside to tell the owner that he had found it wandering around the railroad tracks. For his pains he received a dime and a brush (which he had also stolen). He took the brush to Barton and exchanged it for a quarter's worth of drinks — and was caught.

In 1894 a tramp stole a valuable goat skin from H. Krieger, and for his pains was "whipped good" and spent 30 days in the jail. It was not uncommon to have wooden planks stolen from the bridges, making travel dangerous, especially at night when their loss could not be readily seen. So many train robbers relieved the employees of the Chicago and Northwestern Railroad of their wages that the company stopped paying the men in currency and arranged for the checks to be cashed at the West Bend Bank. In addition the railroad spotters caught 15 of their "oldest and best" conductors pocketing change for fares from customers, and received a 60-90 day vacation without pay.

Highway men plied their trade on the local roads, especially in the early hours of the morning or late at night. One man, James Gorman, was sandbagged at six o'clock one morning, robbed of the one dollar he carried, and thrown over a fence near Myra.

By 1930 a police report listed in descending order of occurence the following crimes, for which the perpetrators paid time in jail: larceny, drunks, driving while drunk, disorderly conduct, drunk and disorderly, reckless driving, insane (committed for "safe keeping"), fraud, burglary, violating fish and game laws, minors running away from home, abusive language, assault and battery, holding up an auto with a gun, speeding in the city, and murder.

Today a modern and efficient police force keeps order in the city, but crime persists, as it always has, and the key lies in prevention, of course, but humans have not solved that yet.

CHAPTER 3

Tragedies

Whenever one hears someone speak glowingly of the good old days, it might be well to consider that until fairly recent times, continual tragedy was a way of life. Death or other disaster filled the pages of the weekly newspapers from the very first editions and in some years it is virtually impossible to read one single edition of the weekly newspaper without tragedy dominating the scene. At one time, the local paper carried a weekly column "Accidents of the Week" and it was always filled.

Among the most culpable were animals. Bulls gored the inhabitants and mad dogs bit people, especially children. But the guiltiest of all were horses. Skittish ones bolted, throwing the occupants to the ground. There were runaways which were exciting for the spectators and brought an interested group of onlookers, but all too often they were tragic for the unlucky riders. Once two horses bolted on the track at the fair and the sulkies collided, hurling the drivers into the air, a nineteenth century version of the thrill of the modern stock car race. Horses kicked their owners, sometimes to death. By 1913 the paper reported horse related accidents nearly weekly.

When the train entered West Bend history, the accidents multiplied. There were train wrecks. People were killed while walking the track, for the track provided easier footing and was often the shortest distance between two points. Children were killed or maimed while playing on the tracks, and for a time, youngsters amused themselves by leaping on the cowcatchers in an early version of "chicken." This was more fun at night when they could not be so easily seen as they leaped off at the last possible moment. Some didn't make it.

Children were especially vulnerable in other ways, too. First of all, there were the standard childhood diseases that everyone was supposed to get, but which accounted for many a funeral. Diphtheria was one of the worst killers. Then, too, young children fell into wells or cisterns and drowned; they tripped over tubs of boiling water as their mothers washed clothes. They fell into tubs of lye during soap making sessions. Sometimes they simply disappeared forever. They were left alone in houses which were destroyed by fire and burned to death. At age twelve or fourteen it was not uncommon for a boy to run away from home.

The beauty of the Milwaukee River was sometimes diminished as it claimed its victims. The first bridges across it were often the narrowest of boards, and at one time the sole bridge for pedestrians was a single plank. One actually crept across it on hands and knees. If one slipped, it was sometimes possible to make a quick decision — fall to the north where the water was shallower, or to the south where it might be easier to swim. Men coming home from the saloons at night were frequent victims. In the wintertime eager skaters fell through the ice before it was properly frozen, or in the spring after the thawing had weakened the ice. In 1921 three sons of the destitute Mrs. Berber drowned on thin ice. Their father had run away.

When the village began to industrialize, the number of accidents in factories was alarming, although often they were hushed up in the local papers. At first in most plants there were no safety devices of any kind. Too, all kinds of machinery at home as well as on the farm removed limbs regularly. People fell from scaffolding while building their houses, as most builders were not carpenters by trade, and if one were inept with an ax, then it was goodnight to a finger, toe, or worse, an arm or leg.

As though all this were not enough, there were other calamities. Suicides were embarrassingly common, and sometimes there was a suicide a week to report. Nitric acid was a common method, but Paris Green did a good job, too. Despondency as a way of life existed for too many; older ones simply walked out into the woods to die. There were dreadful tales of insanity. Rat bites were common, especially to children. Scorpions hid in bunches of bananas at the stores to catch the unwary. If one were in an embarrassing financial position, one might leave town, no matter if the family then had no visible means of support and had to be sent to the Poor Farm. In the eyes of most citizens, that was the ultimate tragedy — to be sent to the Poor Farm.

Yet for decades the most common tragedy was fire. After every storm involving lightning at least one building in the area burned. Over the years, there was hardly a structure in downtown West Bend that escaped fire. Christmas candles on the festive trees ignited the branches or nearby curtains and left many a family homeless or the children dead. Lamps tipped over with regularity both at home and at public functions, bringing further horror.

There were all sorts of odd happenings, too. In 1894 Jacob Herman, employed at Lohr's butcher shop, used to while away the evenings at target practice on objects in the Milwaukee River. One night he shot and killed Louisa Burckhardt. Two school boys held a grudge in 1898. Carl Limbach used a mirror to reflect the sunlight in Willie Glantz's eyes at school and the two had words. One thing led to another until they were persuaded to put on boxing gloves and fight it out. In the ensuing bout Glantz killed Limbach with one body blow. Another time Herbert Emery shot his best friend, Eddie Groth, while hunting and an inquest was ordered. The blue ribbon panel of Henry Rolfs, P. W. Harns, John Treviranus, John Althaus, Herman Mueller and B. Braunwarth exonerated the sorrowing boy.

While car accidents claim lives today, it is doubtful that we live as near to tragedy as those living in the past.

SECTION V

RETAIL STORES, HOTELS, AND OTHER PRIVATE ENTERPRISES

CHAPTER 1

Stores and Other Establishments

While a complete account of the retail stores is nearly impossible to compile, some of them were notable enough to warrant a relating of their story. Truly the first "general" stores lived up to their names, for literally everything that was needed in a frontier community was available within. At first the actual necessities were few, but gradually settlers demanded more variety, and one could find everything from patent medicines to pitchforks, corncob pipes to cowbells, galoshes to groceries. While the very first stores were opened by Yankees, in a few years they were run by Germans, and the bookkeeping was done in German, also.

The egg basket was provisioned by local citizens and farmers who traded eggs for groceries. Rat cheese reposed under a large glass bell, and many still alive recall the trade names of Clabber Girl baking powder, Bull Durham tobacco, Ceresota flour, Oshkosh B'Gosh overalls and J and P Coats thread.

And oh, the barrels! There was a vinegar barrel with its pungent smell, another for mouth-watering dill pickles, one for salt pork, and others for flour, sugar, and molasses. Then, too, there was the prominent cracker box or barrel on which lay the cats which every store owner kept to reduce the mouse population. No costly prepackaging existed — just the merchandise, and you could see exactly what you were getting. A large stove surrounded by comfortable chairs was a wintertime feature, and men sat around it discussing the affairs of their lives while the women shopped.

Wm. Peters Store at the corner of Main and Walnut, now Mehring's.

First Grocery Stores

There was no such thing as self-service, and the customer awaited the attention of the proprietor or his clerks, who moved from measuring yard goods to cutting meat with equal deftness. One of the first such stores of which we have much knowledge was Pick's, purchased by John Pick and his wife Mary Goetter Pick in 1873. The store had been started by a Mr. Vollner where the present Tri-County store is now. After John Pick died in 1881 John Goetter became a partner and the two wives ran the store until 1902, when Mary Pick bought out her partner and turned the management over to her two sons. Edwin Pick recalls how very very hard his mother used to work; she made soap every year in 150-200 gallon barrels. When the farmers brought in the pigs she would cut them up for resale and even smoke the hams. Eighteen hour days were common.

As was typical, if one bought a week's supply of groceries, the grocer donated a sack of candy for the children. One of the

Inside Peter's Store at Hickory and Main, 1905. Left to right, George DeBano, Carl Bernhagen, Albert Heipp, William Peters, unknown, Katherine Wagner Stahl, Emma Peters.

Pick's Department Store, southwest corner of Cedar and Main Streets.

competitors of Pick's was Poull's Department Store, as was Bloedorn's, "West Bend's clothing man for 49½ years."

Another noted early store was known as Peter's. West Bend pioneers Henry and Minnie Peters were born in Germany and came to West Bend in 1857. A son William graduated from St. John's Lutheran School and began work as a clerk in the B. S. Potter store, the earliest in the village. When young Peters was

Heipp's Store (originally Peter's). Fritz Heipp and his dog.

18 his parents gave him $500 and signed a note for a like amount so that he and his brother-in-law Adolph Harms might buy out Potter's store, which was located where the Sears store is today. The family thought this was truly a great country where an immigrant could accumulate $500 in a few years, for back in Germany one might never see that much in a lifetime.

The store was a success from the beginning, for the young Peters had an innate business sense, and never bought more than he could sell. He added a clothing line, sending an agent to New York twice a year to order the latest fashions. At Christmas time, too, he did a booming business in toys and candy, as did his rivals. By 1890 he had developed the much appreciated Peters Rapid Delivery Service, using a horse and wagon; he improved the service still further in 1914 when he exchanged delivery by horse for that by a Model T Ford. Amongs the firsts for which he was noted were the first bananas in the city and the first ice box to keep perishables. When chain stores came to town, the old general store and personal service vanished.

The Bakeries

There were many other types of private enterprise in West Bend, among them, bakeries, the first opened by Francis Schreiber in 1861. Another of the popular shops was that of Emil Krieger (1896), a German who built his brick oven after the

Boerner Bros. Mercantile Co.

fashion of the European bakeries at Main Street and Walnut, and baked bread and rolls primarily. His oven was fifteen feet square, six feet high, and had 20 inch walls for heat retention and proper browning. Gottlieb Schlegel bought the store in 1899, and added cakes, pies and other pastries, a mouthwatering collection of baked goods that are remembered today with nostalgia. When he retired in 1924 Hugo Krueger bought it, and ran it until 1930 when Schlegel's daughter, Mrs. Clarence Kircher, took it over. The baker was Ernst Stellbrink and they had branches in Jackson and Kewaskum.

Many people remember Bauer's Bakery which opened in 1904. Everybody bought semmel rolls then, and Bauer's would deliver them to your door. He built his own ice cream machines and sold ice cream and homemade candy in a parlor at the back of the store. He had two routes, the first from 5:30-7:00 A.M., known as the breakfast route, and the second from 9:00-11:00, the so-called bread route. In 1936 Millard Bauer bought it after Henry's death and sold only baked goods. During World War II he, like all other bakers, had a hard time, for sugar was difficult to obtain, so they used corn syrup, and made do with the limited supply of shortening. Bauer's, too, has vanished from the retail scene, sorely missed.

Druggists

Early duggists prepared most of their prescriptions from a few basic ingredients, but this was not profitable, so they added patent medicines in order to make a living. The first druggist was probably Civil War veteran E. Wolfrum, who strapped a knapsack on his back and walked to Milwaukee once a month for supplies, according to his granddaughter, Camilla Wolfrum. As a father he once opposed the suitor of his daughter Cora, believing the fellow to be lazy, so one weekend when the young man was a guest, he decided to do something about it. While the suitor was making home-made ice cream, Wolfrum substituted marble dust for the salt. After two fruitless perspiring hours Papa relented and brought out the salt. But the young man had the last laugh. He married Cora anyway.

Other druggists included Gerlach and Hesse, who owned a store in 1891, but the drug store that is still recalled with nostalgia was Regner's, for in 1910 he added a fancy soda fountain with syrup containers of solid silver and a fruit bowl of real cut glass. His counter was of marble and to entertain his customers, he played his Victor talking machine, the forerunner of today's ubiquitous juke boxes.

Meat Markets

Another type of early store was the meat market, and one of the first was Junghbut's, established in 1851. When the butcher intended to butcher an animal the following day, he would go into the street in front of his shop and ring a bell to alert housewives. After he had killed the animal he would load it onto his cart and haul the meat from house to house. N. N. Emery opened the next meat market in 1854, but he enlisted in the Civil War in 1861 and that ended his business. Westenberger's and Kortendick's were two popular later meatmen, especially the latter, for he would give a free weiner to the youngsters doing the shopping for their parents.

De Tuncq's Furniture Store

Sometime between 1855 and 1858 Pierre (Peter) De Tuncq came to West Bend to open the first craft industry in the village — that of making furniture. He had originally come from Douai, France, and spent a few years in New York before opening his shop on Fifth Avenue where the Savings and Loan Company is

Residence and first furniture store of Peter DeTuncq.

Arthur DeTuncq, furniture delivery wagon, First State Bank and Weinand Hotel in background.

presently located. An ad in an 1863 newspaper read: "Cabinet maker, keeps constantly on hand all kinds of furniture, bureaus, stands, tables, chairs. The best of lumber used; all work guaranteed. Coffins made upon short notice." In 1865 he added bedsteads and settees manufactured to order.

Because there were few furniture companies in the country as yet, most furniture was made to order, and the demand was great as West Bend grew. Soon he had competition in the form of Rudolph Aschke, Jacob Roecker, the "Frenchman" Le Tailleur, and Frank Deutsch, but only the name De Tuncq remained. His business prospered so that by 1875 he could move to Main Street in a building just south of the present Sears store.

He married Catherine Louise L'Homme and had three sons of whom Adolph joined his father in the furniture business; they added an undertaking parlor and invented a new embalming process which did not require the use of ice to preserve the bodies in the summer.

Peter De Tuncq was a superb craftsman. He went into homes and created such woodwork as the banisters and window work in the Stork house on Eighth Avenue. He made all of his own coffins and could produce some rather ornate ones on demand. When work was especially heavy, as it was in 1880 when he had 70 funerals, he would often crawl into one of his coffins to snatch a few hours sleep late at night, and his wife always knew where to find him. A few pieces of his furniture are still in the city, treasured remnants of a once flourishing business. In 1881 he turned his hand to making a hearse. Besides his craft, he owned all the land south of the Savings and Loan on Fifth Avenue up to and a bit south of the present Badger School, which was a cow pasture when he was living. On some of the land he planted ginseng, an incredibly difficult plant to grow, but one that was (and still is) financially rewarding if one has the time and patience to nurture it to maturity.

After Peter's death in 1900 his son Adolph took his own sons Arthur and Louis into the business, making it a three generation venture.

Haebig's

One of the remaining names from the 19th Century still doing business is Haebig's. Ed Haebig owned a tailor shop on North Sixth Avenue which he started in the 1890's and then bought out the Main Street shop of Knippel's Tailor Shop in 1905. Knippel had followed his father in this business and was a skilled cutter. Ed Haebig's brother Charles joined him two years later and then Charles bought out Ed for there was not enough business to support two families. Ed left for Waupaca, and the haberdashery store he ran there still has the Haebig name on the front of the Main Street store.

Charles' two sons, Ray and Bob, joined their father in the business, but as the years went by it was cheaper to buy ready-made clothes than to have them tailor-made, so the family turned primarily to dry cleaning. Besides, the tailors were getting old and no new ones were learning the business. Within the memory of people living in the city is that of visiting the tailor shop and seeing the tailors sitting tailor fashion as they constructed the hand made garments. Even though there were eventually no more tailors in the shop in West Bend, Ray Haebig was so skilled in taking the personal measurements of those who were harder to fit in ready-made clothes, that the firm sent the measurements on to a Chicago establishment who then finished the suits. When they were returned, they fit perfectly.

Fuge's

Another prosperous early business was that of A. C. Fuge, who had immigrated from Prussia when he was twelve. After spending some time in Jackson on a farm he came to West Bend to join the Wilmot Hardware firm in 1869, and a year later he owned the store alone. Later his two sons, H. A. and A. C., Jr., ran the store and moved to 143 South Main Street. A disastrous fire cost them their entire stock, but they rebuilt and soon became the largest hardware store in the county. They whole-saled Maytag washers, Winchester guns and ammunition, in addition to carrying a large stock of bicycles, sporting goods, floor coverings, etc.

During the prosperous twenties they added John Deere plows, and soon had the largest farm business in the county also. Then A. C. left to sell insurance and Herbert became president. During the depression the store went bankrupt (in 1931) and the stock was sold at auction to Gehl's, who also went bankrupt in 1936, and the West Bend Hardware bought out the stock.

But it was not the end of Fuge's. Herbert A. started a small plumbing and heating shop and was so successful by 1934 he was back at his old 143 South Main Street address. Today his sons run the successful Fuge Plumbing, Heating and Cooling industry at 149 South Main.

Livery Stables

One other interesting type of private enterprise was the livery stable. Salter's had an early one, but it was bought out in 1899 by Julian Yahr who sent a carriage to meet every train, took trunks to the hotels and private homes, and rented out a team and driver, or a horse and buggy that you could drive yourself. He also had fancier carriages for weddings and funerals, and operated with the motto, "Feed well, drive slow, and pay your bills before you go."

Pautsch and Wolf Shoe Store.

Other Stores and Businesses

There were other types of stores, too. Bruhy's jewelry opened in 1885 when the young Bruhy came to West Bend with only a few tools of his trade — no cash and no jewelry stock. By 1903 he could say with pride that he had repaired 10,000 watches and he had a store filled with jewelry to sell.

The first funeral parlor, as such, was that of August Ritger at Eighth and Hickory. Leander Schmidt and Clem Reinders opened one on North Main. Today two funeral homes serve the area, the Schmidt Funeral Home and that of Techtmann--

Myrhum. The change from the word "parlor" is interesting, for today's generation probably does not realize that in the past funerals were all held in the family parlor, so establishments took that name, too. The average house of today is not built with a parlor, so funeral "homes" purport to substitute for the home as a place for funerals.

A type of business that no longer exists is the bath house. Engman's had one with a tin roof, and the sun warmed the water through the roof. A place called Jacob's Well sold bottled water, "the same as Waukesha water." Then there were chimney sweeps; in 1893 there were two such, William Warnke and Rudolf Lemke. With the prevalence of fireplaces, that trade is returning to the scene.

Probably the first major chain store to come to West Bend was the J. C. Penney Company. It continued for a time to use the intriguing aerial cable originally used by Pick's Department store. Little cups carried the sales slip and the cash (it was a cash only store) up to a girl who made the proper change and sent the cup flying down to the sales clerk. G. C. Kessel was the first manager, while Lester Schutt, who came in 1931, was here for the longest time.

Other miscellaneous retail establishments include Ashman's Greenhouse which began when Harrison Ashman came to West Bend and bought out the Kesting Greenhouse in 1916. He had always liked flowers since he was a youngster. He remodeled the greenhouse (located on Ninth Avenue) in 1925, added the conservatory in 1929 and had "over an acre of plants" by 1930. Ownership passed to his son Robert, who is no longer in business.

Midland Cooperative began on a modest scale in 1937, but by 1976 it was doing a two million dollar business in its quarters on Decorah Road. It began delivering oil in 1938, added coal and fertilizer in 1939, tires, paints, and feed in 1940, and among other innovations, a self-service gasoline station in 1976, the first in West Bend.

Culligans started in 1946 under William Claybaugh and George Klumb, with William Buchelt as their first soft water customer. They started in the Fuge building on 147 South Main but expanded and moved to 524 Fourth Avenue where the firm is still doing business.

Barbers

The early barber shops in West Bend had red plush stationary barber chairs with sliding footrests. Hot water for shaving was heated in a kettle on a gas stove. Regular customers had their personalized shaving mugs, and an iron cuspidor sat on the floor to serve those who chewed tobacco. Twenty cents would buy a haircut and a dime would buy a shave, although one could purchase a set of tickets giving twelve shaves for a dollar. The rows of chairs awaiting customers were usually filled with men who came into the shop just to talk.

Some of the early shops had a bathroom attached, so that after the river froze a man could get a hot bath for a quarter; the shop provided the bath towel and soap. Some patronized nearby bathhouses, too.

The first innovation in the barber shop was the electric clipper, but the big change was wrought when women invaded the previously all-male domain in the 1920's and soon about 40% of the business of local barbers was on women's hair. After the beauty parlors came to West Bend, the men had their retreat back to themselves again. Today, of course, it is the men who have invaded the previously all-women beauty parlors. But business was never the same for barbers after safety razors and the later electric shavers were invented; men now shaved at home.

West Bend has had several memorable barbers, two of whom became mayors of the city. William Knippel left West Bend High School in 1898 to become an apprentice to barber John Wendelborn, who had a three chair shop and bathroom. It was not so important, it was felt, for a boy to finish high school then; it was more important to learn a trade. In 1905 he and his brother Joseph (mayor from 1930-1940) bought the Henry Martin shop on the O'Meara triangle and continued as partners for 48 years. William served as City Treasurer, Washington County Democrat Chairman, Treasurer of Holy Angels congregation, and was a member of several clubs, including the Chamber of Commerce, Rotary, Knights of Columbus, Loyal Order of Moose, etc. Joseph recalled clipping the hair of five Joe Hubers.

Ray Behrend was another long-time barber in the city. He became an apprentice at the age of 15 under Immanuel Haintze of Barton. All that was needed at first was an ability to avoid clipping the customer's ears, but he gained the needed skills and passed the state examination in 1925, opened his shop on North Main Street, and hired Lawrence Wickert and Charles Guth as his two assistants. A. C. Franckenburg was another popular barber, employing two assistants.

Ted Holtenbeck barbered at the same time as the Knippels in his shop in the Lemke Triangle (where Heil's Decorating Shop is located). Barney Inkman was a popular barber in the late 1920's and the 1930's, as well as being the organist at Holy Angels. He also had a shoe shine parlor where high schools boys could earn extra money, and he was one of the first to admit ladies to his shop. And then there was Mayor Paul Henke's shop, a place where for years the affairs of the city were discussed. At this writing, at least ten barbershops serve the city.

Beauty Parlors

A later addition to Main Street was the beauty parlor, and of them all, Tillie Hoffman's leads the list. She owned a millinery shop for many years and added the beauty parlor in 1918. She bought Wendelborn's old barber chair from George Kuehlthau for a quarter and was in business. Besides the chair, she owned a sterilizer and a gasoline heater in the basement to heat the water for shampoos and employed a girl to make switches for her customers. By the mid-nineteen twenties, permanent waves and marcels were the rage, so she went to Chicago to learn the art of permanent waving. It cost $20 for a curl, but the price dropped considerably during the depression. Getting a permanent was an exercise in faith in the operator and patience, for the process was a long one, often with uncertain results, but Tillie was the best, and is fondly remembered by many.

The whole topic of stores and private businesses is a fascinating one and one could easily write a whole volume on them alone. This chapter has but scratched the surface. Many other businesses cry out for a historian to record their story before those who know it best are no longer here to narrate it.

CHAPTER 2

Hotels and Saloons

Washington House — 1864, B. Goetter, proprietor.

Hotels

If the walls of the Washington House could talk, what tales they would tell! There would be echos of laughter, reminiscences of countless meetings, aromas of bountiful meals. Among the few remaining accounts of all the early businesses, that of the Washington House is the most complete. Actually, it is in essence the story of a remarkable immigrant, Balthazar Goetter.

Goetter learned the art of brewing in his native Germany and immigrated to Milwaukee in 1846, where he worked in a brewery there for three years. Seeking a site where he might become an independent brewer, he consulted his friends, Steve and Charlie Mayer, who lived south of West Bend, and they recommended the fledgling community on the Milwaukee River that already had a grist mill and would soon have a sawmill.

Christ Wolf Hotel, built in 1869.

Intrigued, he visited the spot, liked what he saw, but feared he would be lonely. The Mayers told him that they had a sister back home in Germany who was a "good girl" and just right for Balthazar.

So he trekked back across Lakes Michigan, Ontario, and Erie, through the Erie Canal and into New York. Then it was eastward across the Atlantic for six long weeks and on to Germany where he located the young Mayer girl. He must have been persuasive, for in three short weeks she said "Yes!" Then it was westward across the ocean, into New York, back through the Erie Canal, and into the Great Lakes once again. From Milwaukee, they came north by ox cart. Goetter immediately put up a crude cabin for his young bride and set to work to build a brewery, a two story frame structure that housed the family upstairs and the brewery below.

Unfortunately for the young brewer, Goetter soon developed a serious eye infection, and so he taught the art of brewing to his two friends, the Mayer brothers, both of whom now worked in the brewery, and Goetter left the business to build a hotel, the second one in the village. Built in 1852, the frame building was to become the Washington House.

Essential to any hotel business then was a good warm stable, and Goetter provided one for the horses and oxen, complete with hay, oats, and clear drinking water. The basement of the hotel contained a natural spring well, so the water was excellent for man and beast. Back of the hotel Goetter grew a vast garden, providing fresh vegetables for the guests. It is said that the proprietor was especially fond of his fine asparagus. He was also proud of his wine cellar, and Carl Quickert, who later lived there, maintained that the cellar enjoyed a reputation as far south as St. Louis.

When we remember that the original purpose of founding West Bend was to serve as a half way stopping place between Fond du Lac and Milwaukee, it is not surprising that all the rooms were soon filled, primarily with traveling salesmen. Because people could travel only during the daytime, and the intercity trip took two days, the traffic into West Bend from both directions was heavy at nightfall. People also came to the hotel just to eat of the bountiful dinners.

Hotel Wiskerchen, built in 1896.

Wightman Hotel barn, built in 1848. Later became Wisckerchen Livery.

The Hotel Fire

Perhaps the most dramatic moment in the life of the Washington House occurred on January 1, 1864. It was a severely cold day, as New Year's days usually are. Every room of the hotel was filled. The many stoves were crammed full of wood to ward off the frigid air, and inside in the cheery atmosphere the men played billiards, cards, or told stories to while away the holiday.

Suddenly the dread cry of "FIRE!" brought everyone to his feet. The roof was afire! Instantly, townspeople and guests set to work to save what they could. There was no local fire department as yet, and the only equipment the village had was a "donkey engine" with 20 feet of hose, entirely inadequate to reach the river, which at any rate was frozen solid. Willing hands pitched blankets, beds, pitchers, washbasins, luggage, and looking glasses from the upper floors to the frozen ground below. After the entire first floor was cleared, men went into the cellar to rescue the sauerkraut jar and carried the heavy burden all the way up the steps and outside to safety.

Other helpers managed to carry out the cumbrous hotel range, with the holiday turkey still in the oven. The turkey promptly froze. Most of the food in the basement was well enough insulated so it did not freeze — the apples, potatoes, etc. When it was all over, the only item remaining on the spot where the hotel had been was the cast iron stove which had overheated and probably caused the terrible conflagration. There is no record of where the guests spent the rest of the day, but probably the townspeople took them in.

Almost at once Mr. Goetter began to rebuild, this time a three story cream colored brick building of local clay that rivaled the famed Cream City brick from Milwaukee, according to local observers. It could accommodate 100 guests and was ready for occupancy by October 15th of that same year. By this time West Bend had its own cabinet maker, a Mr. Roecker, who made some of the furniture for the new rooms.

Over the years the once proud hotel suffered many indignities at the hands of ever-changing owners, who kept remodeling it and changing its name. In 1913 a parlor for ladies was added that boasted of a piano and "pretty rugs on the floor." By 1948 it was renamed the Mermac, and maintained 50 guest rooms and nine apartments. The showplace was still the lobby which boasted of bright oriental carpeting.

Many famous Americans have stayed at the Washington House, including William Jennings Bryan, William Barkley (Vice-President), and John F. Kennedy, and it is the oldest business left in the city, having celebrated both the centennial and the bicentennial.

More recently Paul Ronyak rescued the decaying building by buying it from A. C. Berkholtz and completely refurbishing it, the first effort of a downtown merchant to reclaim the central city. During the reconstruction workmen left a portion of the foundation exposed so that today's generation might see the boulder construction of the solid foundation. Once again the Washington House serves dinners and provides a place for societies to meet, as in the past. Readers might be interested to read the historic marker on the property, the most attractive in the downtown area.

Other Hotels

West Bend has had many other hotels over the years. The very first one was the American House which began life in 1846 as part of the tiny log cabin of George N. Irish where he boarded the mechanics who worked on the mills. Confusion exists whether this became the American Hotel or whether there were two separate establishments, but by 1865 the American Hotel had acquired a brick veneer, the first such in West Bend, and was a full three stories high in the front and two stories in the rear. With its back to the mill race, it was located on the south side of Mill Street where Mert's Bar is now located. It, too, had a famous dining room, and became the meeting place for the rising German middle class, where they met to play cards, tell stories and have a beer or two. It had many different proprietors including Charles Ottilie, Christ Wolf, Ben Boerger and Frank Day. It became the property of Michael Gonring who had visited Germany at the time of the Olympics and had become fascinated with German style architecture, so the new building on the old location somewhat resembles a German hotel with its colorful tile inserts.

The city also had the Wiskerchen Hotel, built in 1890 of Boltonville brick and remodeled in 1909. Among its famous guests were Governor LaFollette and William Jennings Bryan. It quickly established a superior reputation for its dining room, presided over by Rose Wiskerchen, with the food cooked by Mrs. Wiskerchen and Julia. Arthur, Walter, and John took care of the office and the barroom, while another son, Frank, managed the hotel barn and baggage line. The hotel was located across the street from the American Hotel on Mill Street, since 1917 the Geib Hotel, and attracted people from Milwaukee who came on the train for an outing and to sample the famous cuisine of the hotel dining room.

Then there was Weinand's Hotel, built in 1894 where the Schultz store is today. It had forty rooms and was kept busy. Schlegel's Hotel also served the downtown area for years.

The early hotels were generally lighted with kerosene lamps, and because most of the men chewed tobacco, spittoons were everywhere. An interesting sidenote is that many of the men smoked Sweet Caporals, a five cent cigar illegal to sell here because wrapped inside each package was a picture of a nearly nude woman. There were 24 such poses altogether, and the object was to collect the entire set. They had to be bootlegged into the village and were huge money-makers. The recent flap over pornography is nothing new to the city!

German hotel proprietors were famous not only for the quality of their cuisine but also the quantity. A typical hotel breakfast might include oatmeal, cooked for hours at the back of the stove and served with thick cream, followed by eggs and bacon, toast, and buckwheat pancakes which were swimming in good butter and local maple syrup.

So West Bend was well supplied with hotels in its periods of growth. Today the Holiday Inn (1970) and the West Bend Motor Inn serve most of the transient trade coming to the city.

Saloons

Saloons, which we now call taverns, played a larger part in the lives of the earlier settlers than do their modern counterparts, for most of the men in the community went there to share the news, formulate the politics, and solve the world's problems. It was the one spot where there was a real form of democracy; "gemutlichkeit" was the atmosphere, for with one foot on the brass rail one could be friendly with all the townspeople.

Beer came to West Bend with the Germans, and for five cents one could have a glass of beer and a free lunch consisting of sausage, roast beef, baked beans, bread and butter or other goodies. At six beers for a quarter and the free lunch one could conceivably stay all day and socialize. However, after World War II the nickle beer disappeared. On every bar there were both raw and hard cooked eggs to go with the beer. In 1884 West Bend had thirteen saloons, each of which paid a $75 license fee to the city treasury.

The local saloons were strictly for the males, although sometimes there was a women's waiting room where the more genteel soda and lemonade were served as the ladies awaited their men after a shopping expedition. Most of the proprietors ran a decent establishment, although several of the town's citizens remember a few fights that set the town talking. Many a person who went on to greater things got his start in life washing glasses in a saloon.

In addition to the saloons connected with the hotels, there were always plenty of others. One was owned by Jacob Ziegler, father of B. C. Young Ben got his start working for his parents in the saloon, and when his father was elected County Treasurer on the Democratic ticket, Ben did the book work. The office did not pay any salary, so the treasurer would lend the money and collect the interest. Another well-known saloon keeper was former Mayor Lemke. There have been many others.

Gonring's

In a 1971 interview with Miss Edna Schloemer, Michael Gonring recalled the time he worked for Peters and Albinger in

Mike Gonring

C. Illian's Saloon.

the American Hotel. The nearby Schmidt and Stork Wagon Company gave its workers fifteen minutes for lunch, and during that time several boys with a yoke-like arrangement over their shoulders to which were attached two buckets holding up to twelve quarts each would come into the saloon. There young Gonring and John Peters would fill the buckets, one opening the faucet and the other filling the buckets. They would dispense two half barrels in fifteen minutes.

Gonring's workday began at 6:30 AM and ended at midnight. He had to fill the lunch counter before 8:30 when the men who had been at work since early in the morning came in for the first beer and a bite to eat — that bite being a generous one. It took twenty loaves of Bauer's bread and plenty of ten cent a pound sausage and fifteen cent a pound cheese to keep the counter filled. Each day they gave away up to $20 worth of free lunch, but it was not unusual to sell ten half barrels of beer a day and on cattle fair day considerably more. Back of the saloon was a barn with an artesian well, and the saloon owners hired a man to feed and water the customer's horses.

Eventually Gonring bought the establishment and had a working man's table that seated at least a dozen men who ate there regularly. His wife worked from six in the morning to midnight, too, preparing and serving the meals. On Monday it was roast beef and Tuesday a leg of pork and a leg of veal. Thursday was pork chop day and his wife would fry 40 pounds of chops in the morning and then put them in a big roaster and put it in the oven to bake. A customer could have all the chops he wanted and some of them had gargantuan appetites. With the chops she served home-made sauerkraut and potatoes. Friday was fried pike day and it came in fresh from Green Bay on the train in the morning. Gonring would meet the train and take the fish home and clean them. People worked hard for their money in those days. He had started work for Peters for nine dollars a week but advanced to fifteen dollars, a goodly wage in West Bend in the early part of this century. He remembered that Martin Walter, President of Lithia Brewery, came in once a week to collect for the beer, which was always Lithia.

Treveranus's

Another popular saloon was Treveranus's, and it was the scene of many a skat tournament. It was one of the "better" saloons and was patronized by such dignitaries as banker Ernst Franckenberg, for whom a Sunday afternoon game of skat at the saloon was a usual event. He served hot lunches in the wintertime with turkey at Thanksgiving and Christmas. In 1910 Charles Schlegel bought the saloon and preferred to serve pork sausage, bread and butter with the beer. There was always less drunkenness in saloons than perhaps there is in taverns today, for the practice of serving food with the beverage made a big difference.

West Bend always had a goodly supply of saloons, which were renamed taverns after the era of Prohibition had ended. West Bend still has a plentiful supply.

CHAPTER 3

Lighting

(1) Old Pewter Oil Lamp, (2) Alcohol Lamp, (3) "Pastor's" Lamp from Germany, 1848.

Early West Bend Lighting From top to bottom, Perforated Lantern, Candle Mold, Betty Lamp.

An unusual private enterprise involved lighting the city. What to use for light after the sun descends has always been a problem for man and the problem was still acute when West Bend was founded. At first the residents relied on the fireplace or the

Betty Lamp, an iron container filled with either tallow, oil, or lard, with a homemade wick (usually of old cloth) inserted in the middle. Later there were candles, which had to be either dipped or pressed. Because most families went to bed early, artificial light was most needed in the winter, and so families tried to have a minimum of 90 candles, one for each of the shortest days. What an improvement when kerosene lamps* replaced the earlier lights.

The streets of the village were unlighted at first, but by 1879 there were eight oil lamps on Main Street, lighted each night by a man who carried a ladder to climb up the light poles, for which he received $12 a year. Of course, street lights were used only in the darker months of the year. One of the plagues of the lamplighter was a band of mischievous boys who sometimes followed him and turned up the wicks so high that they blackened the chimneys; then he would have to climb up and clean them again. A few citizens had their own private street lamps.

When electricity became fashionable, the Silver Lake Ice Company built a small water wheel on the Milwaukee River in 1890 which provided power for the brewery and a few nearby residents. In two years it reached its maximum capacity of 700 light bulbs. The streets now had 32 candle-power lights, an improvement over the oil lamps.

Kuehlthau

But the demand for electricity grew and the Silver Lake Ice Company system was never completely satisfactory for anybody. In 1896 Adam Kuehlthau built a small lighting plant between Mill and Division Streets on the west side of the Milwaukee River to provide better power. Born in 1876, Kuehlthau was a West Bend High School graduate, had worked in the brewery, was a fire department captain and a life-long lover of both fishing and baseball.

The lighting plant was a small family affair run by Adam's son Walter (Buck) who had to repair and service the equipment, act as salesman, and do all the office work. The most noticeable effect on the city at first was the installation of 21 arc lights in the down town area, for which the city bought electricity according to the number of hours of moonlight. At first, customers

*Examples of these forms of lighting are in the Washington County Museum.

were charged according to the number of lights in a house, the rate being fifty cents a month for every 16 candlepower lamp. There were as yet no appliances.

As demand grew, the Kuehlthaus borrowed money in 1902 and installed two more powerful 48 kilowatt generators. Now the number of customers increased, but not enough power was sold to retire the debt, pay the salaries, and make any profit. To raise the rates would be financial suicide. The trouble was, all the power was used at night, and the plant was idle most of the time, especially in summer. Some cities had installed electric streetcars to increase the use in the daytime, but West Bend's plan for them never materialized. Some way had to be found to sell electricity in the daytime.

Enter: Real Private Enterprise

Now we are treated to private enterprise at its finest. The Kuehlthaus went out and purchased electrically heated glue pots and electrically powered embossing tools and persuaded the leather company to install them. Then they pioneered in urging housewives to buy electric ranges, and slowly, by 1910, they had achieved a balance in the use of electricity so the plant could operate profitably both night and day.

Soon the demand again out-distanced the supply. As the number of homes, churches and business places bought electricity, the demand was too great and sudden darkness was common during the periods of greatest use. On the Thanksgiving Eve of 1910 the light went out at four separate church services. "A 16 candle power light gives less light than a firebug," muttered an editor and the owners were accused of using the plant only to make money.

In 1911 Kuehlthau added a 150 kilowatt Westinghouse generator and converted from Direct Current to Alternating Current. Three years later he added a steam turbine and increased the power to 500 kilowatts, ending the use of the water wheel driven generator, but the demand kept growing. Taxpayers urged the adoption of gas for light and power as blackouts became more numerous, and the aldermen went to Fox Lake to see for themselves how city gas worked; they came home suitably impressed. One of the aldermen remarked that you could "see the time on a watch 300 feet from the light."

Kuehlthau achieved a first when in 1919 he built the first complete rural electric line in the United States, serving 57 farmers in Barton, Addison and Wayne on the 24 mile line from West Bend. He sold the West Bend Heating and Lighting Company to the Wisconsin Public Utilities, one of the largest independent electric plants in Wisconsin. In 1927 the company installed more effective city lights along Main Street when 90% of the people along Fourth Avenue and Main Street petitioned for better lighting.

But the life of independents in most businesses and utilities has an ending, and in 1932 the Wisconsin Public Utility sold out to the Wisconsin Gas and Electric Company for a little over a million dollars, and the company serves the area today.

The only log cabin left in West Bend. Originally a shed, it still serves that purpose in an alley between 4th and 5th Avenue, south of Poplar.

Division Street.

Central Main Street.

Foot Bridge over Milwaukee River.

Mid Main Street.

Main Street on a busy day.

Elm Street Looking West — Catholic Church, Public School and High School.

Main Street looking North.

Snow Storm, January 30, 1947.

SECTION VI

TRANSPORTATION AND COMMUNICATION

CHAPTER 1

Transportation

As did every other early Wisconsin town, West Bend had transportation problems from its inception. At first there were only Indian trails used by horses, oxen and humans. As better roads became necessary, citizens petitioned the state government for aid in constructing them, but all pleas for money for internal improvements went unheeded. Towns had no money for large scale road improvements and farmers along the rural roads were invariably in debt. The financial panic of 1857 brought all hope for assistance to a halt. In the spring the farmers cut brush to fill in the worst spots, but every time there was a thaw the roads became impassible. They were better in the winter, but then there was the omnipresent danger that after one left the comparative safety of the village, the roads would become obliterated by the snow and one could lose the way.

In front of every store was a hitching post; some of them were fancy ones, but most were utilitarian cedar posts. While the horses were tied to the posts in the summer time they stomped the flies so vigorously that huge holes were dug by their hooves. When churches were built, families drove to church in their wagons or buggies and sheltered the horses in sheds built behind every church. The usual weekday lumber wagon was called a "democrat," but many families owned fancier rigs for Sunday. West Bend sported a thriving wagon factory so that it was easy to obtain a good wagon locally.

For a brief time there was a toll road from West Bend to Milwaukee with a fare of 70 cents for one animal and one vehicle. It was a small improvement over the other trails, but it was still full of stumps and roots and holes. In the winter bob sleighs were the rule; at first they were homemade boxes on runners, but Schmidt and Stork made fine ones that could turn corners easily. With hot bricks well wrapped up to hold the heat, and an ample supply of buffalo robes or bear skins, it was possible for a family to nestle down quite warmly.

The big dream was for the town to have a railroad. In 1858 the directors of the Chicago and Northwestern Railroad Company met in Chicago to consider building a railroad north of Milwaukee, and every town anywhere near Lake Michigan aspired to have the tracks go through their town. West Bend awaited the news that they would be one of the lucky ones, but it was not to be. Instead, the line went to Richfield, twelve miles away, for the railroad company felt that that town had a better chance to grow into a thriving city. So all the needed freight had to be brought in to West Bend over the miserable roads by horses or oxen. Typical freight loads consisted of lumber for the homes and other buildings, farm machinery, and all the supplies and groceries for the stores. These first railroad "stations" were mere platforms, and it was necessary to pick up the freight when it arrived. Merchants still preferred to drive directly to Milwaukee when the weather permitted, however.

Farmers had to drive their cattle either to Richfield or to Milwaukee, and it was an increasingly common sight for people in West Bend to see single herds being driven down the Main Street on their way to the railroad, followed by several farmers who combined their cattle into one large herd to share the hazards of the long trip.

Later a stagecoach line came into West Bend from Cedar Creek, only seven miles southeast of West Bend, but the hills were steeper and harder for the teams, so loaded wagons kept to the longer Richfield route. What trials! Often merchandise sat in Milwaukee or Richfield for up to three weeks until the roads settled so goods could be picked up. Farmers and merchants often travelled together to help each other out of the gigantic potholes on the road. Sometimes each wagon had to have all its goods unloaded while the team pulled the empty wagon over the bad spot, and then the goods had to be laboriously reloaded. As this might occur several times on a typical trip, clearly a railroad was needed.

West Bend Depot.

West Bend Gets its Railroad

Unfortunately for the historian, all copies of the newspapers are missing for this crucial period. It is recorded that in 1870 L. F. Frisby, C. Ecstein, G. H. Kleffler, L. Findorff and John Potter formed a committee to try to bring the railroad to West Bend. Whatever happened in the interim is not known, but in 1873 there was wild rejoicing for at long last the railroad came to West Bend. By this time there were the first seeds of industry in town, and it appeared as though the town might grow further. As yet most of the building was on the west side of the river, but when the railroad bought land on the east side (because it was cheaper) and built a depot, water tower, stock pen, and switch track, two stores promptly built grain elevators there, coal companies built bins to store coal, and a stave factory was erected. The lumberyard was nearby, and the mere handful of homes there was soon the nucleus for others to build to the east.

By 1884 there were six trains daily, with service beginning as early at 1:30 A.M. One could buy a round trip ticket to Chicago for $4.95. The only blight on the joy in West Bend occurred when people of nearby towns, now connected by similar freight lines, no longer brought all their business to West Bend. Then, too, the railroads charged high rates to compensate for the expense of building the tracks, but when the construction was fully paid for they so enjoyed the income that they kept the rates high until bus and truck competition forced a lowering.

West Bend's first freight office consisted of one room with a hard coal stove, and a large coal bin. The depot was strictly utilitarian and rather ugly. There were benches inside for the customers, and spittoons to take care of the tobacco chewers. Those first station agents, one of whom was Tom Farmer, had to be telegraphers, freight managers, ticket agents, firemen and bookkeepers. The depot was enlarged by 1900 to include two waiting rooms, one for women and children and another for men, and to protect the weaker sex one could not get from one waiting room to the other unless one went outside. No smoking was permitted on the ladies' side, and no men were allowed, even though they might be in the same family, a rule which remained until 1910. A night operator was hired so that there was continual service at the depot. A bucket and dipper supplied drinking water until 1925 when running water was installed; and stoves served until 1929 when a furnace replaced them.

When the railroad sold a booklet of 25 rides to Milwaukee for $10.00, it was a boon, but as always, people found a way to cheat the system. Stores loaned out the tickets to their favorite customers and families swapped them. Inasmuch as this defeated the purpose of the reduced fares, the railroad ceased to issue the cheaper tickets and everybody lost.

In addition to the choices one had to get to neighboring cities, something sadly lacking today, a horse-drawn carriage used to meet every train. Inside there were lengthwise benches seating up to a dozen people, carrying the passengers to town for a quarter. There were even side curtains in case of bad weather. A livery stable provided direct service to the hotels until taxis came to town and met every train.

The other advantage of the railroad, not only to West Bend but to the entire country, was standard time. Before that people used either local time or solar time. In the latter case it would be 1:10 in Madison, for instance, 1:16 in Milwaukee, and 1:17 in Chicago. When all time was converted to standard time, local citizens used to go to the depot to set their watches, for the telegraph periodically sent a time signal over the wires.

Bicycles

About this time bicycles were becoming commonplace and West Bend had its share of them, too. The first ones were the kind with the large front wheels and the tiny rear ones, requiring quite a sense of balance to ride and it was also an art to even mount one, let alone stay on. Usually one walked them up hills and it was always possible to tell who owned bicycles because they wore bicycle guards on their pants legs, a precaution against entanglement in the sprockets of the wheels. Bicycle racing became a local sport, too.

Automobiles

Eventually automobiles came to West Bend and transformed the town, for cars demanded better roads. Horses reared at the approach of the "newfangled" things and many a car driver was heartily cursed as he was responsible for sending the horse into an uncontrollable gallop, or, worse, into the ditch. But horse owners had their revenge when the cars became mired, as was frequent, or had innumerable flat tires, as was more common. The horse drivers sniggered audibly and cried "Get a horse!" to the discomfiture of the proud new car owner. S. F. Mayer owned the first car in town in 1905, a Grout Steam touring car made in Massachusetts, "an elegant machine." By June C. C. Henry had a Mitchell touring car with four cylinders capable of going 20 miles an hour. The city had to pass an ordinance immediately to limit speed to 12 miles an hour, while surrounding areas limited speed to 25 miles an hour. In West Bend one was further compelled by law to stop his car whenever meeting a horse to avoid causing an accident.

Some of the men had to practice steering in the secrecy of their garage, for they had been brought up with horses, unlike today's youngsters with all their tricycles and other wheeled toys. It took some doing to learn to drive. Local tales abound of the first time car drivers shouted "whoa" in vain as they approached their shed, only to fly through the wall before remembering to apply the brakes. Besides, the horse always knew its way home. Many were the dire predictions that those autos would replace workers in the harness industry, for example. And what would the buggy whip manufacturers do? Soon, of course, the number of people employed in the new industry in West Bend outdistanced the number of workers catering to the horse trade.

The era of those first cars was something to behold. When they roared into town they raised clouds of dust. Riders had to wear linen dusters, goggles and scarves for protection. It was necessary to arrive home by nightfall until kerosene lamps or the later acetylene lights became standard equipment on cars. The number of different makes of autos was astonishing, too. At one time there were 50 different brands made in the state of Wisconsin alone, one of the more popular being the Kissel car made in nearby Hartford, but by 1930 the big auto companies controlled the market and the small firms vanished into history.

As late as the first years of World War I, cars were rarely driven in the winter. H. B. Foster, the local Ford agent, put his car away in December, 1910, after making a "remarkable record of 7,000 miles since May with only one flat tire and no blowouts." He noted that Ford had made no changes in its cars since 1907, and that there was no reason to change, for they were "sound just the way they are!" If one waited until spring to buy a touring car it would cost $780, complete with all the latest gadgets: an extension top, speedometer, gas lamps, brass windshields, and a generator. A roadster would cost only $680. Later it was possible to buy a Ford for approximately $400 as mass production lowered the cost.

One proposed change in West Bend transportation came when the Milwaukee Railway Company sought to secure a franchise here for an electric railway, and in 1931 the citizens were all excited about it. A committee including G. A. Kuechenmeister, A. Pick, John Gehl and A. C. Fuge was appointed, but the railway never materialized. During World War II a local bus company served West Bend and Barton for a time, but by the 1970's all that is left is the Wisconsin Coach Lines bus twice a day, as a passenger train no longer serves the city. It is not always true that everything improves with time.

Airport

The first airplane to make an appearance in West Bend came to the County Fair in 1912. The highly touted plane flew forty feet — and crashed ignominiously. But planes became safer, and local businessmen began to agitate for a city owned airport, yet there was no state law empowering cities to buy land outside the city limits. So in 1929, B. C. Ziegler, Dr. William Urkart and Frank Groom bought 100 acres two miles east of town to hold until the state law was changed. Later that year the legislature duly enacted the enabling law and the city bought the land from the original investors for $15,000, becoming the first city of its size in Wisconsin to own land for an airport.

One of first planes at Airport.

By November the airport installed a rotating beacon, boundary lines were laid out, the land was tiled and leased as a landing strip to the Fox River Valley Airmail Service. On the 25th of May, 1930, a big celebration was held when the airport was dedicated; airplane stunts and other events entertained the large crowd. The first plane to land at the airport from out of town was a Ryan cabin monoplane, from which Governor Kohler stepped to pick up the American Legion and Legion Auxiliary membership cards as a stunt to help the new airport.

After the metal hangar was built and celebrated with a 40 plane parade, lessons began for local people, some of whom eventually served the United States Air Force in both World War II and the Korean War. Miss Lillian Puestow was the first young lady to take flying lessons. By 1942 there was a long 3000 foot airstrip as well as a shorter one, and the property was leased to Al Haen and Earl Stier.

By the 1970's local business firms used the airport regularly and Lear jets are a common sight. Helicopters and the newest sport, gliding, also use the airport, and land purchases are proceeding for future expansion.

Left to right, Jos. O'Meara, Joe Knippel, and unknown.

West Bend Transit Company

Fred Karsten and S. Henry started the firm as a sideline while working for the Standard Oil Company, but sold it in 1905 to George and John Hetzel who used three teams of horses to carry materials for customers in the area. Six years later Henry P. and Henry E. Schloemer formed the West Bend Drayage Company with three employees. By 1916 they had their first truck, hauling milk for the White House Milk Company in the morning and for private business in the afternoon. They would come directly to one's home to pick up packages. At first they made daily round trips to Milwaukee only in the summer time, but when the state highway was built they made the trip the year round; local merchants were elated over the door to door delivery. In 1921 the firm became the West Bend Transit Company with a warehouse on Forest Avenue, after which it grew until it had a fleet of trucks. It is now the West Bend Transit and Service Company. The city is also served by bus parcel service and United Parcel.

CHAPTER 2

The Telephone

Only two years after Alexander Graham Bell demonstrated the wonders of the telephone at the 1876 Centennial Exhibition in Philadelphia, the marvelous machine made its debut in West Bend at the local Fair Grounds. According to an editor, everybody seemed to want to "shoot off his mouth" in the wonderful instrument. That same year Franckenburg and Karsten put one to its first commercial use in the village when they connected the grain elevator to their Main Street store to save countless steps. Depot agent Thomas Farmer, son of one of the first inhabitants, made the installation.

In 1883, the Wisconsin Telephone Company selected Andrew Pick to secure enough subscriptions to warrant an office in West Bend. This proved to be difficult, but nevertheless 16 men were hired to dig post holes on Main Street in the frozen ground and to erect posts to carry the wires. By May, Pick had persuaded Goetter's store, Weil's law office, the brewery, and the Barton Depot to install phones, but it took another two months before two more customers could be found. In five years there was a total of only 16 phones.

"Central"

"Central" was located in various business places for the first 17 years of its life in West Bend. Mrs. Muenzer's millinery shop, Weil's law office, the Fairbanks creamery, Opgenorth's book store all served, among others, to house the central switchboard. When the magic number of 25 subscribers was reached in 1900, the village could have a central office. By then all the doctors had a phone, as well as a few private homes, including those of S. S. Barney, G. A. Kuechenmeister, C. P. Moores, and the Franckenburgs. Elmer Barnes was the first telephone manager, and either Bessie Goeden or Emma Pick Muenzer was the first "hello girl." (The record conflicts on this point.) When a call came through for a non-subscriber, "Central" would have to walk to find him and bring him to the phone. On July 1 a night operator was added and the craze to own a phone grew. Fannie Barnes served in the daytime and Katie McQueen manned the post at night.

By 1901 the office was in the First State Bank building on Main Street, and if there were a call for the police, the operator would switch on a red light on the top of the building; when a policeman saw it he would phone in to the operator for information.

Mrs. Emma Boden Altendorf recalled that her mother Emma Pick Muenzer came to West Bend as a widow in 1883, and supported herself as a seamstress and piano teacher before she became the operator. During an electrical storm the office would be filled with bluish haze and electrical sparks would play about the switchboard, frightening the children so that they hid under the bed.

With that humble beginning, progress was more rapid. In 1917 a battery operated system was installed. There was a temporary setback when a severe ice storm incapacitated the community in February of 1922; the wires were torn down, and it took months to repair them all. The phone company's Christmas present to West Bend in 1927 was to saw off all the poles on Main

Street at ground level and install underground cables. A year later there were 1200 phones.

By 1978 there were 79 local telephone "families" serving the public and the more than 8000 subscribers sent out over 60,000 calls a day. The payroll and local purchases grossed more than two million dollars for the local economy.

CHAPTER 3

The Radio

After radio was invented, people in West Bend awaited the appearance of their own local station. Long before that, though, a United States government operator came to West Bend in 1926 for five days in March to set up a portable station in the Mermac theater to show people how shows were produced. (Many local citizens had their own sets by that time, battling with ear phones and static to hear the precious sounds from a distant locale.) He called the station WHBL and used local talent to demonstrate it all over the state with a noonday program, a show for kiddies at 5:30, and came back on the air at 10:30 at night with West Bend's leading dance band, Heinies' Feet Warmers. Wires were strung from the steeple on Holy Angels church to the Mermac Hotel to broadcast music from the church organ there and help make the name of West Bend known throughout the state. August Berkholtz was the prime mover in bringing the demonstration to West Bend.

Milwaukee's WTMJ had community hours on its station and in 1928 it was West Bend's turn. The Moose Band, under the direction of A. G. Hron, performed. Baritone Al Homuth sang a solo, Lauretta Johannes whistled, Eugene Lucas played the organ, Mrs. LeRoy Poull soloed, Frances Flaherty entertained at the piano, and Charles Raloff played the violin. The air was filled with static, but it was a satisfying program for it further broadcast the name of West Bend throughout the state.

Some people were as suspicious then about the ill effects of radio on children as others are today about the ill effect of television. In 1934 a speaker came to a PTA meeting to rail against

WBKV Radio Station, 1979.

radio programs as detrimental to children's health — for it excited them too much!

But the real day in West Bend radio history began in November 1950 when WBKV began to broadcast. Paul Mueller had been working for a radio station in Milwaukee when he became ill and had plenty of time to dream of owning his own station some day. Locally, August Berkholtz had the same dream and the two joined forces and secured the only remaining open spot on the AM dial — 1470.

They bought a five acre plot on Decorah Road, and awaited a license. This was no easy matter. It took them three months to gain even a conditional license, and then the FCC monitored them daily for another month before granting them full licensing in December. Today WBKV operates a 1000 watt station at 1470 KC and its sister station WBKV-FM at 925 MG with 32,000 watts of power, but it is no longer home owned for in 1970 it was purchased by the Gazette Printing Company.

SECTION VII
THE PROFESSIONS

CHAPTER 1
Medicine — Physicians and Surgeons

Health

Early settlers had to be tough and healthy. No doctor lived in the village, but what an assortment of ills could befall one! First, there was the omnipresent danger of contagious diseases: diphtheria (the victims were buried the same day as their death to avoid further contagion), typhoid fever, smallpox, cholera, and the more common childhood diseases of measles, mumps and chickenpox. Each child was expected to run the gamut of the common diseases to insure future immunity.

People became ill with the "blue cough," quinsy, catarrh, fits, lumbago, galloping consumption (as well as regular consumption), humors — all words that have largely passed from our vocabulary. One might have hemorrhaging of the lungs, lung fever, la grippe, a paralysis, or die of "old age." Rheumatism was common. An attack of erysipelas was usually fatal, as was appendicitis until doctors mastered the art of operating properly. Then, too, there was the possibility of pneumonia, worms, snake bites, or a host of diseases under the general term "nervous diseases," often affecting and killing young children. And always there were the "female complaints," due partly to the constant pregnancies and nursing of babies.

West Bend did little to reduce the danger of contagion. Garbage was tossed into the river, or worse, allowed to gather on the streets. Animals roamed the streets freely, leaving their droppings to attract flies and germs. Every home had its privy which was often so placed that drainage ran directly into the

1890 Medicine Man.

drinking water, for each home had its own well. In the spring of 1866, the local editor admonished the people to clear out their garbage before all the snow melted, or there would be pestilence and malaria. Cholera appeared periodically, and was particularly rife that year.

Milkmen brought milk to the homes in open pails swinging from a yoke carried over the shoulders. They measured it out by the quart into a crock on the kitchen table or on the front porch, and if a finger were necessary to remove a fly or other filth, well, it kept the milk looking clean! Sometimes generous milkmen poured a bit of milk on the front steps for the friendly family cat.

Screens were unknown. Inasmuch as screens are still largely unnecessary in Europe to this day, the immigrant population was unused to them. Wells were left uncovered. There was neither hospital nor trained nurse, just women who had a "knack" for caring for the sick, and midwives to deliver the numerous babies. Until doctors settled in the community all ill persons had three choices: leave the illness alone in the hopes it would cure itself, submit to the numerous home remedies, or resort to patent medicines. There was a home remedy for everything. Did you have a corn? Merely soak a piece of bread in vinegar and apply. The corn would vanish. Did your rheumatism flare up? Just add saltpeter and turpentine to a pint of cider vinegar and drink. Was cholera feared? Ward it off by putting a teaspoon of flowers of sulphur into each stocking daily. And to stay healthy one must never, never go outdoors on an empty stomach or eat fresh hot bread or any sour fruit.

Did you have a common cold? Merely boil some onions in new milk, add some oatmeal and a little salt, sip, and go rapidly to bed. Throat sore? Soak some salt pork in hot vinegar and sprinkle it with black pepper and apply. There was a remedy for everything; what need had they of doctors?

Damp air was considered dangerous, so people stayed indoors during damp seasons. Particularly unhealthy was night air, so the bedroom windows were kept shut. Imagine the steam baths on hot summer nights!

But if home remedies didn't work, there was the shelf in the general store that held the marvelous patent medicines — wonderful concoctions that could cure everything. Ayers Cathartic pills in the 1850's were "so composed that diseases within the range can rarely withstand or evade them." Ayer's Cherry Pectoral would cure even "desperate diseases of the lungs." Dr. Robert's Scandinavian Remedies could cure dyspepsia, liver troubles, and a host of other afflications. Lydia Pinkham would cure the most stubborn of female complaints. All were advertised in the local papers.

Indian medicine had a peculiar fascination for the early West Benders, and one Indian Root Pill box informed the reader that all diseases originated from impurity in the blood, and these pills would root out all such impurities. Of course, the chief ingredient of the pills and all the other medical wonders was alcohol. No wonder there were testimonials of instant relief.

West Bend Receives its First Doctor

In 1859 there was general rejoicing, for a Dr. Willenski was coming to town "permanently." His credentials were impressive; he had been the regimental surgeon in the British Army during the Crimean War! Typical of most doctors at that time, he had little training. Doctors in this part of the country were merely apprenticed to an older doctor, following him around in his practice and learning what they could by observation and first hand experience. Early doctors usually arrived in town with a horse and buggy, or perhaps a horse and saddlebags, and a minimum of equipment: some balance scales, a stethoscope, mortar and pestle, a few instruments such as forceps and some obstetrical tools. They made their own splints and bandages and concocted their own medicine. How thankful we are that most people survived.

An interesting early tool for healing was a cupping knife. This consisted of 16 tiny sharp blades on a spring. When the contrivance was pushed down on the arm, 16 tiny incisions were made in the skin; then a glass tumbler in which alcohol had been burned was pressed down on the incision to extract the blood. (One such knife is in the Washington County Museum.) Curiously, they drew blood from the ill, while today's doctors give transfusions.

The above named Dr. Willenski apparently did not stay long, and a succession of advertisements by other doctors appeared in the local papers. In the 1870's the doctors were rarely German, while most of the local residents spoke German, often almost exclusively; one Dr. Hunt hired a citizen to interpret for his German-speaking patients. He was noted for never sending a bill, a relatively common practice then. An interesting comment in the March 5, 1879, *West Bend Democrat* mentioned that the doctors were joyful; "They are kept on the go."

Local Board of Health Established

Gradually conditions began to improve. Doctors came to West Bend to stay. But the physical conditions of the city did not improve until the State Board of Health insisted that West Bend establish a local board of health. That was finally accomplished in 1891, and Dr. W. Lynch became the first health officer. His 1891 report mentioned that there were 36 deaths that year; 15 from old age, 4 from pneumonia, 2 of consumption, 1 of scarlet fever, 1 of typhoid, and the rest dying of chronic or "complicating" diseases. West Bend was touted as a healthy town in which to live.

Dr. Lynch got busy at once. He had wells tested and those unfit for use had to correct the pollution or cease to use the water. He and many townspeople were horrified at the open sewers, so culverts had to be covered. Meanwhile Lynch tried to convince the people that a city well and sanitary sewerage were essential to the city's health. In 1895 the State Board of Health noted the unsanitary condition of the Milwaukee River with all the raw sewage in it, and its members were horrified at the

Dr. D. W. Lynch office and residence, built by B. S. Weil. Stork residence in background.

proximity of the slaughter house to the river, into which all the offal and blood were drained. And all this time the river was used for swimming! The Board also chided the local physicians for failing to report contagious diseases properly.

The State Board of Health began its practice of issuing bulletins to warn citizens of unhealthful conditions. They especially spoke about consumption, which rampaged here for years. While the disease had been recorded as long ago as 1000 B.C. by the Hindus, man had done little to arrest it, but the bulletins warned of the dreadfully impure air in schoolhouses, factories, and public buildings, all due to improper ventilation. Sleeping together in crowded and unventilated rooms, drinking the milk from or eating the meat of tubercular cows, and prolonged nursing beyond twelve months were all inveighed against. The cure for disease was fresh air and sunshine.

Fly-by-night doctors often came to town for short stays, usually setting up a temporary office in the Washington House. One of these dispensed nothing but colored water, proving that faith is the primary part of the cure. During prohibition Regner's Drug Store was dispensing drugs that called for Rye, Whiskey or other spirits to be taken by the half wineglass or a tablespoon every three hours.

Health Ordinances Passed

Meanwhile the village fathers were passing ordinances to correct some of the more obvious evils. In 1891 they decreed

Dr. Edward Boesewetter, Veterinarian.

that no children from homes where contagious diseases existed could go to school, a law that at least partially slowed contagion. If there were a death from a contagious disease, funerals could no longer be held in the schoolhouse, as had been done, nor could any child legally be a pallbearer or be present when the coffin was open. In June of 1905 they banned spitting on the sidewalks or other public places and fined some of the guilty. Would that such an ordinance were enforced today!

A popular idea that provoked much local conversation but never got off the ground was the one about the Chinese doctor from New York who charged an individual $35 a year to keep him healthy; a family paid up to $150 for the same privilege. The doctor would come around daily, and for every day the person could not get outdoors, the doctor forfeited 10 cents, so it was to the advantage of the physician to keep his patients healthy.

The mills of the gods surely do grind slowly, but West Bend became more health conscious in the second two decades of the twentieth century. The State Board of Health gave teachers permission to send home all students with colds, coughs, severe itches, lice, body filth and clothes vermin. By 1919 a heart and lung clinic was set up in one of the rooms of the First National

Bank, and a school nurse spent five weeks there and was appalled to find malnourishment and 30% of the children underweight, by state standards then. In one home she found that a mother worked nights and her brood was eating pancakes, syrup, and salt fish for supper, with the pancakes all but inedible. She fumed, "A mother rearing a family has no business to go out and work!" and proposed that West Bend provide milk twice a day for its school children. Of 482 pupils who were examined, the nurse found 287 with tooth defects, 76 mouth breathers, 109 vision problems, 160 with enlarged tonsils and 149 cases of malnourishment. Two years later a nurse tried to force some action by reporting that the ones who did not get milk were at the bottom of the scholastic list.

Tuberculosis was a persistent problem; seven cases were discovered at once during an examination by the Anti-Tuberculosis personnel in 1920. Persistent efforts to have the garbage collected on a regular basis paid off in 1923 when the Woman's Club, among others, backed it.

The periodic issue of sex education in the schools was highlighted in the schools in 1920 by a visit from a State Board of Health speaker who told the parents that it was parents who needed the sex education (by implication that it was not the students), and that their children were "innocent until age 12!" How times change!

During the flu epidemic of 1919 that affected West Bend as adversely as it did the rest of the nation, Dr. W. J. Wehle noted that of the 50 patients at the asylum, the high fever restored reason to some and that a few who had not talked due to "insanity" now did so as the high fever elevated their pulse and sent more blood to their brain, according to his theory. No record could be found as to his use of that discovery.

Gradually, contagious and other diseases abated. By the 1930's milk was sold in the more sanitary bottles, with Peter Gutchenreiter being the first to do so. In the 1940's a polio scare occurred; one year the schools opened late, and in 1946 an epidemic closed the fourth, seventh and eighth grades. The epidemic recurred in 1947 while in 1950 a ten year old boy died of the disease. Several local citizens suffered lifetime crippling.

West Bend was hard hit by the Asian flu in 1956. In 1958 an attempt was made to reduce the rat population by cleaning up all the old yards and buildings and ordering all animals except cats and dogs removed from the city. No particular epidemics or other public health problems have visited West Bend for years except periodic lesser flu epidemics.

The Doctors Heidner

The story of the Heidners, father and son, is one of the pleasant stories in West Bend medical history. The father, G. A. Heidner, was born in 1864 and graduated from Plymouth High School, after which he taught school for two years to earn the money to attend Rush Medical School in Chicago. He began practice in Waubeka, came to West Bend in 1896, and built and operated the first hospital in the city, according to his daughter Edith, and was the surgeon. While in practice he helped to found the Washington County Medical Association, and was its first secretary.

Among his endearing personal traits was a detestation of anything that was sham or smacked of ostentation. He believed that if everybody would practice good manners every day in the family, they would become an inherent part of one, and there would be no need to put on any airs for company. Good manners in the home would also reduce family tension, he said. The advice is as sound today as it was then. Another of his beliefs was that a man would never amount to much if he were known only by the deeds of his ancestors. "Live up to the good reputation of your forbears, not on it" he would say. He lost his wife in the typhoid epidemic of 1910 and subsequently remarried.

Typical of his unheralded bits of service to the city was his wont of raking the stones from the road in front of the Catholic cemetery, and smoothing the rough spots so that the road might be fit for automobile travel. That was long before the cement highway made such an action unnecessary, of course, but he never lost his belief that the individual should step in and do his share and not leave everything for the government. He died in 1918.

His son Albion was a graduate of West Bend High School and the University of Wisconsin (1911), after which he attended his father's Chicago alma mater, graduated, and came to West Bend in 1915 to practice medicine. He trained as a surgeon and planned to go to Europe for further study, but World War I intervened.

During his many years of service to West Bend he served on the School Board as treasurer for 25 years. In 1952 he was Kiwanis Man of the Year. He served as President of the Wis-

Dr. Albion H. Heidner

consin State Medical Society in 1951-52 and was on its Board of Directors for 28 years. While president, he initiated a flexible Blue Shield plan and expanded the Wisconsin Journal of Medicine. At one time he said, "The medical profession must join in solid ranks to assure people of qualified medical care, untrammeled and unfettered by bureaucratic control of the government." Because his advice has not been heeded, bureaucracy seems about to invade the profession even more.

He was happily surprised in 1959 when a special dinner was given in his honor by the Wisconsin Medical Society at which chief spokesman, Dr. Fox, said, "It is given to but few men to have participated so long and so fruitfully in the affairs of his fellow men."

During his years as a physician and surgeon he dreamed of an adequate hospital to serve the community. His dream coincided with the needs of modern industry, for the appalling rise of industrial accidents affected the insurance the manufacturers had to pay, and B. C. Ziegler, particularly, was able to mobilize the West Bend Aluminum Company and the First National Bank, which he also controlled, for the drive. He and his supporters knew who had the money to give and many an arm was twisted in the process, but Dr. Heidner's dream came true. He died in 1962.

Chiropractors

In 1905 the first chiropractor, Dr. Frederic, opened an office in West Bend, after which there have been a succession of others. At the present time three chiropractors serve the city.

CHAPTER 2

Medicine — the Hospitals

The road to the present hospital was a long one. At first there were no hospitals of any kind, and all work was carried on in the doctor's office or at home. Many of the first operations were performed on a dining room table. Then there was a succession of small hospitals in private homes, supervised by practical nurses. Among the early ones was one at 815 Cedar Street managed by Mrs. Jacob Herdt, in whose home the first operation was performed. In 1916 Mrs. Carolyn Merten opened a hospital at 231 North Eighth Avenue with four beds in three rooms and another room for operations. Five doctors used that hospital: Doctors Driessel, Weber, Lynch, Bauer and Heidner. When Mrs. Merten quit, Dr. Heidner bought the beds.

Between 1915 and 1918 there was a Columbia Hospital at Seventh and Elm with Mrs. M. Hopper supervising it from 1916 to its closing. To insure its success, the Aluminum Company donated kettles and other utensils, the M. E. Church provided some preserves, the *West Bend News* sent its weekly paper, and Martin Walter donated ham, flour, sugar, canned goods, coffee, bacon, etc. But there were not enough patients to go around, and it had to close, for doctors could not agree on the use of any one hospital.

In 1907 Dr. Heidner had his own hospital at 229 Fifth Avenue, with Mrs. George McCormack as the first patient. Heidner's office was on the first floor, the family living quarters were at the back, and the six room hospital was upstairs with five beds and an operating room. He trained his own nurses and supervised a correspondence course for them from Chautauqua, New York. One of them, Anna Butzke, became the second Mrs.

Heidner. Mrs. Etta cooked for the patients and boarded the nurses. In 1913 Dr. Driessel bought the hospital, but by 1915 it was back in the hands of Dr. G. A. Heidner, and his son joined him there.

In 1920 Mrs. Steve Bradley used the second floor of her home at 909 Cedar Street for a hospital and it remained in use until the new hospital was opened in 1930. It was started by Dr. Lynch when Mrs. Merten's Hospital acquired too many patients. Bradley's could accommodate up to eight patients at one time, and was supported by all the doctors, so "the rock was removed on which former attempts of this kind foundered."

City Sanitaria

Three years later Dr. Webster Lynch opened a sanitarium at 418 North Eighth Avenue especially for patients with diabetes and Bright's Disease. Mrs. A. H. Klumb was his office girl and Edna Klumb went to California to learn to prepare proper diets for his patients. When the sanitarium closed he donated his equipment to Mrs. Bradley; much later it was sent to St. Joseph's Hospital and used in the tonsillectomy room.

In 1911 Dr. Urkart opened a sanitarium on the second floor at 157 North Main Street. He had six beds, a sterile, light operating room, one or two nurses, a housekeeper and an office girl. When he died in 1935 the san closed. He was known as a generous donor to the city hospital and cooperated fully with the staff there.

St. Joseph's Community Hospital

Long before this, however, there was sentiment for a proper city hospital, but the post war depression in the early 1920's forced postponement of any plans. By the late 1920's, though, the inadequacies of all the local hospitals were patently evident, and besides, rival Hartford already had a community hospital! A prize was offered to the student who could write the best essay on the need for a local hospital, and Louis Ottmer won the award.

Finances were, of course, the issue. After much investigation, the planners decided that a sisterhood would be the cheapest way to operate a hospital; the Sisters of Divine Savior would take no wages for their services, other than room and board, and they pledged 50% of the initial cost and all the operating expenses if the city would provide the rest of the funds.

The drive began in 1928-1929; 150 workers canvassed every home in the area and held mass meetings of factory workers. There was an intensive three day drive to obtain the needed $68,500, with B. C. Ziegler providing the bonds for the rest of the community's share. A quota register was placed in Schoof's Music Store to record the donations. Committee members pledged $24,200 of the amount before the drive officially opened, and at the end of the first day, the register showed that another $24,000 had been pledged. The second day brought in $11,000. Could the third day provide the remaining $13,000?

People were in suspense all day as the quota register showed no changes. Would they make it? When night fell, the first of West Bend's community drives showed that not only had they made it, but they had gone over the top and eventually $88,000 was pledged. Some local residents recall that pressure was sometimes exerted on the populace to obtain the funds, but they were obtained. The early years of the Great Depression slowed up some of the giving, and several donors could not meet their pledges.

The Lt. Ray Dickop Post donated five acres of land for the building and by 1930 the fireproof 25 bed hospital was ready for dedication by the Milwaukee Msgr. But before the official opening, Mrs. Walter Gumm had given birth to a daughter, becoming the first patient. Five years later the yearly patient number grew to 1064. Twelve sisters of the Order of Divine Savior provided the service, under the supervision of Sister Galla. If one wanted or needed a private nurse, the service was also available.

By the late 1970's the hospital has undergone several renovations and additions and is a source of civic pride.

CHAPTER 3

Dentistry

If anything should make us glad that we do not live in the "good old days" it should be modern dentistry. For most of the early years of West Bend there were no dentists in the village. People had three choices: suffer, rely on home remedies, or walk to a neighboring town that had a dentist to help them. And help was crude indeed. Tales of horror abound concerning the dreadful pain inflicted by early dentists and many a patient vowed never to return for a tooth pulling.

Early extraction was often done by doctors or barbers, who used forceps to yank out the offender. When dentists arrived, the cure was little better. They often clamped a turnkey on the painful tooth, and twisted a key as one might turn a key in a lock until the tooth was either torn out by the roots or ground down, killing the root and stopping the pain. Few dentists cared to fill teeth; the universal remedy was — if it hurts, yank it out!

The first dentist came to West Bend in 1875 but did not stay long. In 1877 Dr. Campbell practiced three days a month but stayed only a couple of years. Dr. Flaherty opened an office over Bruhy's. The latter dentist was somewhat of an inventor, for he invented a pressure machine to deaden the nerves of the infected teeth. By depressing a foot lever, the pressure forced an anesthetic into the teeth, but when nerve blocking became popular he abandoned the pressure system. He also invented a sterilizer, quite an improvement in principle. Most early dentists merely opened the unwilling patient's mouth and plunged their fingers in without any thought about washing their hands.

Dental advertisements are interesting to read. Dr. Campbell advertised "extraction without pain or danger." An 1877 ad read: "If your tooth is making you dance against your will, or inclined to draw profanity, call at Dr. Hunt's office."

The most personally popular early dentist was Doc Cameron, who arrived in the early 1880's and then left for a time, to return for one week every month, but he eventually came back to full time practice in his Main Street office.

Historically, people have always neglected their teeth. A report in 1935, for example, stated that West Bend school children had: spongy gums, poor enamel, staining, large cavities, teeth discharging pus which might affect their health later, etc. The free examination was an eye-opener to many.

In 1959 the dentists led the movement to add fluoride to the city's water. After a battle between the pros and the cons, with all sorts of information and mis-information, the pros won in a city-wide vote by 1377 to 1276. However, the reluctant City Council claimed the referendum was purely advisory and did not bind them to the addition of flouride to the water system, but

City Attorney Thomas O'Meara told them that the referendum had the force of law and the Council had to accept the decision.

When the city finally added the flouride they did not announce that they had done so, for they feared a rash of complaints about the taste of the water. When after several weeks no complaints were received, they announced the addition, which upset all those who had been prepared to remonstrate.

The most famous family of dentists in West Bend has been that of the William Hausmann's, and at the present time William Hausmann IV is practicing in the city.

By 1979 West Bend is served by more than 20 dentists and orthodontists and the number grows steadily.

CHAPTER 4

Education — the Elementary and High Schools

Elementary and High School Education*

When one walks into the fine school buildings in the city today it is hard to reconcile their condition with the following description of old South School written by Carl Quickert, who quoted the old *Democrat* as calling it "a house with whitewashed walls and uncurtained windows, through which the sun's rays streamed all through the long summer day upon blistered necks and sweating faces and aching spines, because the soil was too niggardly to nourish a tree to mitigate with its shade the suffocating blinding heat; with seats so high from the floor that the feet of their tallest might not hope to reach the floor for years — seats with backs made of plumb line, and confronted by horizontal desks, hacked with jackknives of no-one-knows-how-many

*The subject of West Bend education is such a vast one that there is room for very little of it in this volume. Interested readers are referred to a comprehensive account of it in *A History of Secondary Education in West Bend*, a Master's Thesis by the author and available in the West Bend Public Library.

owners, and besmirched with enough logwood ink to cover with pot-hooks every sheet of foolscap in Wisconsin; a house whose builders must have thought that the young intellect could grow without water as well as air, and so with wonderful sagacity placed the ventilating machinery in the roof; a house whose playground was a wilderness of sand and whose apparatus consisted of an oaken ferrule and Walker's Dictionary."

Further imagination will picture that same school in the winter time, when those who sat nearest the meager source of heat roasted, while those in the back of the room acquired chillblains. And this school was called a "better building" than the first shanty in which Miss Cynthia Sinn taught in 1846, just a year after the village was founded, when the state provided $22.00 for the 22 pupils ranging in age from four to twenty. The school was used for every public function at first: church services, political meetings, spelling bees, etc. Inasmuch as adults would never fit into child-size seats, the children had to suffer with dangling feet.

It was the first settlers, the Yankees, who brought with them the principle of public responsibility for education. Believing that Satan opposed learning, it would be possible to weaken Old Nick by learning to read and write. They also saw the public school as the place to further Americanize the incoming Germans. On the other hand, the Germans looked upon education as a means of achieving more esteem and social mobility, especially for their children. So there was early motivation for a school, but there was opposition, too. Farmers wondered why it was necessary to go to school to learn to farm, and there was a dreadful to-do about the question of "mixing" in the public schools. How was it possible, some wondered, to "mix" good American Yankees and the uncouth Germans in the same school? Heaven forbid it!

Money for education was not the immediate problem in West Bend that it was in some areas, for the plentiful trees had to be cut down and there was a ready market for them: locally there was the ashery, and Milwaukee needed railroad ties, potcharcoal, cordwood and pearl ashes. So in the clearing of the land there was an immediate profit. That money, the poor condition of the public schools, and the fear of "mixing," made it possible for the wealthier to send their children to private schools. The voters, of course, were those who owned property, and while they were in favor of general education, they were not anxious to spend vast amounts of money on the public school. Then, too, Germans had a predilection for parochial schools, for they were primarily either Roman Catholic or Lutheran. So a variety of choices was available for education. In September of 1866 an editor could ask, "Who in the vicinity hasn't an opportunity of going to school? Who? Here we have primary schools, District Schools, High Schools, Select Schools, German Schools, Sunday Schools, and in short, lots of schools all well taught and well attended if we may judge by the smiling looks and piles of books carried past our window daily." One might call this hyperbole!

Father Rehrl

Father Casper Rehrl was the founder of parochial education for Catholics in the West Bend area. He founded a Roman Catholic Academy in Barton in 1858 which some of the young ladies of the village attended. At first his efforts were hampered by lack of funds, but by 1861 Sister Mary Agnes Thecla wrote that they taught "healthy and crippled, Indians and white, anywhere between the ages of seven and thirteen. We were all very happy. The parents brought us wheat, flour, meat, vegetables, and groceries, somtimes in lieu of tuition, at other times in gratitude for what we did for the children. We suffered no want." Parents were anxious that their children receive the blessings of Christian doctrine in addition to retaining the German language, but Father Rehrl was also interested in preparing teachers to supply the growing area. He accepted non-Catholics, too, and defined "parochial" as meaning that "no salaries were paid by the state." Tuition at one time was 12 cents a month. Parochial education has played a large role in West Bend and that is a whole story in itself.

Other Private Schools

Another type of private school in West Bend was the Academy. The first one was founded by Professor Frederick Regenfuss, who moved to West Bend from Milwaukee, after founding an academy there. He came from Batavia, having been educated in a German seminary. Select schools were also common, especially for girls; Miss Francis Wightman founded the first one in 1859. She was the daughter of a large West Bend landowner, the graduate of a female college in New York; her students met in the German Methodist church, paying between three and five dollars a term depending upon the course of study. In 1860 Miss Wightman moved to Boston and Miss Pluma Holcombe taught the second Select School in the district in the public school house when it was not in session. After this, a succession of such schools appear, sometimes several at one time, but none of them lasted more than a few terms. Miss Wightman returned to West Bend and she and Regenfuss ran a Select School jointly for a short time (1863) but by 1875 Regenfuss had his own German English Select School in the Court House.

The boys had their own private schools, too. A law student, N. S. Gilson, organized one for 20 boys after a highly touted Doctor Hayes "fizzled out." Later (1864) Gilson and Thomas Farmer taught the primary department in the District School. One of the most interesting, and possibly the best, of the private schools was that of August Babille, who came to West Bend in the 1850's from France. He built an unusual house with shuttered windows, an innovation in the village, on a triangle of land in the middle of town and had an unusually successful vineyard in his back yard, for he was a skilled naturalist. It was easy to recognize Schoolmaster Babille, for he wore a long brown robe tied at the waist with a cord, somewhat in the manner of a monk; a skullcap completed his costume. Evenings would find him in his garden wearing a fancy dressing gown. The fathers of both Florence Stork and Thecla Richter attended his academy; they recall that their fathers were excellent mathematicians, and believe that Babille was a fine math teacher. The best families in town, including the well-known Weils, sent their children to the Babille Academy. Miss Stork still has two books from that school, a *Science for the School and Family* and *Sanders Fifth Reader.* A glance at the titles of the readings in the latter reveal the caliber of the topics, and provide a comparison with today's anthologies: "Proper Direction of the Intellectual and Mural Powers," "Antidote to Despondency," "Damon and Pythias," "Search for Wisdom," "The Speech of Blackhawk," "The Evils of Ignorance." None of that sterile Dick and Jane education for his primary pupils, either. The graduates of his school went on to other schools of higher learning.

Statistics about the number of pupils in all sorts of private schools is "patently unreliable," according to a State Superintendent of Public Instruction, so we will never know how many students attended them. Many such schools were started by "enterprising individuals" and were purely temporary.

Old South School

The Public Schools

There was plenty of room, therefore, for the public schools, whose first need was for qualified instructors. Early school laws did not provide for compulsory attendance, and the legal school term was just three months out of a year. The Town Supervisor was responsible for education, and he could do rather as he pleased until 1861 when County Superintendent Frederick Regenfuss took over the duties. West Bend had two school buildings, Old North at Eighth Avenue and Elm and Old South at Fifth and Poplar. At first Old South was the only school, but later it functioned as a primary school while older pupils attended Old North.

Early education was nearly all rote; it did not matter if the material was understood — just parrot it back to the teacher. The generally ill-prepared teachers had no other way to teach, for most of them had no more education than the highest grade in the school in which they taught. To keep order they were strict disciplinarians. This was the era of spitballs and slates, of dipping the braids of the girls in the inkwell, of high topped shoes and black stockings. Whispering was often the chief relief from the monotony — either that or carving on the desk tops by the lucky boys who owned a penknife. In spite of the rigor, however, most boys preferred school to staying at home, for those who stayed home had to work all day, and at school at least there was a recess for some playtime. Books were whatever a pupil could procure, and mothers covered them in cloth to make them last for the rest of the family. Washing the mouth out with soap was the common punishment, in addition to the rod.

While Miss Cynthia Sinn (daughter of founder "Blacksmith Sinn") was mentioned as the first teacher, she taught only one term and then William Ramsey became the "first male schoolteacher." He was followed by Judge L. F. Frisby, who had an agreement with the School Board that whenever court was in session, school would be dismissed.

People sometimes failed to turn out for school meetings in the early years; let the editor of the *Democrat* speak about 1859. "School elections are too generally disregarded, while nothing so vitally and intimately concerns the dearest interests of the whole people. It is criminal neglect that enables a few to foist upon the district men utterly unfit for district offices, no matter how good citizens they may be in other respects. And then the whole school system is brought into disrepute, bitter quarrels, vexations, litigation, unworthy teachers employed, and the children deprived of the proper facilities for acquiring an education. When there is scarce one in a hundred who goes to a university, college or academy, how vastly important it is that our common school should be watched over with zealous care." By 1879 school expenses were $20.00 a "head," and school was made compulsory by state law for three months a year for all between the ages of seven and twelve.

The High School

Just when West Bend had its first high school is a matter of conjecture, for the term "High School" was used loosely. At first the district merely added some seats to the upper room at the Elm Street site and called it a high school, taught by the

Old High School. Later Krieger Saddlery, 1894.

The Public School, 1889.

same upper grade teacher. By 1872 there were 53 in what they called a "high school department", and by 1887 the first mention of a high school appears in the School Board Minutes as a "regular high school department" offering as courses of study: Classical, English and Scientific. The Principal, Prof. Congdon, taught 7th and 8th grade, too. Pupils who attended those first high schools declared them an extension or glorification of the grades. By 1878 there were three "grades" for the high school listed in the newspaper: 1st, 2nd and 3rd, together with the composite academic grades for each pupil. What a furor would arise today if the grades were to be printed! Yet for all this, when the *History of Washington and Ozaukee County* was printed in 1880, there were four high schools listed in Washington County: Hartford, Schlesingerville (Slinger), Kewaskum and Farmington. Not one mention of West Bend, and the author lived in the city. A State Superintendent of Public Instruction called the term "high school" "misty, vague and incongruous" as late as 1902. By 1885 the *Democrat* listed 35 in high school with ten studying "high school branches," which is surely an ambiguous statement.

Incidentally, Professor Regenfuss, whom we met as a teacher, founder of an academy and County Superintendent, by 1880 was mentioned in the School Board *Minutes* thusly: "Mr. Frisby moved to employ Mr. F. Regenfuss for three months with the understanding that said Regenfuss conduct himself properly, and at expiration of said three months to be rehired for the rest of the term if he gives satisfaction." Two years later the School Board Minutes mention a salary of $80 for the principal and one of $45 for F. Regenfuss, Assistant. By 1882 he was hired on a monthly basis. Let the reader imagine what tragedy befell him to account for his downfall. Or perhaps it was his increasing age. He died in 1885 and was buried in West Bend.

Growing pains afflicted the school system, especially after the demise of the private schools and with the influx of new inhabitants. But it was the non-resident who created the space problem in high school; at one time (1887) 31 out of the 53 students in the high school were non-resident. The Old North School had become the High School, and it was in that year that the School Board resolved that the "one free High School shall be established in the school district in the city of West Bend. At a March public meeting 25 electors voted unanimously and the high school was "real."

When a new grade school was built at the Old North site in 1889, it also housed the high school department, but by then they had graduated the first class in West Bend High School history. On this momentous occasion three boys and five girls received diplomas in an impressive ceremony held on the Court House stage, gaily decorated with garlands and greens and the class motto, "Education and Liberty Inseparable." P. O'Meara gave the address on the topic, "The Value of an Education to the Nation." J. A. Buckley and Herman Lueders constituted the entire staff.

Progress was slow but steady while D. T. Keeley served as the first principal and L. E. Amidon as the second one. In 1892 a music course was added, taught by "Professor" William Borchert, who was prominent in community musical activities, and the two high school literary societies provided the public with "cultural" entertainment during the winters. The teaching of German commenced in 1894 and four years later the Phy Ed department had some "decent apparatus," which cost $50.00. When the first West Bend football game was played in 1894 against arch rival Hartford, jubilation was high as West Bend won by a score of 11-0, and the $10 profit bought needed laboratory equipment. That same year the first High School Alumni Association was formed. By 1897 the last of the stoves had disappeared from the classrooms and all the rooms had a "heating system." The staff was enlarged to four high school teachers in 1899, "two males and two females," and when the 20th century dawned there were 101 pupils in their building on Elm Street, in what is now the Recreation Building, with other rooms for the seventh and eighth grades. The primary students were still in Old South.

School Problems

Sometimes each generation seems to feel that it has a school or youth problem for the first time. History shows that the problems of the day had their counterparts in the past. For instance, there is the eternal problem of the academic ability of the pupils. In 1903, for instance, a course in English and History was added for "those not fully prepared and who act as a drag on those more advanced students." In addition to the ones who had academic difficulty, there were the farm boys who were kept home until November each year to help dig potatoes, husk corn, etc.

Clara Jones — member of first graduating class, 1888.

Dennis Keeley — first Principal.

L. E. Amidon — second High School Principal, 1892-1897.

James A. Buckley — teacher, High School, 1888.

Professor Borchert — teacher of music.

Gertrude Forrester — first commercial teacher.

When they arrived for classes the school had but two choices: stop the class and let the latecomers catch up — or put them back a full year. Sometimes one course was adopted — sometimes another — and neither choice was a pleasant one.

Truancy was a problem in the past, too. The habitually truant were ordered to go to a Truant School, but the sole reference to such occurred in the School Board *Minutes* of September 15, 1882, when the three members of the School Board met to discuss truancy with the parents and guardians of the miscreants; no parents appeared, the matter was dropped.

Lest that one think, also, that the discipline issue is a modern phenomena, the 1898 commencement address was entitled, "Discipline and Opportunity" and the only youngsters allowed to attend the ceremony were the younger brothers and sisters of the graduates, for there had been "previous disturbances at other formal occasions." The yearly meetings of the Teacher Institutes *always* dealt with the problem of discipline. Similarly, the smoking issue was ever with the School Boards. In desperation in 1912 School Board members Edwin Pick, C. F.

Leins and F. W. Bucklin met in December to promulgate the following rules:

#1 No smoking in public places or the street on the way to or going from school.

#2 No cigarette smoking at school at any time.

#3 No dice, playing cards, no slot machines were to be played, either for money or gain.

#4 No habitual loafing or loitering in public streets or public places.

The penalty was suspension, losing the right to compete for any honors or prizes, or to participate in any public entertainment or athletic contest or event. The measure was just as effective as those of today — a few were apprehended and punished, but the kids kept right on smoking. There was no mention of drinking, but the "old timers" noted that students indulged then, too. The chief difference today is in the increased number of students in the schools, so the number of drinkers and smokers also rises.

Many of the students were from parochial schools and were unprepared for high school; a five year course of study was adopted, so that the first year could be used for those students to catch up to the graduates of West Bend's eighth grade. Most of the teachers in the parochial and rural schools were barely eighth grade graduates themselves, while West Bend was by then hiring Normal School or higher graduates. Such parents as Mrs. Thomas O'Meara became incensed over their children's inferior education, and they forced the authorities in Holy Angels to procure better teachers and upgrade the curriculum.

Early Victories

Rightly or wrongly, it is by the high school that the community judges the caliber of its education. West Bend residents became increasingly proud of their high school. In 1901 Emma Leins won the state declamatory contest, more of an individual and school honor than it is today, for then only one pupil represented a school in a division and there was only one winner at each of the district, sectional and state meets. To win at Madison was a real boost for West Bend, and upon Emma's triumphant return she was met at the depot by a band and the cheering student body, and rode in triumph down Main Street. The president of Milwaukee Downer College and a professor from Milwaukee Normal both agreed that West Bend High School had a reputation for the caliber of its graduates, and the college president offered the highest ranking senior $100 to attend his school.

Tragedy

The first tragedy involving the school directly occurred in 1908 when Arthur Miller was killed in a football game with Marquette Academy. After the game he complained of a headache, but he managed to join his teammates at the depot in Milwaukee and arrived home, dazed. In ten days he was dead. Marquette denied that he had been hurt during the game; locally, the coach was accused of not taking him out of the game soon enough. Feelings ran high. He was given an impressive funeral with many of the town's leading citizens as pall bearers: A. DeTuncq, Chas. Mooers, V. O'Meara, M. Regner, R. Rolfs, W. Schmidt, A. Bruhy and P. O'Meara.

Changes Occur

In that same year only 79 grade school pupils out of 134 passed the Common School exam. What would happen today if that small percentage "passed"? By 1913 the high school was fully accredited, and its curriculum expanded to include Manual Training at the insistence of the Woman's Club, who paid for the equipment and the instructor, although at first the courses were only offered on Saturday morning. In 1912 the girls had Domestic Science, again courtesy of the Woman's Club, a kindergarten was started, and the students held a benefit to get electric lights in the high school building.

It may seem surprising, but pupils from Jackson rode the train to West Bend to high school daily. One day three boys hiked home, and when the train overtook them, they hitched a ride — gratis. Because the conductor thought there were no passengers to alight at Jackson, he did not stop the train; the panicky boys jumped, and one was severely hurt. "The flipping cars can be dangerous.'' Other pupils from rural areas rented a room in town for the school week.

Changes in the method of teaching were slow, but steady. In 1898 a lecturer advised both teachers and citizens that a new day was dawning. The latest concept was that one should not think of education as cramming knowledge into a head; rather, it was to develop the child's social, mental, and physical capabilities. It was now more important to teach the child to see himself

Public School Teachers, 1908. Standing, left to right, Roxanna Knapp, Marie Weller, Margaret O'Connell, Anna Gossel, Elizabeth Dunham, Barbara Mueller, Mary Mueller; seated, Irvin Coates, Tessa Hickish (Mrs. Edwin Pick), D. E. McLane, Bella MacArthur, Lola Woodford.

and express clearly in his own language what he saw. He was also supposed to be taught to be independent. Whereas the center of knowledge had heretofore been knowledge, now it was to be the child. Society still grapples with that dilemma.

Honored School People

Over the years a few of the earlier twentieth century grade school teachers have been highly revered. The first of these was Miss Elizabeth Dunham who taught here for 25 years and received a purse of $128.50 when she retired. Anna Gossel taught third grade and upon her retirement her former pupils collected money for a long-awaited trip to California, but death intervened. Her will left money to West Bend for scholarships, and the fund is still being used. Roxanne Knapp, a 6th grade teacher, was highly honored, as was Daniel McLane, principal of the grade and high school for 37 years (1905-1942), and for whom McLane School is named.

An account of West Bend schools would be incomplete without paying tribute to Hubert Becker, a school custodian for 49 years who retired at the age of 76 in 1959. No teacher or administrator ever exerted a greater influence on more students than did "Hubie." Until the high school became too large, he knew

Hubert Becker — Chief Engineer West Bend High School system for 49 years.

each student by name, and he would take a recalcitrant boy to the boiler room and talk him into doing the proper thing.

He always did more than was expected of him and his example affected many a young person. The school was always clean. Everything was in repair. In the winter sidewalks were shoveled before the arrival of students and staff even if he had to enlist students to help him. Because he had no hobbies and school was his life, he would often return to the building in the evening to fix something for a teacher. In 1938 the school dedicated its annual to him. He might turn over in his grave were he conscious of the change in custodial services.

A New High School Building

After World War I the need for a new high school building was evident, but it was difficult to persuade the voters. The first step was to acquire land, and the most suitable site was south of town on lots bordering Fourth Avenue and Oak Street. Opposition to that site was vocal. It was too far from town. Why do we need so much land? Etc. But the voters were persuaded that the walk of a mile or so would be good for the pupils, and besides, it was modern to build a school further from the business district. Farsighted leadership under such men as D. J. Kenny knew that it would be cheaper to buy the land then, so they would have room for future expansion. The land was purchased for $20,000. Incidentally, it was once part of the old Dekorah Road (variant spelling) which cut diagonally across the property to avoid a swamp, and also the homesite of the first settler, Anson Verbeck.

Next came the question of the building. The first committee asked for $250,000 — the referendum was defeated. A new committee tried to reduce the costs to $200,000 by suggesting that the school be built facing Oak Street away from the increasing traffic on Fourth Avenue, and that the land facing Fourth be sold. Eventually (1924) the voters approved by a vote of 130-103 a compromise cost of $220,000.

In 1927 the big news was that the new high school ($220,000 plus $40,000 for equipment) was ready for occupancy. It also housed the 7th and 8th grades until 1939. The school now boasted of football, basketball, baseball, track, tennis, an intramural program for boys, a glee club for girls, and forensics for both. This was the fourth so-called "high school" building, from "old South" to Eighth and Elm, to a three story building in what is now the recreational building, to the site on South Fourth Avenue.

There was further progress in the Thirties. Ruth Hess won the state declamatory contest and in 1931 Ed Manthei won a national forensic contest. The boys were the state track champions in 1934, in a school that had 530 pupils. A big problem in the grade school was that the subject of art was not being taught and no matter how often the parents requested it, the School Board did not add it to the curriculum. So in desperation the many interested parents appealed to principal McLane, who sympathized with them, advertised their cause and held a public meeting to which the state secretary of the PTA came and offered advice on how to organize parents to improve the schools. Local parents were impressed, and by September the city had a viable PTA organization under the leadership of Mrs. George Kuehlthau, the first president, with Mrs. C. Peters the first secretary. Other early presidents included Mmes. E. Eberhardt, Aaron Johnson, Albert Gensman, Robert Grogan and Leroy Cooley.

McLane School is Built

It was in 1939 that McLane school was built on land previously owned by Walter and Dorchen Ottmer and the adjacent lots of the Bennin, Rolfs, Novak, Pick, Leins and Albrecht fam-

D. E. McLane — Principal, 1905-1940.

McLane School, 1939.

Badger Middle School.

Decorah Grade School.

ilies. The hill was originally much higher than it is today, so thousands of yards of dirt had to be removed before construction could start. At first it was called the West Bend Grade School, but when Principal McLane retired in 1942 the school was renamed in his honor and served West Bend as the only grade school until 1954-55 when both Decorah and Fair Park were opened to relieve the congestion.

There had been the usual difficulty in voting the money for the school, which was so patently needed. When a far-sighted citizen asked the voters if they would be willing to raise $165,000 now or postpone the matter for a few years and pay $318,000, the opposition melted.

Later Improvements

Over the years other additions and other buildings have been added. In 1952 and again in 1957 there were additions to the high school, the latter including a double gym and a swimming pool for the 1049 pupils, a "large school." In 1960 Barton was attached and in 1961 Oak Knoll was added. The district encompasses 90 square miles in 1979, one of the larger geographic areas in Wisconsin, has a seven member school board elected for three year terms, seven elementary schools (Barton, Jackson, Silver Maple, McLane, Fair Park, Decorah and Green Tree), two Middle Schools (Badger and Silverbrook) and a twin high school on 55 acres of land with four gymnasiums, a community auditorium seating 1300 and a new (1979) Olympic-sized swimming pool. When the school was opened in 1970 (at a total cost of over seven million dollars), it had 111 teachers and just under 2000 students; top capacity was judged to be 2500, at which time the idea was to build a third high school on another corner of the complex with eventual plans for the fourth high school when the city reached it full population sometime in the future. In 1978 East High School had 1351 students and West had 1257. According to Superintendent of Schools Duane Ehrlick the school employed 425 teachers in the entire district for its 6991 pupils in '78-'79; it had 31 administrators, 44 clerical employees, 125 full and part time custodians and ran 56 buses for a total cost of $13,064,353.

In addition to the public schools, there are three large Roman Catholic grade schools (Holy Angels, Cabrini and St. Mary's at Barton), two Lutheran grade schools (St. John's and Good Shepherd), and the Kettle Moraine Lutheran High School in Jackson.

Catholic Parochial Schools

A large part of the elementary education in West Bend takes place in the parochial schools. It has had a Catholic parochial school since 1866 for the Holy Angels congregation, but no one seems to know where the school was located. Its first recorded teacher was John Lindl. By 1878 they had 85 pupils taught by the Sisters of Notre Dame.

In 1880 the need for a better building was obvious, so the school held a three day fair and festival to raise money, and parishioners brought in bricks, stone and lime for the new building on Hickory Street. The old building was purchased by John Knippel who moved it and used it for his business. The new one in 1880 was remodeled several times.

As the congregation grew, that, too, was inadequate, so when the public school district built McLane in 1939, the Holy Angels congregation purchased the old Elm Street public grade school and used it until they could build their fine new building in 1963. Today both lay teachers and the Sisters serve on the staff for a large school. St. Francis Cabrini has a beautiful school which serves a large number of students, too.

Lutheran Schools

Parochial education for St. John's really started in 1860 when the pastor taught both Sunday School and school, all in German, of course. The purpose of Lutheran parochial education was to "join earthly knowledge with heavenly wisdom." As early as 1872 the congregation had a Christian Day School in one room in its church on Sixth and Walnut. They "called a male teacher"; over the first 30 years they had 16 different teachers, some of them students from Northwestern College at Watertown. The second school, a two story building, was built in 1891 at a cost of $1500.00, and by now their enrollment had grown to require two teachers.

In 1894 it was typical of the times to want only male teachers, but they could not find one so had to have a female, Miss Henrietta Wagner, for two years, but at the end of that time they hired a man and "a woman under him." In 1901 they had grown to 126 pupils; as late as 1916 there were up to 83 pupils per teacher. Then they built a new school at Sixth and Walnut in 1918 which became inadequate in the 1950's, so now the congregation has their fourth school next to their church, built in 1958 at a cost of $319,000. The Good Shepherd Evangelical Lutheran Church also maintains a growing school for Lutherans.

CHAPTER 5

Education — the University Center

The story of the problem in obtaining a University of Wisconsin Washington County Center in West Bend illustrates the difficulty of elected bodies to progress; what progress there is is always the result of men of vision and perseverance.

When the demand for more higher education facilities after World War II reached Wisconsin, Governor Thompson called a state wide conference to study the expansion of higher education, and West Bend had two interested members: Judge Robert J. Stoltz and Mr. J. R. Brown, President of the West Bend Company. They became enthusiastic over expansion and served on the local citizen's committee later. The plan was to place an institution of higher learning within easy reach of 95% of all the population in the state; more than the recommended number of annual high school graduates (1000-1250) lived within a 30 mile radius of West Bend. The other possibility for an area school was Port Washington, but it was limited geographically by Lake Michigan, so The Coordinating Committee on Higher Education recommended that West Bend be the center for the area.

But nothing happened until Waukesha, Janesville and Rice Lake announced plans for campuses in their communities. This seemed to be an impetus to West Bend; where were the plans for a school there? In spite of inaction, West Bend was still being considered and received a "second priority" rating for the 1967-69 biennium. Mayor Paul Henke was instrumental in October of 1963 in influencing the City Council to endorse a meeting between the members and the officials of the University. After a December meeting Councilmen became enthusiastic for the project, and the problem was to sell the community and the county. Custom in West Bend dictates the appointment of the inevitable citizens' advisory committee, which consisted of the following influential people: James R. Brown, President of the West Bend Company, Chairman; Joe Zadra, Treasurer of Gehl Bros. Mfg. Co.; Mrs. Jac Anderson, President of the West Bend Chapter of American Association of University Women; Judge Robert J. Stoltz, Washington County Court; Leonard Oelhafen, Labor representative; Paul Loofboro, Superintendent of West Bend Public Schools; and A. P. Staral, Washington County Clerk.

Now the *West Bend News* added its editorial voice to the idea. The Hartford Common Council was enthusiastic. The Allied Industrial Workers of America backed the school. But as 1966 wore on, not one word had been heard from the Washington County Board of Supervisors, whose support was necessary. Finally in late June Mr. Brown was able to meet with them and explain the plan, after which they, too, decided to appoint a study committee. But they did not do so immediately.

Pressure for the campus was mounting and time was fleeting. In desperation, a joint city-county study committee was formed and the group conducted an active newspaper campaign, as well as meeting with more than 70 public groups throughout the county. There was no question now about whether there *should* be a university center in West Bend. The only question was: could the powers whose approval was required be convinced?

By October the West Bend City Council approved cooperation between it and the County Board, and the Board heard its first reading of a resolution to split funding on a 60% county and 40% city basis. The City Council agreed. The *West Bend News* urged the County Board not to "muff the golden opportunity which had been presented to them." It voted to delay action until December and asked: Why could not the state fund the school 100%? Would it not be cheaper to send the children to another school? Would not out-of-county students use the facilities? Etc. But at the December meeting they put aside their doubts and voted to support the school unanimously. West Bend agreed to provide a site for the campus. The Wisconsin Board of Regents agreed to equip, staff, and operate the campus, which was to open in September of 1969. Success at last.

The best site out of the twelve possible ones was the Carl Pick farm, but the 187 acre farm was too large. Baltus Rolfs, chairman of the Washington County Citizen's Committee for park acquisition, urged the County Board to buy the land for a county park, and J. R. Brown urged them to then set aside part of it for the campus. To make the proposal more appealing, he personally pledged $25,000 toward the purchase price. If any one person deserves credit for the West Bend Center it is surely James Brown.

By October the County Board agreed to purchase 100 acres of the Carl Pick farm for the county park at $950 an acre, and the West Bend City Council quickly purchased the remaining 87 acres for the center at a cost of approximately $84,000, of which another $25,000 was contributed by the West Bend Company. In the summer of 1967 ground was broken for the three buildings to house an instruction building, student center, and a library at a cost of $1,355,000 of which over $300,000 was paid with a grant from the federal government. When the campus was opened in 1968 the expected enrollment of 250 students turned into an amazing 397.

While the campus has proved an impressive asset to the county, and the enrollment is fairly constant at between 500-600, there have been problems: classroom space, indoor physical education facilities, and the controversy over the union of the center system with the vocational school.

As part of its mission, the University Center is dedicated to serving the citizens of the community by providing professional and technical expertise, by serving as a cultural center, and by meeting continuing education needs of the area. Many who would not otherwise be able to do so take classes conveniently close to home. The 31,000 volume library serves anyone in the area who needs reference material, while the Fine Arts and

Lecture series entertains and educates the community through their program of music, drama, dance, lectures, etc. The fully accredited school offers 180 courses leading to the Associate Arts Degree or Associate of Science Degree. West Bend and the surrounding area are the richer for the presence of the Center in its midst. (Present enrollment is at an all-time high of 616. This includes full-time and part-time students of all ages.)

CHAPTER 6

Education — the Vocational School

Moraine Park Technical Institute.

In addition to its K-12 public school system and the University Center, West Bend also has an outstanding vocational school. The school had its rudiments in 1920 when one opened for eight hours a week for the 14-17 year olds who were not enrolled in regular school. Some feel it was the first night school of its kind in the United States. The big impetus for enlarging the school came primarily from the American Legion which was concerned about the World War I veterans. But the school was not a true vocational school until 1938 when its first building, attached to the high school, was dedicated.

Wisconsin has had the dubious distinction of being next to the bottom in the number of rural boys in high school, and Washington County had the even worse honor of ranking #71 out of the 72 counties in the state. So there was a push for some action. Why was this true, West Bend asked? Was it the nationality of the people involved? Did the dairy farmers need the boys at home? Had the high school failed to make the course of study attractive? Were the facilities inadequate? (Laboratories were admittedly poor). The merchants did not want to anger the farmers of the area for fear of losing their business, and Mayor Schoenbeck believed he expressed the feelings of 95% of his constituents when he opposed vigorously, but in vain, the law to keep 16 year olds in school. The law, passed to raise Wisconsin's dismal record in the number of youth in school at age 16 or so, is in just as keen debate today.

The prime motivator for a decent vocational school program in West Bend was D. J. Kenny, Clerk of the Public School Board, who appointed a group of citizens to oversee vocational training in the city. What was needed was a building.

The Vocational School Board had Walter Malzahn as its president and Mrs. Joe Huber as secretary. There was strong opposition to a separate vocational school, but the School Board, the Woman's Club, the PTA and other groups wrote to Washington to acquire funds from PWA and eventually secured a grant for 40% of the cost of the building. The citizens voted to build the building and a vocational school was a reality. Bernard Rice was appointed the Director.

The school primarily served (1) the out-of-school dropouts who were still legally required to attend school, and (2) the adults interested either in advancing their own education or participating in do-it-yourself projects as an avocation. There was very little for women at this time.

But World War II changed the emphasis to war production training and Mr. Kenny's foresight proved its worth, for the actively involved manufacturing plants needed trained skilled workers. After the war the emphasis shifted to adult education, a new course in agriculture for veterans, and to apprenticeships, in addition to high school dropouts. By the late fifties the high school assumed the primary role of farm training, while the vocational school gradually offered more adult education courses, more supervisory training, upgrading of job opportunities, hobbies, use of leisure time, etc. Irving Johnson was the long term vocational school director during its period of greatest growth.

The problem was always space. Each time there was an addition to the high school, space was allotted; in fact one of the factors in getting the referendum passed each time was always that of space for the vocational school. But each time the high school kept growing and usurped the areas previously allotted to the vocational people. They were forced, therefore, to seek rooms in such diverse sites as the City Hall, the Library, Masonic Temple basement, etc.

A big change occurred in the 1960's when the West Bend Board of Education accepted responsibility for educating all its youth up to the age of 18, or through high school graduation, whichever came first. This relieved the vocational school of working with the academic rebels and allowed them to concentrate on adults. Both Art Wiener and Dick Roberts became adept at early identification of the potential high school dropout.

The next big thrust came in 1965, when the state legislature attempted to equalize vocational education throughout the state by placing every part of the state in a vocational district by 1970. Washington County joined Dodge and Fond du Lac counties to form District 10, the Moraine Park Technical Institute.

Now begins a long period of political jockeying. Fond du Lac already had a vocational school and was in the best position to get public funds. Beaver Dam was building a school. West Bend had nothing to offer at this time except a small group of dedicated people determined to rectify the deficiency in West Bend, among them Dick Klumb. The problem was to convince the County Board. The City Council supported the school and in 1968 bought approximately 30 acres of land, of which about 25 remain as some of it was sold for Green Tree Road, etc.

The real crunch was that simultaneously with this demand for a vocational school came the movement for a university center in West Bend while the public schools were campaigning for ten million dollars to build a new high school and upgrade the other buildings. How would each fare as they jockeyed for the tax dollars?

The public agreed to the ten million dollar public school referendum, the university center was approved, and the Washington County Board finally acquiesced, and approved the vocational school, so in January of 1969 construction began on West Bend's first vocational school. By September students were enrolled in five programs: Machine tool operation, clerk-typist, stenography, merchandising, and mechanical drafting, with space rented from the high school for auto mechanics.

During the political jockeying, the West Bend School District Board of Education and the Board of Vocational Education cooperated fully. So did the District School Board and the University Center. The differences lay between the vocational school and the center system; the old argument between academic training and vocational training muddied the water. Each rebuffed the idea of shared facilities for fear of losing its identity, although joint facilities would be cheaper. Finally the Vocational Board abandoned the idea of joint planning for fear of delaying the coming of the University Center. (Those differences, incidentally, no longer exist between the two school directors, Dean Robert Thompson of the University Center and Director Lee Flanders of the Vocational School, who cooperate fully).

Any attempt to correct the error of two separate campuses, if error it was, came to naught when the need for expansion of the Vocational School grew and the five governing bodies needed to give the assent could not agree. The Board of Regents of the University System, the State Vocational Board, the Moraine Park Board of Education, the City of West Bend, and the Washington County Board of Supervisors all had to agree. The last two could not, so any joint planning was abandoned and an addition to the Vocational School was approved in 1978 and completed for the fall term of 1979. The school presently serves over 5000 different individual students or the equivalent of a full time enrollment of over 400. Because most of the classes are held at night, it has been necessary to rent at least 18 different locations in the city. This has been somewhat reduced with the latest addition, but West Bend East High School, Badger School, West Bend Recreation Department, Police and Fire Department, Court House, Open Door, The Samaritan, St. Joseph's Hospital, Cedar Lake Home, Linden Inn, Holiday Inn, Fifth Avenue Methodist Church, Trinity Lutheran Church, West Bend Company, Gehl Company, and Amity all provide classroom space for the growing concept of vocational education. This generates an administrative headache, but West Bend has every reason to be proud of its vocational program.

CHAPTER 7

Law

In the earliest years of the village there were no trained lawyers nor any buildings to hold criminals. When a case needed trying it was usually done by an untrained person who had the gift of talking well. "Court" was held in a local tavern or the kitchen of the Justice of the Peace until the first schoolhouse was built, after which cases were tried there. Early trials bore little resemblance to those of today; the audience, usually a sizeable one, would consist of the men of the village who attended to watch the fun, for there was inevitably some entertainment. The language of the trial was in the vernacular of the citizens, and the lawyers shamelessly played on the sympathy of the audience and the jurors. ("This man is just like one of us, a plain farmer.")

The first lawyer in West Bend was Ira Spencer, who was also the first postmaster. In 1850 Leander Frisby arrived and for two years was the only lawyer in the central part of the county. Other early lawyers were: John E. Mann (1853), I. N. Frisby (1853), B. O. Thorpe and John Sheeley (1854), N. W. Tupper (1855-1859), Ansel Tupper (killed in the Civil War), Paul Weil, and Col. N. S. Gilson who served for six years in the Civil War. Lawyers usually did not stay long in any one community in this era of Wisconsin history.

The most familiar name in law has been that of O'Meara, and the firm is reputed to be the oldest law firm in Wisconsin bearing the same name. It all began in 1870 when Patrick O'Meara came to West Bend to practice law. His brother Thomas joined him a decade later and in turn his son Thomas Jr. joined the firm. When Patrick died in 1934, the two Tom O'Mearas continued the firm until Tom Jr.'s brother Stephen entered practice with them and the three carried on the family name.

The long time residence of the firm was the building on the O'Meara triangle, the shortest business block in the world, according to Bob Ripley's "Believe it or Not." That building became the victim of progress when the O'Meara triangle became a small city park. Today three O'Mearas, Thomas, Jr., Stephen, and Charles carry on the family tradition.

Many are the amusing law cases in West Bend. Justice of

the Peace John Haase heard a case in which a man was brought into the court for calling another man an SOB. Haase dismissed the case with the words "Everyone knows he is one." One couple asked a judge to marry them and then backdate it. In 1931 Ken Marsden went with Sheriff Holtebeck to serve papers on August Steinbrenner. When the entire Steinbrenner family attacked the pair with brooms, fists, fingernails, and teeth, the hapless pair fled, to return with reinforcements and arrest the man.

Another of the famous lawyers of West Bend is Clyde Schloemer. In addition to his services as a lawyer, he has presented a lecture on the trials of Jesus several thousand times to fascinated groups.

Today nearly 30 lawyers have their offices in West Bend and serve the city.

SECTION VIII

RELIGION

CHAPTER 1

Religion — General

Many of the early founders of West Bend had been church members in their Eastern or European homelands, and when they came to the wilderness they missed the rituals and the fellowships. There were many difficulties facing a wilderness congregation: buying property on which to erect a building, finding a clergyman willing to brave a frontier life, raising the money to build a church and in some cases, a school nearby. And all this at a time when many of the settlers had little or no cash, surely not enough to sustain a viable church, so all the early churches in West Bend were missions at first, with the mother church supplying much or all of the cash. In time some of the churches became so used to having support from the outside that they tried to prolong the pleasant state, but funds were always eventually cut off.

As they faced the problem of living in a churchless territory, settlers began to worry about the keeping of the Sabbath; when the weather was good, people tended to work as there was so much need for physical labor on a frontier. Could they labor on the Lord's Day and still remain Christian? Was it all right to hunt and fish on a Sunday? And how about drinking and swearing, both common on the frontier? Was it all right to covet money, now that immigrants were living in a land where there was a chance of upward mobility? Was it Christian to charge interest? These questions began to disturb Christians. Besides, they missed the one excuse most of them had to clean up and dress in their best clothes, for church would provide the chief social contact and relief from the daily monotony of hard labor in the earliest years.

At first there were no churches, per se, in the sense of a

church building. After a congregation had outgrown meeting in a settler's home, it either built crude log buildings, often a mere shack, or met in the equally crude first public school. All of the labor on the buildings was performed by willing volunteers, and most of the materials came from the nearby farms of members. As more settlers arrived, the churches began a spirited rivalry for members, hoping for new supporters of their church. Inasmuch as local Protestants were more prosperous at first than the Roman Catholics, rivalry among the Protestants became an impetus to get busy and construct a building which would attract new members. There were other rivalries, too. One involved the virtues of "High" versus "Low" Episcopalians. The "new" Lutherans disagreed with the "old" Lutherans, and all churches had to survive the temperance question as the "natives" battled the incoming Germans over the drinking issue. Then, too, there was the divisive issue of slavery, with the Christian concept of love and brotherhood drowned out in prejudice.

As more and more settlers poured into West Bend, rivalry for membership in the churches became intense, and much of it was reported in the newspapers. Preachers inserted brief items in the paper promoting the virtues of one church over another; for example, one item read "We preach the Holy Scripture and

First Sunday School, 1879, 5th Avenue Methodist Church. Seated: Unknown, Willie Wolfrom, Alvin Pfeiffer, Fritz Althaus and brother, a Frisby boy. Standing: Gustave Haase, Albert and Henry Glantz, Fred Hunt and an unknown.

ONLY the Holy Scripture," a direct dig at the churches who believed it was possible to make this a better world here below through social action. Some churches advertised their faithfulness to the rituals that Christ founded. In the 1850's and 1860's the Free Will Baptists (not to be confused with any modern-day Baptists) proved among the more hardy, for they baptized their members in Waller's Lake (now Wallace Lake) where their minister lived. One winter 11 were baptized in water which had to be reached by chopping a hole through the thick ice, and then hurried to a tent wherein a roaring fire warmed the bodies to match their newly warmed hearts.

Feuds over theology were common. The most publicized culminated in June of 1859 when the Reverend Mr. Goodrich of the Methodist Church publicly invited the Reverend Mr. J. C. Crawford, a Universalist, to "review" his sermon, and the latter gentleman accepted the invitation. There had been words bandied back and forth between them in the local newspaper for some time, and it is interesting to contemplate the verbal fireworks that ensued after the sermon "review." This was the same Mr. Goodrich who returned the weekly free copy of the local *Democrat* marked "Refused" when he disagreed with the editorial policy. The editor invited him to use the columns of the paper to air his thoughts instead of refusing the gift, but the author can find no such rebuttals.

Among the other differences of opinion that created many a lively discussion in the local meeting places was the German Evangelicals' view that they could help create a heaven on earth right here in this natural paradise, while the Catholics were more accepting of their lot, expecting life to be difficult. The German Lutherans, on the other hand, were not particularly concerned about solving earthly problems, but were united in being anti-Catholic. In addition, Lutherans usually came from countries where they had been accustomed to state churches, for all had to belong to the church of their prince. So the various local Lutherans had different rituals and slightly different theology, according to their state of origin, and they were difficult to unite. In fact, they kept splitting farther apart as the years passed, while some of the other denominations drew closer together.

The issue of the presence of a Hell invaded West Bend in the 1870's and the *Democrat* reported that "the hereafter discussion has struck West Bend and preachers are drawing full houses." Reverend E. R. Ward "replenished the future fires last week," in the evening Episcopal services, and "Reverend W. Fisher will warn sinners to repent and thus evade everlasting punishment."

The local paper tried to enliven the grave subject of the proper way to worship by including religious jokes in its columns. In 1861 one story told of the minister who was consoling a young widow with the words, "Such a jewel of a Christian! You cannot find his equal, as you well know," to which the bereaved lady replied, "I bet I will."

Early West Bend history contains few references to religion other than that found in newspapers. In the June, 1859, issue of the *Democrat* there is this: "Ministers are not more addicted to dissipation than men of other professions. A few take gin toddies and liberties with females, but the great majority are as good as lawyers and doctors." It would be intriguing to know what local events occasioned that reporter's comment! Because few ministers were educated, often not even ordained, and some were merely itinerant, there was much to be desired in the men who came to West Bend as pastors. Often they were full of all the "Thou shalt not's" and made Christianity a solemn religion. Because there was little if any money to pay clergymen, they survived with handouts, including firewood, homemade sausages, cheese, butter, fresh meat at butchering time, local garden produce, and an occasional jar of jelly. Most denominations had donation parties to sustain the poorly paid preacher. Fifty cents for a baptism and up to a dollar and a half for a funeral was a common price, but all too often there was no money in the home to pay a minister for such services.

Now let's pursue the story of the individual churches.

CHAPTER 2

Roman Catholics — Holy Angels

The real origin of Catholicism in West Bend goes back to 1844, a year before the city's founding, when the Milwaukee Bishop Henni began to urge southern Germans, who were primarily Roman Catholics, to migrate to eastern Wisconsin, so that he might build up the territory as predominately Roman

Catholic. One who answered the call to become a parish priest here was Father Casper Rehrl, who was to become the single most important influence on early West Bend Catholicism.

Often called "the Apostle of Washington County," he was born in Austria, earned the degree of Doctor of Divinity in 1835, and soon thereafter answered the call to the great American mid-west, in which he was to serve out the rest of his days. Arriving by boat in New Orleans in 1844, he took both the stage and boats on his slow trek to Milwaukee, where he strapped some of his precious books, a crucifix, and a blanket on his back and set out forthwith on his self-appointed round of duty. It took him three days to get to West Bend from Milwaukee, for he kept getting lost, but before many years passed he knew every Indian trail in his large parish, which extended all the way north to Green Bay.

He spent his first night in West Bend near a fire before the crude hut on Isaac Verbeck's property. Verbeck was the only Roman Catholic here at the time, and his shanty and a few Indian tepees were all that Rehrl could see. Three years later there were 12 Roman Catholic families in West Bend out of the 30 families here at the time, so West Bend qualified as a mission station. Father Rehrl also spent years teaching and Christianizing the Indians. He believed Barton would become a larger city than West Bend, so he concentrated his efforts there, even though he had as many as twelve charges at one time. He spent years at Fond du Lac, but returned to his first love, Barton, where he had built a convent to train teachers to propagate the faith and to teach the rudiments of education to the frontier community. Before he died in Barton in 1881, he asked to be buried there and his wish was granted. However, his body was moved twice, once to the new parish cemetery and the last time to St. Agnes Convent in Fond du Lac on September 3, 1968. When his goods were auctioned off in 1882 the editor of the West Bend *Democrat* acquired the type from Rehrl's private printery and Mr. Bruederle bought his rare 1574 Martin Luther Bible. One wonders where it is today. In addition, Father Rehrl had written two books to be used in worship services, but he had never had the money to have them bound. Bruederle bought them, too, bound them, and profited from their sale. One of the volumes is in the Washington County Museum. Many missionary priests served the area, but none of them left the mark that Father Rehrl did.

By 1849 missionaries were arriving more or less regularly to say mass in private homes; the first regular priest was Rev. Beittner of St. Lawrence. By now Barton had a flourishing congregation and many local residents were climbing the hill to Barton to go to a "regular" church. Two years later, the local Catholics bought a lot from Moses Weil for $15 for a church at the corner of Hickory and Seventh Avenue, and by 1853 there was a 23′ x 34′ beamed frame building that cost $1,000 and was named Mary, Mother of Sorrows. When Father Rehrl began to devote all of his time to Barton, which had also adopted the name of Mary, the West Bend parish changed its name to Holy Angels. Barton pastors were to serve West Bend for 34 years before the parish became an independent one.

A key event occurred in 1862 when the parish imported a 600 pound bell from St. Louis at a cost of $220, and rang it three times a day, at 6 A.M., 12 noon and 6 P.M. The local editor expressed the sentiments of the community when he wrote: "What a seeming change does the first bell give the place." West Bend was slowly acquiring the sounds of a true village.

That first church proved totally inadequate for the rapidly growing congregation, and by 1866 a second building was started at Seventh and Elm Streets. The old building then became the parish school, but it soon proved as inadequate for a school as it had for a church, so by 1880 a new $7000 school (and convent) was built at Seventh and Hickory, in which four sisters who taught the school also lived. The building is still there today, having served for a variety of purposes over the years.

By 1882 there were 66 Catholic families in West Bend, and the small church now had a 125 foot steeple on which was a large clock with a four foot diameter dial on all four sides, enabling one to tell time from each direction. This handsome addition to West Bend was soon the pride of the village. These changes occurred under Rev. Ruckengruber of St. Mary's in Barton. All services were in German.

In 1892 Messrs. D. W. Lynch, C. S. Lang, and Math Regner went to Milwaukee to persuade the Bishop to make West Bend a separate parish, so in 1893 West Bend acquired its very own parish priest, Father Stupfel, and ceased to be a mission church. It had been a long wait, but a rewarding one. But now the same old space problem arose and again a larger church was desperately needed as the congregation grew rapidly. Where would they ever get the money for a new building? The land they

Laying the cornerstone of Holy Angels.

Holy Angels Catholic Church

Father Stupfel

desired was the rest of the original Wightman property and bore a price tag of $20,000. One day while Father Stupfel was playing shafskopf with Jake Ziegler he mentioned the need for financing. Young B. C. Ziegler had just started a small farm loan business, and when his father told him of the need of the Roman Catholics for a loan, B. C. promptly loaned Father Stupfel the entire $20,000, the B. C. Ziegler Company was born, and Holy Angels had a fine church.

In 1913 a grateful congregation celebrated Father R. J. Stupfel's 25 years of service to West Bend. His father had come from Alsace and his grandfather had been a maker of wooden shoes, a trade that Father Stupfel had also mastered before he entered a seminary. During his ministry here, the church had grown to about 200 families. He was an unusual man, and respected by all, regardless of their rèligion. When in church he maintained he was a priest, but when he was out of church he became a plain citizen "like the rest of us."

A new twin-towered Tudor Gothic church was built in 1914 and dedicated in 1915. The lovely stained glass windows were imported from Munich, and the total cost of the Bedford limestone and concrete brick building was $125,000. The church began to grow rapidly, as more and more immigrants arrived in

West Bend; by 1930 they were baptizing 65 youngsters annually.

As West Bend continued to gain more inhabitants, Holy Angels could no longer serve its people, so in 1955 plans were laid for a new church in the southern part of the city, and while Holy Angels continues to grow, the new (1969) St. Francis Cabrini serves another large congregation on South Seventh Avenue.

CHAPTER 3

Fifth Avenue Methodist Church

Exactly when the Methodist church began in West Bend is a mystery, but as early as 1848 a church was listed in the Eastern Wisconsin Methodist Conference minutes as a mission church, so it may have been West Bend's first actual church. A scrap of an old record lists two charter members, Abraham and Clara Van Epps, but there is no date remaining on the aging paper. Circuit riders were the first preachers; with books and a blanket in their saddlebags, they traveled a wide circuit, often sleeping in the woods between charges. The first such circuit riders in West Bend were P. W. Frink and H. M. Train, but which was first is pure conjecture, because the dates for both of them are unrecorded. The first regular appointed minister was Rev. A. C. Pennock, probably in 1848, with Reverend John Bear following some time around 1850; the first one with a recorded date was Rev. David Lewis, 1853-1855.

How welcome those circuit riders were to the settlers! Mr. Frink had a 600 miles circuit ranging from Green Bay to Chicago and all points in between, so he could not have arrived at any one charge very frequently. He, along with the other brave men who served the west as circuit riders, would ramble along trails, seeking a log cabin here or a small settlement there, stopping to see if services were needed. One such preacher spoke of fording streams six feet deep to get to the next settlement.

Weddings, funerals and baptisms all had to await the preacher's arrival, which was seldom known in advance. There

Fifth Avenue Methodist Church, 1872.

were often long waits for one to come to "say a few words over a grave" or marry an impatient couple. Living together without benefit of clergy was simply not done in rural Wisconsin in the mid-nineteenth century if the people wished to retain the respect of their neighbors. Most of these early Methodist ministers were ill-educated, depending upon the spirit to guide them, but this in no way detracted from their intelligence and zeal. After all, this was America, where everybody was as good as everybody else.

The conference minutes for 1853 mention a church building in West Bend but its exact location is unknown; the best assumption is that it was just north of the courthouse. Then the minutes are blank until 1875. The first couple to be married in that earliest church was John Rusco and Elizabeth Perry, while Laura Lewis received the first recorded baptism. A mere scrap of paper dated 1859 mentions Preacher Holcombe, Leader Francis Everly, Presiding Elder P. S. Bennett, Steward William Norton, and a partial list of members, including Polly Fulz, Emily Wolfrum, Jane Verbeck, and William, Sarah, and Hester Norton. The names indicated that the members were transplanted East-

Fifth Avenue Methodist Church.

erners, rather than immigrant Germans, and all services were in English.

As was typical of so many rural areas, the assigned ministers often had several charges to serve at the same time. Thomas Potter, for instance, had eight such charges in 1869, so he conducted four services a Sunday. A typical Sunday would find him at Kewaskum at 8:00 A.M., Farmington at 10:30, West Bend at 2:30, and the County Farm at 5:00 P.M. The next Sunday he would serve the other four charges. And all of this on horseback! But difficult as it was, it was a gigantic step forward from the 600 mile circuit of an earlier day.

By 1872 the Methodist church claimed 54 members out of the total population of 700 in West Bend. (One must always be very careful in comparing membership in churches, for each denomination counts its members differently. Some figure only adults as members; others count them after a ceremony held during childhood, while still others start enumeration as soon as they are baptized.)

Apparently the old church ceased to exist, although no one knows what happened to it, so the congregation met in the village school on alternate Sundays with the St. John's Lutheran congregation. But the members wanted their own building, so William Hamlyn donated the first $100 to start a new church, and inasmuch as he had been a railroad construction worker, he had learned the principles of building. Other major contributors were listed as Peter Knapp and David McLaughlin, while all the men of the church went into the woods to cut the timber. The approximately 50x75 foot building was built in 1872.

Local editors carried news of forthcoming sermons. One notice, just before Memorial Day 1870 read: "Let all the old soldiers come and bring their muskets. The best hour of the best day and the best place in my church is none too good for the veterans who served the nation. A. L. Tull." One of the most graphic notices occurred in 1895: "I would like to have all of the officers and members of my church present next Sunday morning as I desire to make a complete report of all work done, material purchased, moneys expended and the condition of the church exchequer. Don't forget to bring your long faces as you will feel the need of them. But please do not let anyone stay away for fear of the extra collection, as I have promised I will take no collection before Monday."

By 1884 another lot was purchased for a parsonage, which was erected in 1892 as "cheaply as possible, without any modern conveniences." Money was still scarce and it was common to read of donation parties for the various pastors, but improvements on the church followed. The stained glass windows were donated by "some Chicago and Milwaukee parties" in 1894, more comfortable oak seats were purchased in 1900, gas lights were installed in 1901, the bell from the defunct Presbyterian church in Barton was hung in 1902, electricity was installed in both the church and the parsonage and hard wood maple floors were laid in 1906. A furnace made services more comfortable. At one point the church exalted that they had acquired a blackboard to assist in the "finest Biblical teachings."

Rev. J. B. Noyes

One of the more interesting ministers in the 19th century was J. B. Noyes, about whom there is some information. Because his story is typical of many Protestant ministers at the time, it is worth reporting. He was born in 1855, and converted at a camp meeting at the age of 16. His father died the following year, leaving five mouths to feed and not one dollar to support them, so the son had to go to work. In 1889, he joined the Methodist church and received a local preacher's license, after having tried his hand at farming, brick laying, and publishing. At first he worked under another pastor, walking from five to twenty-five miles each Sunday, the latter distance once a month. Because his salary was so small, he turned his hand at teaching shorthand and printing books in West Bend to eke out a living. Slowly the church grew and he noted that he had baptized 10 souls within two years. In order to get a cistern, he dug the 60 barrel hole himself and bricked and plastered it with his own hands. When the church needed electric lights, he presented a series of stereopticon slide shows to raise the needed $75. Versatility was needed in those days for survival, and all organized religions to this day owe these hardier earlier souls an incalculable debt of gratitude.

Little mention is ever made of the wives, but many ministers were married, and their life was one continual round of trying to "make do" on a totally inadequate income.

Over the years, the Methodist church became interested in social issues and members were ardent supporters of the Temperance Society and the Freedman's Aid for Southern Education. Leading movers of these causes were Mrs. Heidner, Mrs. Mooers and Elizabeth Dunham.

A new and larger church was planned in 1929, but the depression struck, so it was not until 1934 that an additional lot was purchased and another eight years before they razed the old church and laid the cornerstone in May, 1942, for their new building. It cost $60,000 and was completely debt free when dedicated, the members having given dinners and solicited for years. The church was enlarged in 1968 and presently has over a thousand members.

CHAPTER 4

The German Methodists

One of the first churches in West Bend was that of the German Methodists; perhaps it actually was the first church building, but records are fragmentary at best. At any rate, while most other churches were being served either on a part time basis or by missionaries, the German Methodists were meeting regularly with a pastor of their own, Rev. Frederick Heinz, as early as 1855-1856, although one "memory" letter gives a date of 1854. In three years they had purchased a lot across from the courthouse square and erected a frame church. The farmers in the congregation donated the wood, hauled it to the sawmill, and then handplaned it. Everything inside was handmade, too, for a joiner named Ganzel fashioned the pulpit, a Mr. Schneider made the pews, and others constructed an altar rail and a bookcase. There was no need for an organ as no one in the congregation could play an instrument.

When Clara Kuechenmeister came to town the church had a musician at last, and her father, G. A. Kuechenmeister, helped

Rev. and Mrs. C. F. Neitzel, German Methodist minister, 1885-88.

her form a choir composed of W. Eberhardt, Emma Heidner, Will Hosig, Joe Nickel, Bertha Heidner, Katie Blaeser and Charley Blaeser. The first hymnals had only the words and all singing was A Capella, with no one being exactly sure of the correct tune. When several of the young ladies went to Milwaukee to work (Milwaukeeans prized help from "good German girls") they heard the correct music in the Milwaukee churches, and when they came back to West Bend they taught the tunes to the other young people, who, in turn, taught them to the congregation. A daughter of one of the first settlers, William Wightman, taught the first Sunday School, and because the Episcopalians and the English Methodists still had no regular Sunday School she taught them too, in English, which was unusual for all the regular services in her church were in German, while the Episcopalians and English Methodists had services in English.

The German Methodists were the first ones to hold summer camp meetings. At first they were held in the Francis Ganzel woods (later the Lang farm and now the site of homes west of 18th Avenue). What a time they had! This was the high point of the church year for many. Two families would often camp together, fashioning a tent out of yards and yards of unbleached muslin or of spare sheets. There is no record of what happened when it rained. Those who could not stay overnight walked the "short distance" for the services, held daily from Wednesday through Sunday. In typical camp meeting style, there were prayer meetings, testimonials, singing and preaching intermixed with camaraderie around the table as people cooked together and shared food. This made a fine break in an otherwise hard life for most of the parishoners.

To encourage Bible study among the young, each student was given a "ticket" on Sunday on which were printed the Bible verses to be learned for the following Sunday. When a certain number were learned, they could trade their tickets in for a "pretty picture." Because there was almost no art on the walls of early settler's homes, and pictures were scarce, these rewards became highly prized and eagerly sought.

Money was largely unknown, so in lieu of cash the minister received lodging, a garden, and a horse and buggy to call on parishoners, who almost always gave him oats for his horse, or a chicken, smoked ham, or sausage when he called on them. Otherwise, his diet was mostly vegetables.

In 1892 the German Methodists acquired the former Baptist church on Seventh Avenue, but by the end of the Second World War interest in the German language had waned and the congregation had dwindled, so in 1950 the Reverend and Mrs. Otto closed the doors of their church and led the 65 members of their congregation down the street to join the Fifth Avenue Methodist Church. Three sons of the congregation joined the ministry: William Nungesser, Conrad Eberhardt and Bartel Lambert, but the days of the German Methodist Church were over.

CHAPTER 5

St. John's Lutheran Church

Every school child learns that the Pilgrim Fathers came for religious freedom, but it is not so easily learned that the first Lutherans in Washington County came for that same reason.

St. John's Lutheran Church — 6th and Walnut, 1864.

The Prussian leaders were notably intolerant of Lutherans, trying to force them into the Reformed faith, but many Lutherans would have none of that and left Germany for America, and some of them eventually arrived in the fledgling West Bend community. Records of St. John's church go back to 1849, when they joined fellow Lutherans from Trenton in asking Slinger Pastor Meis to conduct services here and in Trenton. But he soon preferred to stay with the Trenton congregation, so West Bend Lutherans called their own minister, Pastor Oswald, who could come only every two weeks. By 1850, however, they had their own regular minister, Reverend Heis, who served until 1853.

At first the small band of about 15 families met in the home of Carl Wilke, and when they outgrew that, they met in Barton, and then moved to the District School House. Among the legible names on the early roster are those of Wernicke, Bastian, Jung, Jeklin, Althaus, Wilke, Ludwig Ottmer, Carl Fritz, Wm. Schroeder, Voss, Eberhardt, H. Treviranus, Engleman, Schmidt and Hornig. According to the records, Emma Bastian was the first baby baptized in the congregation (1850) followed by five others baptized that first year. There is a record of three funerals, the

St. John's Lutheran Church — present church.

first an eight year old boy, Thomas Nungesser. The first confirmation was in 1851 when 27 children were confirmed.

The members of the congregation began to differ among themselves and split into two separate congregations in 1853, but that made financing difficult and in a short time they resolved their disagreements and rejoined under Pastor Roell so that they could formally organize into one congregation in 1858 at the Rusco schoolhouse. St. John's absorbed most of the Trenton congregation and took the formal name of German Evangelical Lutheran St. John's Society of the Unaltered Augsburg Confession. A year later they changed to the German Evangelical Lutheran Church of Wisconsin, which was more in keeping with their familiar German heritage.

Christmas had always been a favored holiday for Germans, and the church had a big Christmas eve program in 1863, charging 20 cents for adults and 10 cents for children, but they promised the "wonders of an illuminated Christmas tree." It was not uncommon for churches to charge for church or Sunday School programs, as funds were meager. They had saved $3000 by 1864 and built a church at the northwest corner of Sixth and Walnut, with Newburg resident, T. E. Vander Cook, as the architect for the building. The entrance of the congregation into their first church was dramatic, for on the 15th of December, 1864, the members met at the district schoolhouse and marched proudly en masse to their new building where Rev. Vorberg unlocked the doors and the congregation beheld for the first time the crucifix on the altar, the Bible, communion cup and new altar covers. The energetic Vorberg had a sense of history and recopied all the church records he could find, in addition to serving three other charges, teaching Sunday School, and starting what was to become the parochial school.

By 1872 they could add an 800 pound bell to call the faithful to church and toll for the dead, and an active Ladies' Aid raised money to buy such things as carpeting, stoves, etc., for comfort, as much had been lacking in the first difficult years. Another split among the members occurred in the 1880's over the dual question of the right to join lodges and the doctrine of election by grace. Surviving that, they built a parsonage, added an organ, installed new bells in 1886 and celebrated the 25th anniversary of their church in 1889, at which time each farmer brought in a load of ground to use as fill on their property, and the congregation planted trees. Typical of the male chauvinism of the time, the records show that in the 1890's "single members" were reported in separate voting statistics. In 1908 one vote reads: "146 voting members and 86 ladies," for women were denied the right to vote. A custom at the time was for the men to sit on one side of the church and the women on the other. The children sat with their mothers.

Even as late as 1914, the services were still being held in German, except for one evening a month, promoting discontent among those who felt it was time to conduct more services in English, so the latter group split off permanently in 1923. It was not until 1950 that German services were dropped completely. Meanwhile membership increased, and they were ready for their third church in 1958. Built on land they had purchased in 1952, this modified English Gothic style church is one of the most handsome in the city, with its Moeller organ and Willett stained glass windows in 13th century style. When the church was dedicated it had over 371 voting members out of a total membership of 1381. It cost $300,000 and was remarkably debt free in 15 months.

In June of 1963 the members voted to leave the Wisconsin Synod of the Lutheran Church and joined the more liberal Missouri Synod.

CHAPTER 6

The Episcopal Church

Episcopal Church, 1908

The last of the "old line" churches in West Bend to leave the status of mission was St. James Episcopal church of the Worldwide Anglican Communion presided over by the Bishop of Canterbury. The church began as a mission of the Diocese of Milwaukee in 1870, although visiting priests had brought the sacraments to local Episcopalians before this, for there is a record of the marriage of William and Elizabeth Wightman in 1852. As the Wightmans were large property owners, they donated land for an Episcopal church building with the proviso that the land never be sold, thus insuring the continuity of Episcopalians in the village.

Before they built the church in 1870 on what was known as "Yankee Hill" (because the families of Potter, Miller, etc., lived there) the members had met in various places, one of them being the Methodist church on alternate Sundays at 10:30 with Reverend Beckel leading the English services. Their wooden church became the victim of an overheated furnace in 1932, just a week after new hymnals had been purchased and shortly after a new heat-resistant roof had been added, which hampered firemen and kept the fire inside. The fifteen families voted to rebuild and met temporarily in the Masonic Temple while their new larger church was being constructed on the old foundation. No regular fulltime priest served the church until sometime after 1932.

One interesting item in the *West Bend Democrat* of 1896 reports the beautiful Easter service which had over 50 plants and 8 vases of cut flowers and an unusually large collection of $29.90. But the church had grown dramatically, and the happy day of full independence for the church came on October 30, 1974, when Father Leeson was installed as the parish's first rector for the more than 200 members, after 104 years as a mission.

CHAPTER 7

The Immanuel Church of Christ

Among the last of the churches to organize in the 19th century was the Immanuel ("God with us") Church, a part of the Evangelical and Reformed denomination. In 1890 the local Lutherans became embroiled over the subject of continuing the parochial school system, and a minority opted to leave the church rather than continue to support a parochial school, although there were other doctoral differences as well. Their first services were held in the old Baptist church, but later they moved to the German Lutheran church on Sixth Avenue until they could build their own. Rev. F. P. Leich came from Jackson to lead the organization and he alternated services with Rev. Freidrich Wagner as their first resident pastor. All services were in German. The nine charter members were: Carl Quade, Frederick Krieger, John Lohr, Henry Krieger, William Fisher, William Freur, John Treviranus, Valentine Muenk and Philip Heipp, who patterned the church after the German Reformed Church in the United States.

By 1902 they had built their own church building at the southwest corner of Fifth and Walnut, a frame building costing $1,000. As the congregation grew they expanded the original structure, but by the 1920's the building was totally inadequate, so the present russet tile building, built along Gothic lines, was dedicated in 1923. It is somewhat similar in classic design to that of Holy Angels church, but its tower has the battlemented copings of the old English churches, a reminder of the days when churches were used as forts against invasions by the savage tribes who swooped down periodically from the north of England. The towers had no spires, so they were excellent high points from which to watch the enemy. Remodelings in both 1943 and 1955 to accommodate continual growth resulted in the present structure, and by then Dr. Henry Baumer had become the pastor, Norman Schowalter the treasurer, and C. Schneiss, C. Wendt and R. S. Grogan the elders. One of the fine additions to the church is the superb Schaefer organ, made in Slinger.

Immanuel Church of Christ

It was in 1940 that the congregation abandoned the German language and conducted all services in English. When they merged with the Evangelical Synod of North America they became known as the Immanuel Church of Christ. During World

War II they started the custom of a continually lighted cross as an invitation to prayer and as a testimony that they were constantly in prayer for the soldier members of their congregation. At least five of the sons of the congregation have become ministers: Edward Manthei, Robert Vornholdt, Wells Grogan, Paul Baumer and Martha Baumer. Over the years they became noted for their good election night suppers, and the large congregation joins other churches for annual Good Friday, Thanksgiving and World Day of Prayer services.

CHAPTER 8

Trinity English Lutheran

For many years there had been a group of Lutherans who wanted to have their church services in English, instead of the German language, and so on the first of April, 1923, Messrs. and Mmes. Henry Nagel, Herman Claus, William Kocher, C. I. Nielsen, G. Emmet and Walter J. Gumm wrote the charter that organized the first English speaking Lutheran church in the city. Inviting 40 others to join them in becoming charter members, they met at first in a room over Poull's Department store (Security Bldg.). Field missionary Rev. William Stump came to West Bend on weekends to visit the homes and organize the group, but members soon called Rev. Paul Wetzler as a full-time minister to the "church for which Luther contended" and one which promised to preach "the Bible, the whole Bible and nothing but the Bible." C. I. Nielsen was the first Sunday School Superintendent with classes for 22 pupils from the 26 families and 49 members who became the charter members. They bought a lot on the southwest corner of Seventh and Elm, the site of the old Catholic church, and moved their services to larger quarters on the mezzanine floor of the Masonic Temple, but fire destroyed it and they had to return to Poull's.

Another tragedy struck when Rev. Wetzler decided to leave shortly after the church was founded and they were unable to call another pastor for seven months. But the faithful remained

Trinity Lutheran Church

and the church grew so that in three years they had 43 families and 88 members and could approve the building of their own church at a cost of more than $16,000, half of which the members pledged and the other half they borrowed from both the First State Bank at a low rate of interest and the Board of American Missions at no interest whatsoever.

By 1932 they owned a pipe organ and after four years the Mission Board, which had been supporting them, stopped the funds and they were on their own. This had been the pattern for most of the churches founded in the 19th century in West Bend, but Trinity sustained the loss by cutting Rev. R. W. Groth's salary in half. Membership increased and by 1937 they built a parsonage, and in 1943 were debt free and had a membership of 319. Growth was continual and constant, requiring another lot in 1952 and an enlarged church in 1957. A recent addition makes it one of the largest and most attractive churches in the city.

CHAPTER 9

Christian Science Church

Christian Science Church

Among the later churches to enter the religious life of West Bend is that of the Christian Scientists. After a young local girl had been healed without benefit of a doctor, a small group of perhaps a dozen people began to meet regularly in homes in 1910 to study the teachings of their founder, Mary Baker Eddy. By 1920 they had bought a lot on Fifth Avenue from Adolph DeTuncq and built their church. Architecturally, the church follows the unadorned style of the old Pagan and Greek temples at the time of the Roman's conversion to Christianity, with its four simple Doric columns in the front. Inside is an auditorium seating 280 people. By 1929 the church was freed of debt and was dedicated.

CHAPTER 10

Roman Catholics — St. Francis Cabrini

As West Bend continued to expand southward, and as farm land was converted into a new subdivision, Holy Angels grew seriously overcrowded. The school plainly could not take more pupils and young parents dreaded exposing their children to the "dangers of secular education," so on July 3, 1955, a meeting was held in the McLane school gym to start a new congregation. Their first need was for a school, so they built one in 1957 for 240 pupils. By 1969 there were already 450 families in the congregation and it was time to build a church, a strikingly handsome modern circular structure on South Seventh Avenue. Pastor Edmund Haen was the founding father and Archbishop William Cousins was present at the dedication. The church is one of the show places of West Bend architecture and it and its school serve an increasing congregation.

St. Francis Cabrini Church

CHAPTER 11

Other Churches

Church of Jesus Christ of the Latter Day Saints

Good Shepherd Evangelical Lutheran Church

More recently, the Assembly of God worshipped in Moose Hall in 1948 until their church was built on East Decorah Road. The Good Shepherd Evangelical Lutheran Church began in 1950 in the Barton Fire Hall with Pastor George Boldt. They moved to the Leigh Carrol Dancing Studio, but it burned in December of 1950, so they had no place for their Christmas services that year. They next worshipped in Veteran's Hall but in 1951 they became the Good Shepherd Evangelical Lutheran Church officially, with 8 voting members pastored by Rev. Wilbert Gawrish. Members of the congregation privately financed a parsonage on Indiana Avenue. They held the first German service in 1951, broke ground for a chapel in 1953 and dedicated it in 1954. They built a school and had 55 children by 1963 but it has, of course, grown since then. In 1974 they joined in supporting the Kettle Moraine Lutheran High School. When they celebrated their 25th year in 1976 they burned their mortgage and in 1979 built a beautiful new church on Decorah Road and Indiana Avenue.

The Pilgrim Lutheran congregation built a church at Cherry Street and Meadowbrook. Begun in 1956, the cornerstone was laid in 1958. Still another Lutheran Church is Our Savior's, which began life as a Home Mission Evangelical church in 1959 at Sixth and Walnut and is now at home at 1044 Silverbrook Drive. The Church of Jesus Christ of the Latter Day Saints erected its building on Paradise Drive in 1965 and has seen an addition for its growing membership. In 1973 the Church of God also chose Paradise Drive for its location.

In addition to the above named churches, the following congregations meet regularly in West Bend: First Baptist, Emmaus Bible Church, Jehovah's Witnesses, Church of the Nazarene, Hope Reformed, Church of Christ, Church of God, Full Gospel Church, Christian Living Fellowship, the Baptist Bible Temple, and St. Mary's Catholic Church in what was formerly Barton. There would seem to be a church to fit the needs of all in the growing city of West Bend.

St. Mary's Church — Barton

CHAPTER 12

The Cemeteries

Closely allied with religion, of course, are cemeteries. A philosopher once said that you can best judge a people by their cemeteries. The oldest one in the city is Pilgrims' Rest on Chestnut Street. Founded in 1851, it was originally the old Lutheran Evangelical Cemetery, but the name was changed in 1902 to honor the man who had given the land. The oldest birth date on a marker there is 1784.

The first Catholic cemetery was located a half mile south of what was then the village and 500 feet back from the road. The first body buried there was that of Margaret McHugh in 1856; she may have been the city's oldest resident at the time of her death at the age of 81. The last one to be buried there was Katherine Ollinger in 1886, for the church bought land for a new cemetery on the corner of Decorah and South Main Street. By 1891 the graves from the older one were moved to the present location, and a newspaper account of the moving tells that relatives, curious to see what was left of a corpse, had several of the caskets opened. It was reported that one boy who had died at the age of eight had grown a full beard before the casket was opened nine years later.

The city-wide cemetery was built on land donated by Wightman on what is now Tenth Avenue. This Union Cemetery was founded in 1857 on land that was dry and relatively free from stones. Besides, it was on that preferred location, a hill. By 1885 it had a well, had repaired the original rickety fence, and began to plant trees, but the plan to include a fountain never materialized. By 1920 it was enlarged, and when it outgrew that, the new 25 acre cemetery was built in 1932 at the corner of 18th Avenue and Paradise Drive.

SECTION IX

INDUSTRY AND LABOR

CHAPTER 1

General Information and Earliest Industries

West Bend's Industries

The motto of West Bend is: "The City of Varied Industries." Now, what made West Bend such a successful industrial city? We must recall that businesses require many elements: dependable labor, capital, leaders with business acumen, wide markets, a ready source of power, and access to transportation. As for the labor, early West Bend attracted capable craftsmen from both the Eastern states of the United States and from Europe, and they opened the first one-man shops where everything was handmade. Immigration increased and the companies were assured of an ample, dependable labor supply, primarily German. As the following portions of this chapter will show, businessmen of unusual ability were either born here or came to West Bend, made money, and re-invested it in larger ventures, providing the needed capital. Early power was supplied by the Milwaukee River and that same river provided a convenient gigantic refuse tank for the spoils of manufacture at no cost to the owners. The abundant nearby forests and fields furnished the first raw materials and some of the fuel, and the proximity to Milwaukee made it possible to get goods to market. So West Bend had it all, plus a large prosperous nearby farming community to buy the manufactured goods.

At first, however, West Bend was a commercial rather than an industrial center. Because of the successful grist mill that soon provided for the local areas as well as with a surplus to ship out of town, and the prosperous sawmill that produced all the lumber, West Bend was considered a trading center almost from its inception, and continued to be so for its first half century. Stores appeared immediately along the main street (River Road) right next to blacksmiths, tanners, harness makers and cabinet makers and sold every conceivable need for pioneers from ammunition to muslin. Farmers brought in their milk, honey, maple sugar, wheat, chickens, eggs, hogs, cordwood and cattle. Fifteen years after the first cabin was erected there were four blocks of stores (admittedly not very close together), along with five lawyers (temporary ones — they came and went), two doctors, a visiting dentist, a printer, insurance agent, gunsmith, marble worker, and at least three hotels, so settlers for miles around came to West Bend for supplies and services.

The key year that begins the change from a commercial city to an industrial one seems to be 1895 with the entrance of the Enger-Kress factory. By then West Bend was no longer dependent upon local raw materials, for the railroad brought in needed supplies. Although the flour industry was still the largest industry with a capacity of over 40,000 barrels of high grade flour a year, the fledgling leather industry was a close second. Seven department or general stores sold everything including pianos and sewing machines. There were nearly 1800 people in town, and it is difficult for us to realize that 173 of the original 720 acres were still in active cultivation, while another 90 acres were still in woodlot or unimproved land; one of the sights was the weekly entrance of farmers into town driving their cattle down Main Street to the local stock yards for transportation to Milwaukee. The monthly fair was still so popular that wagons and buggies were parked two deep for blocks and blocks, creating a traffic jam of magnitude.

In spite of the rural atmosphere, the heretofore one man businesses were now employing several people, and by 1912 West Bend was supplying the world with pocketbooks, aluminum ware, cheese boxes, canned peas, barn fixtures, silage cutters, lumber wagons and buggies, Lithia beer and wool yarn. But of all the early industries — which included a grist and a saw mill, an ashery, stave factory, harness making, straw cover manufacture, wagon and buggy making — only the brewery and the production of farm machinery remained into the second half of the 20th century.

Fred Schloemer's Blacksmith Shop

Fred Schloemer

Warnkey Tin Shop

Louis Lucas's Foundry

The Ashery

In 1848 Henry Becker and John Potter started one of West Bend's first industries — an ashery — on the spot where Geib's hotel now stands. While a brewery was a German business, the ashery was distinctly Yankee in the village which now had 30 families.

The source of the ashes was the thousands of trees that farmers cut down so that they might clear the land for farming, along with a lesser number hewn down in the village so that there would be space for buildings and gardens. Sometimes men brought the whole trees to the ashery and then the workers would burn them in immense piles; at other times the farmers burned the trees and brought the ashes in to town, usually by ox cart.

Little equipment was needed for an ashery, and Carl Quickert cites this as a perfect example of Yankee ingenuity and thrift. The basic equipment consisted of large boxes on 4′ x 15′ slanted troughs running down to the river. A thick layer of straw was laid on the bottom over which a generous layer of ashes was placed. The water from the river was poured over the ashes and allowed to run out of holes in the bottom in a process called leaching. The product thus obtained was raw lye which was then boiled in large iron kettles, strained, boiled a second time and allowed to evaporate. This left a finished product — potash — from which local housewives made saleratus (baking soda) and soap, with enough left for glass companies who used potash in making window panes.

The business was short-lived, for when the trees were all destroyed there were no more ashes, and like so many frontier industries, the owners had to either move farther west or change occupations.

Gehl Bros. Manufacturing Company

Gehls

The world renowned Gehl Manufacturing Company began its life as Louis Lucas's Foundry away back in 1850. Born in 1820 in France, Lucas had Huguenot ancestors persecuted for their Protestantism and who became refugees. At the age of 14 he became a coppersmith journeyman and completed his training at the age of 20, but he was impressed into the French Navy at the age of 23 and spent three years in unhappy compulsory service. He had enlisted as a private and rose to become a battery commander.

After marrying, he emigrated to the United States where he established his foundry in West Bend. His service to the community was interrupted by a stint in the Civil War when Governor Solomon commissioned him Captain of Militia in 1861.

In addition to his necessary work in the foundry, something the community badly needed, he served two years as Justice of the Peace and a year as Village Clerk. Friends said of him that his word was as good as his endorsement and he was known as a philosopher, accepting his lot in life.

Because he was a fine tinsmith and coppersmith, he was kept busy in his small plant on River Street in which he also found time to invent a feed cutter to cut dry cornstalks. In addition he made and sold fanning mills, plows, rotating churns, etc. His feed cutters became increasingly popular, and during the rush season he employed five workers to help him.

The factory changed hands several times, going in 1876 to Jacob Young who took in Charles Silberzahn and it became the Silberzahn Manufacturing Company in 1890. Silberzahn manufactured wood sawing machines, hay tedders, corn shellers, plow points, kettles, clothes line reels, etc. He employed 20 skilled workmen and he and some of the men invented a few of their products.

Charles Silberzahn, age 90.

Silberzahn was another interesting person. Born in the Grand Duchy of Baden in 1828 he left school at 15 to become an apprentice to a blacksmith for three years and helped build ships. During his forced tour of duty in the military artillery in the 1848 revolution, when the Germans were demanding a free press, the right to trial by jury, etc., for themselves, he fled and became a fugitive in Switzerland where he worked in a wagon factory for a time. He saved some money and with the help of the President of the Swiss Republic bought a ticket to the United States. He was a political refugee, and there was one Prussian aboard the ship who would not let him put his pot on his (the Prussian's) stove to cook his meal, so young Silberzahn went to the Captain for redress. Other passengers took a liking to him and a thorough dislike to the stuffy Prussian, so they shared their food with him.

Hitching posts made by Silberzahn — 1890 (may be seen in Washington County Museum).

Landing in St. Louis, he stayed there for a time, then worked on a river boat on the Illinois River, among many other jobs, and landed in Memphis in time to witness the battle of Memphis during the Civil War. He did not want to join the army but he did help the north repair their fleet after the battle, shipped on a ram to Vicksburg and helped bring starving prisoners north to safety. He was offered a commission, but refused, and later found his way to West Bend.

Gehl's enter the scene in 1879 when Silberzahn sold his plant to the firm of Berris, Gehl, and Thoma, Inc., who quickly increased the work force to fifty men as the quality of their new manure spreaders and wheel barrows became known.

By 1917 they were making silo fillers and tractors, and one great day in 1923 an order came from Iowa for 300 silo fillers.

Another highlight was the winning of a contest in Marshfield which pitted all rival feed cutters against each other, and theirs won in both time and quality. Growth continued until they were employing 500 workers in 1942; they were to see the greatest period of growth in the 1960's, when they employed over 1200 men, with more than 1400 dealers worldwide.

By then, however, there was greater competition, so Joseph Zadra moved from Office Manager to President and stressed research and development. The company has never had a complete line of farm machinery, preferring to specialize. One of their latest big sellers has been the mammoth hay baler, the Gehlbale, that makes bales up to 1500 pounds in weight and has proved a labor-saving device to farmers. Other labor-saving devices that they have perfected include a grinder-mixer that has captured 20% of the United States market, a hammermill, harvester, and a silo filler; they are noted for several "firsts" of their kind in the industry. In addition to being one of the largest industries in West Bend, employing 1300 workers, they have another plant in South Dakota and the name of "Gehl's" stamped on farm machinery is visible all over the world.

Leather Industries

From the earliest years, West Bend was involved in one way or another with the leather industry. Among the first plants were the tanneries, of which West Bend had four at one time, located along the river because of the vast amount of water needed in the processing of hides. The largest tannery was that of Hass and Fussweller, located behind the current Schultz store in downtown West Bend, but it burned to the ground as did so many of West Bend's early industries. Another tannery was owned by Ottman and Baldwin. A Mr. Mueck tried a tannery on Sixth Avenue across from the Court House, and in 1891 Fritz Stein opened one in his house, but the other occupants complained bitterly of the stench!

The process of tanning was an engrossing one. First of all the hides were put into a large vat containing lime water to loosen the hair; then they were scraped by hand. Meanwhile red oak bark from the sawmill wastes, as well as from the plentiful supply of oak trees in the area, was ground to a pulp and rolled under heavy stones. Alternate layers of the oak pulp and the hides were then placed in vats which were at least five feet deep and four feet wide. Water was added and they were left for

Krieger Collar and Harness Manufacturing Company, 1895.

six to nine months, after which they were hand rubbed with tallow to soften them, dried and stretched. Then they were ready for the shoemaker or harness maker.

The second leather industry in early West Bend was the harness maker, who arrived almost as soon as the first settlers.

Frank Everly had a harness shop on Fourth Avenue which was bought out by William Hildebrand, but Hildebrand, who was also the Village Treasurer, misappropriated funds and landed in Waupun. The last harness maker was Henry Krieger, whose firm at one time turned out 800 single and 400 double harnesses a year. Among other products he made were buggy whips, sweat pads, horse collars, saddles, bridles, and halters. What a to-do was raised when the motor car appeared, for it was feared the invention would cause massive unemployment among buggy whip manufacturers!

Shoemakers were the third of the early leather workers in the village, and they would often leave their shop to come directly into one's home to cut and fit the shoes. Many settlers could not afford to employ a shoemaker to repair the shoes, so they owned equipment to repair their own. Buying a shoe was no light task, for shoes were expected to last for years. Work shoes were usually put together with wooden pegs which lasted longer than nails, but dress shoes had their soles nailed on. Often a customer would bring his own tanned leather to the shoemaker because leather was expensive; boots would cost up to $10, a princely sum at the time. The first shoemen were Yankees, but they quickly sold out to the Germans, some of whom bore the names of Tscheipe, Schaeffler, Gerlach, Jaeger, Althaus and Englehardt. C. A. Schaefer employed six men in 1888 and needed more as he sold his shoes all over Wisconsin.

The entrance of the big-time leather companies occurred in 1894 when George Enger and August Kress came to town. They had come from Germany, Enger from Altenburg, Saxony, in 1869 at the age of 27, and Kress from Ogdenburger-on-Main, Bavaria, in 1879 at age 21. Both worked for leather companies in Milwaukee until 1885 when they joined to manufacture their own products. But fire was no stranger to Milwaukee either, and their factory burned to the ground in 1894. Hearing of this, several enterprising local men, including E. Franckenburg and Math Regner, induced them to come to West Bend. The company needed $20,000 for the move, and the local backers were able to subscribe $14,000 of the money in the first week of their efforts.

Their first shop was in the old South School at Fifth and Poplar, and the work force consisted of 12 skilled workers from Milwaukee who brought their families with them. Enger and Kress then trained local people to fill the staff; in 13 years they were employing 50 persons, and were the first company in town

Enger Kress — 1894, in Old South School, northwest corner of Poplar and Fifth.

Enger Kress girls. Back row: (1) Linda Vincent, (2) Katherine Goeden, (3) Emma Vogelsberg, (4) "Toddy" Mrs. Ted Kugler, (5) Frances Bertram Barwick, (6) Irene Koenings Schwichtenberg, (7) Emma Warnkey, (8) Jean Buss Jaeger, (9) Ann Geminden Nehrbass, (10) Gladys Koenings Krueger, (11) Melinda Faver. Front row: (1) Viola Hecker, (2) Sybilla Schaeffer Heinecki, (3) Susan Schmidt, (4) Viola Jobs Marquardt, (5) Veronica Berres Becker.

to employ women. Officers of the plant, in addition to the owners, were G. A. Kuechenmeister, Andrew Pick, and Ernst Franckenburg.

Most of the leather for the pocketbooks came from the east, and consisted largely of hides from horses, oxen, cows, and buffalo, as well as skin from calves, sheep, dogs and goats. The preferred leather was calfskin. By now the once plentiful oak was scarce in the surrounding area, so hemlock and sumac provided the material to tan the hides. After it was treated, it was shaped, embossed (or patterned), stamped (sometimes with gold), cleaned, sewn and inspected. If the leather were to be colored, it was sprayed. At first one of the most time-taking of tasks was the hand riveting, but Al Gilbert of West Bend invented a machine to do the work faster.

Among the memories of the old time workers is that of the beer breaks, which occurred twice a day when two boys would bring plenty of beer to supply all hands and the factory would close down for the rest period. Another memory concerns the morals of the workers, as it was difficult at first to induce women and girls to work in a factory, for their work was traditionally at home. To preserve the moral atmosphere, the girls worked only in pairs, entirely separated from the male employees! The firm always needed more girl workers than it could employ in the early years, but there were not enough local girls to meet the demand and the lack of suitable housing inhibited girls from out of town coming to the city for employment.

When George Enger died, Anton Guenther bought the controlling interest from Mrs. Enger and became president, with Frank Lehman vice-president and Robert Rolfs, secretary. The latter had been the bookkeeper.

By 1911 they had outgrown the old schoolhouse and moved to Schlitz Park, but lightning destroyed the plant, their second disastrous fire and a tragic one for West Bend for "half the town depended on it for employment." Undaunted, they started anew at the vacant home of what became the West Bend Plating Company, after which they built the attractive brick and concrete factory on Wisconsin Avenue. They had "farmed out" some of the work to local women. In the cornerstone they placed accounts of the fire, a Bible, several current and Civil War era coins, pocket books, billfolds and photos of the old and new plants. A motto on the wall read "Labor Omnia Vincent" — Labor Conquers All. When the day came for the company to start operations in the new building, the employees marched en masse from the old factory to the rhythm of the West Bend City Band; the company celebrated by offering refreshments. West Bend knew the value of the leather industry to its economic welfare.

It might be valuable to learn a bit about the intertwining of the history of money and the billfold industry. The size and shape of purses and billfolds is directly related to the use of coins and paper money in our nation's history. At first most of the money was in coins, so coin purses were more popular. Gold coins were more delicate than silver ones, so Enger-Kress made one purse with a chamois pocket. As more paper money was used, the company made two and three fold billfolds, but when the government changed the size of bills in 1928 from 7½″ x 2⁹⁄₁₆″ to 6³⁄₁₆″ x 2⁹⁄₁₆″ the company switched over to a fold-over hip pocket wallet. They made pass cases and special trainmen's cases when the railroad became popular in Wisconsin, tobacco pouches, music bags, collar and tie cases, and handkerchief cases, which illustrates further the changes history makes on the industries, as all such products are practically non-existent now.

Amity Plant, 1925.

Amity

The second major leather company came to West Bend in 1915 under the leadership of Robert Rolfs, and quickly became the largest manufacturer of personal leather goods in the world. Rolfs began the plant with an idea that billfolds could become

Amity Plant today.

a fashion accessory, which was a new idea in 1915. When he sought a name for the company that would express both friendliness and confidence, he settled on "Amity," which means friendly understanding, and so began operation in September of 1915. His factory was one room over Peter's store (now Sears) with one employee, but during World War I he moved to the third floor of the Hangartner building and employed 15 workers to make leather jackets for the army. Soon his business grew to encompass all three floors and 50 employees.

In 1924 he built his own factory at South Main Street and enlarged it in 1929 to include one of the landmarks of West Bend, the Amity tower. Robert Rolfs continued as President and General Manager, Baltus Rolfs became Vice President, and Harry Rolfs the Sales Manager. Their slogan was, "If it's stamped Amity it's leather."

At first their main product was billfolds, but they added ladies' handbags and opened a factory at Sturgeon Bay. In 1937 their Director billfold with its secret pocket and space for spare keys was a run-away success. During World War II they furnished the handbags for the women in the armed forces, and both Mrs. Franklin Roosevelt and one of her predecessors had carried Rolfs bags. In 1938 they capitalized briefly on the popularity of the pandas in the Brookfield Zoo and produced a billfold made from a panda skin which was for sale at $5000.

The company is the only one in the industry that still finishes most of its own leather, which it does in its West Bend plant. There is a second company with the Rolfs label headquartered in New York. Today the company is run by two sons of the founder, Thomas J., Chairman of the Board, and Robert T., President. Their over 1200 employees are among the highest paid in the industry, which requires fine craftsmen, and they have some of the world's finest leather specialists. Much of the machinery is of their own design.

Presently, they have plants in New Mexico, San Lorenzo, and Canada. Three large distribution centers are located in West Bend, Albuquerque, and Goldsboro, North Carolina, and branch sales offices operate from New York to California.

Early West Bend brewing company.

Breweries

For 124 years beer was one of West Bend's most famous products. The story began when German immigrant Balthazer Goetter, a cooper and brewer by trade, arrived in the United States in 1846 from Hesse, Darmstadt, Germany, worked in Levi Blossom's Milwaukee brewery for two years, and then came to West Bend to found a brewery on the site directly across from the present building. With the almost daily arrival of more German immigrants, most of whom brought with them a "Teutonic" taste for beer, the brewery was a success from the start. When Goetter fell ill with an eye infection, he left the business to his two brothers-in-law, Carl and Stephen Mayer, who had been his fellow workers.

By 1875 they had seven employees and were brewing 3500 barrels of beer annually, but brewing was possible only in the winter, for science had not yet perfected a method of keeping a constant temperature the year around. The Mayers prospered and bought many lots in the city, including the land where Enger-Kress, Cooley's, Gehl's and Regner Park now stand, but they both died young and the brewery passed into the hands of Carl's son Stephen F., his sister Emma (whose husband Andrew Pick had run a department store in Slinger until the Panic of 1873), and Adam Kuehlthau who owned the smaller Eagle Brewery* on the site of the present Lithia building. The new owners also operated a malt house on the site of the original Lithia plant, a cooper shop to make and repair barrels into which the beer was poured, and an ice business in the winter time.

The name of Lithia beer became widely known; a West Bend newspaper reported in 1893 that "many families in the northern part of Washington County use little tea or coffee, for Lithia beer has taken its place."

In 1911 Stephen Mayer became ill, and Andrew Pick died a year later, so the business was sold to four Appleton men, Martin F. and Charles W. Walter, Julius Kerber, and Henry A. Schmidt. The Walters were from a family of brewers; their father George headed the George Walter Brewing Company of Appleton, one of his brothers (John) operated a brewery in Eau Claire, and two other brothers, Christ and Joe, operated a brewery in Menasha. Martin had owned a brewery in Pueblo, Colorado, so the family brought considerable expertise to the local industry. The new owners became involved in other successful local enterprizes, Martin F. Walter becoming a director of the First National Bank and an officer and director of the West Bend Equipment Company and Charles W. becoming president of the West Bend Mutual Fire Insurance Company and Vice President of the First State Bank.

---

*This brewery had been built in the 1850's by Chris Eckstein on the site of the present Lithia building. Eckstein sold it to Adolph Arzbacher, who employed Adam Kuehlthau who had learned the brewery business in Germantown. Later Arzbacher leased the brewery to Kuehlthau and a partner named Johnson for five years, after which it was sold at sheriff's sale and acquired by Kuehlthau. The Eagle Brewery brewed 2000 barrels of beer annually and had six employees.

Julius Kerber, who was their brewmaster, had learned the trade in Germany and when he eventually left West Bend, he founded his own firm in San Franciso. Adam Spaeth became his successor and worked for the Walters for 46 years. The brewer that preceded the arrival of the Walters had been Ben Roedel, who moved to Menasha to take the position Kerber had had there.

The early brewing process is fascinating. The malt, hops, and other ingredients were placed into a large kettle heated by the plentiful cord wood in the area. From there it ran into a large mash bin with a board walk over it, on which men stood and stirred the product with long-handled laddles. After it flowed through the bin it went into the cooling room where it stood on the floor in amounts up to four feet deep until it settled. Then it ran into vats and the sediment was washed away.

In 1900 the firm bought a York ice machine which made year-round brewing possible. An artesian well in the basement supplied pure water, and incidentally, furnished the name of the beer, "Lithia," because of the presence of small amounts of lithium carbonate in the water. Barley for the beer was grown by the area farmers.

Horses delivered the product to nearby areas until 1910 when a Kissel truck was purchased, with the exception of the years when an epidemic killed off the horses, and oxen were used for delivery. One of the drivers was a local legend. William Waechter was nicknamed "Old Faithful" because he was so dependable and prompt that people set their watches when he passed by on his daily rounds. He left and arrived according to schedule and brewery workers used to make small bets as to just when he would be seen coming over the hill after a long day's work.

It used to be customary for employers to give their employees an annual picnic, and the brewers were famous for theirs, complete with musicians, food, beverages, games and sports. In 1911, for instance, they served chopped beef, ham and cheese sandwiches for lunch in the morning, fried fish, roast pork and potato salad at noon, and roast beef, baked and boiled potatoes for supper, together with an ample supply of the company's products. In between all this there were races and games. When the tired but happy employees returned about seven o'clock at night, they agreed they liked to work for "these bosses." Something valuable has been lost in the impersonalization of modern businesses.

When news of the impending Prohibition reached the brewers, they notified the public that they had ample amounts to last the locals until July 1st when the ban would become official, so there would be no need to "break off beer drinking suddenly." They also prepared ample amounts of "Christmas brew."

Prohibition nearly ruined the company even though they tried manufacturing a product known as "Lithia Be Sure," containing not more than ½ of 1% alcohol. They had to ship most of it to Milwaukee, for West Bend citizens preferred their own home version to the ersatz product. This area was particularly bitter about the Prohibition era; Congressman Voight told a local audience at the inception of the ban that the Constitution never intended the government should have the right to regulate the habits of people. Why, he continued, a doctor could no longer prescribe beer for a patient legally, although he was still free to prescribe wine or alcohol, and he feared the nation would resort to law breaking — en masse — which of course is precisely what happened. Local stills were being unearthed in the area decades after the end of Prohibition.

After Franklin D. Roosevelt won the election in 1932, there was no doubt that beer would soon be legal again, so Lithia applied for a license, one of the first Wisconsin companies to do so. (There were 27 breweries in the state then.) Martin Walter, who had been local postmaster during the long "drought" resigned that post and returned to brewing. By working 18 hour shifts the cellar was soon full again, and by the 7th of April, 1933, they had 10,000 cases and nearly 5,000 barrels of beer ready for the first comers, when beer's legality was ushered in at 12:01 A.M.

By ten o'clock that night cars and trucks began to roll into West Bend and line up. Several hundred people milled in the yard and at least 100 cars lined Main Street. When the magic hour neared, the treasury agent assigned to the plant to see that they did not sell any beer prematurely gave the word, and the beer slid down the chute. Amid happy cries at the sight of their favorite beverage, nobody minded the snowstorm that night. Former president S. F. Mayer bought the first beer and a plentiful supply was carted to the saloons which were renamed "taverns."

Orders for carloads of Lithia poured into the plant after the end of Prohibition, but the owners realized that they could not produce beer in this quantity and keep the quality high, so they decided to produce only for the local customers who had patronized the brewery before the ban. "Our success will be measured not by the volume of our sales, but rather by the quality of our product and the service we give to our customers."

In recent years, giant industries have controlled more and more markets, and this became true of the brewing industry also, so in 1972 the West Bend Lithia Company reluctantly closed its doors in West Bend and moved to Eau Claire, one more victim of the giants. Lithia and Old Timers are still being produced there. The Lithia building was purchased by John Kenny and John Koeske and awaits the day when someone with imagination and the financial backing can convert its unusual resources into a new use.

One indication of the financial value of the brewery to the community, for instance, was that in the 25 years after the end of Prohibition, they had paid the city $200,000 in real estate and property taxes, bought a million and a half dollars worth of barley from the area farmers, had nearly a three million dollar payroll and had paid nearly nine million dollars in state and federal taxes. They were missed.

CHAPTER 2

Other 19th Century Industries

Cigar Manufacture

One of the more interesting early industries in West Bend was that of cigar making. As early as 1872 a V. Kohost (sic) was producing 200,000 cigars a year and five years later the firm of Selinger and Luckow added 150,000 yearly. First of all, they made the filler of the cheapest tobacco and rolled and pressed it in a wood press. Then a binder of the more expensive tobacco was hand wrapped around the filler, glued at both ends and laid out on a table to age 48-72 hours. Each cigar was then hand wrapped in cellophane and boxed, each box being placed under a heavy press for two days. Any scraps of tobacco that were not used were sold to a large company for use in cigarettes.

The most famous cigar maker in West Bend was Henry Rolfs, an authority on leaf tobacco after twenty years on the road for a tobacco house. He came from Milwaukee in 1899 and opened a shop at the corner of Elm and Main Street where he made better cigars than his competitors, for he would not use Wisconsin tobacco, considering it too grainy for cigars. Three of his more popular five cent brands were "Blazer," named after the local baseball team, the "Nabob," which became the name of a nearby town, and the clergyman's favorite, the "Harvest Moon." He also made a quality ten cent cigar, touring the state with his product and selling all he could manufacture. In 1905 Herman Techtman also had a factory for a brief time, but as with so many other products, large tobacco companies eventually put an end to the one man operations and cigar manufacturing left West Bend forever.

Grain Elevators

As West Bend's rural area, which had concentrated on growing grains at first, became more and more of a dairy industry, it was time to add grain elevators to the local businesses. The first one was built by Wm. Franckenberg and Charles Karsten in 1874, across from Enger Kress on Wisconsin Avenue and Depot Lane, and was handling 125,000 bushels of grain yearly. They bought grain directly from local farmers and transported it to Milwaukee elevators via the railroad. They also stored wheat and barley, and in a few years added wool, clover seed, flour, potatoes, apples, etc., to the products they handled and stored.

The business was sold several times; names and dates of the various owners conflict. By 1875 there was another one, the West Bend Elevator, owned by B. Goetter, managed by Peter Hetzel, and built next to the first one. Both companies bought cordwood from local farmers to power the steam machinery, although the first one had used horse power for a brief time. Soon bran, linseed and dairy feeds were added.

Today the West Bend Elevator has a prosperous business at its home on Wisconsin Avenue.

Soda Bottling

West Bend is surely a city of varied industries. One of the nineteenth century ventures was the soda bottling business, started in 1890 by Herman Degner, but he sold out to Ed Koepke in 1892, the same year Math P. Boden started the West Bend

Bottling Company, so there were two rival companies. Koepke sold out to the Sturm Brothers, and Boden sold to his former rival Degner, but he was burned out in 1912. Then there was just one renamed the West Bend Bottling Works, which moved to East Water Street.

The nineteenth century recipe called for "plenty" of sugar, extracts, water, chocolate #1 (a chocolate sweeter and cheaper than sugar and soon made illegal), citric acid and foam. Workmen would heat the sugar, add the water and other ingredients so they would "work," then put the liquid mass into a huge drum and turn it with a hand crank as they added the "poison" foam, and then bottled it. Bottles had to be laboriously washed by hand, so they hired school boys to come after school to do the washing. If the bottles could not be cleaned, the company lost money, so the boys would put BB's into the bottles and shake them by hand, a most tiresome process. All bottles were capped and cased by hand. The company produced 100 cases of soda a day, just as many as their wagon and two horses could deliver in one day.

Soda cost five cents a bottle, but the saloon keepers could buy it for 60 cents a case and make a 60-cent profit. It was a popular product. Ingredients cost the owners a half cent a bottle and after all their other expenses, the company planned to make 40 cents a case profit. As was the usual story in West Bend, the factory and machinery burned in a disastrous fire in 1912 but it was rebuilt. By 1945 they could produce 90 cases of pop an hour, and soon had an automatic washing machine which could wash 100 cases per hour. Today the Seven-Up Bottling Company operates on Kilbourn Avenue.

Schmidt and Stork Wagon Company

In 1855 a German immigrant named Fred Schmidt built a factory in Little America north of West Bend to manufacture wagons, but the building burned, and when he took in his brother-in-law Frederick Stork* of Kewaskum in 1892, they moved the plant to West Bend where they added carriages and sleighs to their line. In 1895 Schmidt invented a machine to drive spokes

*Fred Stork was born in Boston and came to West Bend to become one of the city's first aldermen, helped on countless committees, and was responsible for such improvements as the stop and go lights on Main Street, the War Memorial, etc. He loved history and typified the finest spirit of West Bend.

Schmidt and Stork Wagon Company

into the rim which made their manufacture easier. He was quite an innovative gentleman in many ways. The company produced wagons, not only for the local trade, but also for sale in the nearby states, for if one owned a wagon by Schmidt and Stork, one owned the best. The wagons were painted green and had red wheels, so they were easily identifiable. One of them is on display at Wade House.

By 1898 they had orders for 35 carloads of wagons and had to expand. Wood for the wagons came from local farmers who brought the wood to the factory, but as the supply dwindled, the firm bought a portable sawmill and went from farm to farm to saw the hardwood, saving the farmers a trip to town.

Built on the "island" just behind the present First National Bank building, the 18 foot high building which they erected in 1921 was a model of efficiency, for raw material came in one end of the building directly from the dry kiln outside, and then moved through the factory to the woodworking, blacksmithing, and painting departments emerging from the other end of the building as a handsome, finished product. They were one of the biggest manufacturers of wagons in the state until the automobile appeared and the need for wagons declined.

To preserve their business, they changed to making wooden specialties for Enger Kress, display tables, fruit presses to be used in the growing home wine industry, grates for furnaces, truck bodies and in 1931 they started to manufacture caskets, founding the West Bend Casket Company. They used cedar and cypress for the caskets, and an editor wrote, "It seems a pity that one must be dead to be bedded so royally in silk and satin

First Cooperative Creamery. Left to right: Mr. Fullerton, Mr. Winninghof, Adolph Perschbacher, Buttermaker.

in costly fragrant wood." None of these ventures proved financially successful, so the building was eventually sold to the Pick Company, but it had served its purpose and helped to give West Bend an honored name in the manufacturing field.

Creameries

Before the era of creameries, the early settlers made their own butter by letting the cream from excess milk rise to the top of an earthenware pan, after which it was transferred to a stomping jar of either wood or earthenware with a stick that resembled a broom handle attached to a disc. When the handle was moved rapidly up and down, the churning motion made butter. The churner, usually a young member of the family. had to watch very carefully, for when the first thin grains of butter appeared at the top it was time to stop the churning. The butter was then scooped into a bowl, preferably wooden, worked with a butter paddle to remove all the excess buttermilk, and salted. Sometimes the ladies put it into fancy molds for table use. All the excess buttermilk (note the origin of the word) was thrown to the hogs as it was considered too sour for human consumption.

Until separators were invented, all butter was made from sour cream; sweet cream butter was possible when the separators speeded up the process so that the milk would stay sweet, as did the buttermilk. After this invention, the butter making process

Wallau Dairy Company, 1914 (facing Chicago Northwestern RR).

was a bit different, for a large barrel-like churn was used with a crank, and the buttermilk ran out a spout at the bottom. People who had excess milk often made butter to sell to those who did not have cows.

The first creamery was built in West Bend in 1898 and was under the ownership of A. C. Fuge, A. Lindbach, C. A. Schroeder, Louis Ottmer, Peter Campbell, Carl Quandt, William Hamlyn, and J. B. Ahlers, with Hamlyn the President and A. Lindbach the manager. The men incorporated and sold shares for a dollar each, had a wide market for their butter and sold the buttermilk for hog feed. Adolph Perschbacher was the first buttermaker; he had gone to the University of Wisconsin and taken the short course to learn the technique. Samples were taken daily of each farmer's milk, and they were paid by the inch of butterfat, so if the sampler would tip the stick a bit, the farmer made more profit.

This business was sold to the Wallau Dairy Company and remained in business until Mr. Wallau's death, reportedly a suicide over financial troubles. It was replaced by the White House Milk Company which was started in Strube's Park by Martin and Charles Walter, Jos. M. O'Meara, and S. F. Mayer, with Frank Mooney as plant superintendent. By 1924 the A and P Company had a large local condensery which shipped out 101 cases of four-dozen cans each of evaporated milk every 24 hours. There were 125 local workers, one of the largest plants of its kind in

White House Milk Products Company

the world. It, too, has vanished from the industrial scene of West Bend.

Ice Harvesting

There were several uses for ice in the 19th century. Taverns needed it to cool the beer; people used it to make ice cream. Mortuaries required it to keep the bodies cool until the day of the funeral, and railroads wanted it for their diners. So West Bend began to harvest ice. Andrew Pick, Sr., used the cradle of West Bend industry for an ice house around 1900.

Ice Harvesting

This was a seasonal occupation beginning in January and continuing for the four to six weeks of the coldest weather. When the ice was at least 24 inches thick on the Milwaukee River, the ice was marked off into two by four foot cubes, after which a horse drawn plow cut it, first in one direction, then in the other to score it deeply. Men then moved onto the ice and broke it up with saws and picks, and the chunks were floated down the open water to the warehouse near the railroad track. Coarse hay was spread all around the chunks to insulate them.

Tragedies abounded. Going to the river to watch the harvesting could be exciting, for there was always the chance that someone would fall into the icy water. As this was a rather frequent occurrence, a roaring fire was kept burning on shore to dry off the unlucky ones. Sometimes a cable would snap under a heavy load, and a frightened team would run away. When the only place to run was into the open water they would drown. One observer later compared the excitement at the river to watching stock car races, where the fun is to see an accident.

By 1930 the Silver Lake Ice Company had improved the operation to lift and elevate ice to fill 20 railroad cars an hour, but when electric refrigeration became popular, the once lucrative ice business vanished.

Miscellaneous Factories

Other factories included the Straw Bottle Cover Factory, which manufactured straw covers to insulate bottles in transit, the only one in the United States. It burned in 1904 in its location in the "Cradle of West Bend Industry" and did not reopen. The Pearl Button Factory brought clam shells from the Mississippi River to its factory in the same location as the above, and mechanically punched out the buttons. By 1896 it was producing 250 gross of buttons a week, but it closed in 1900, for the scale of operations was too small to assure a satisfactory profit. The workers felt they were drastically underpaid, too. Two years later the plant installed automatic machinery and produced up to 1300 gross weekly, but in 1904 the owners moved to LaCrosse to be nearer the source of their raw materials. Today, of course, most buttons are made of plastic.

An interesting sidenote occurred in the summer of 1979 when workers were improving the city parking lot at Fifth and Walnut. Dean Einerson of Richfield dug into a plentiful supply of the old used shells while digging postholes; they had been used for fill there many years ago.

When word of the impending loss of the Pearl Button Factory reached the West Bend Advancement Association, it raised $1500 in fifteen minutes to start the West Bend Knitting Mills in the same location. There had been an earlier knitting mill (1890's) run by Ames Friedlander and Adolph Weil, as well as the Dennhardt Knitting Company and the National Knitting Company, but no information about them was readily available. None of these still exist.

Another fine industrialist, Patrick Harns, came from New York, went to Iowa to learn the marble cutting business, and settled in West Bend. By 1875 he had his own business and his work was of such high caliber that his monuments were widely sold, making him one of the largest marble works in Wisconsin. A hustler, he also owned a resort on Little Cedar Lake and the Palace Livery.

CHAPTER 3

20th Century Industries

Cooley's Cheese Box Factory

One of West Bend's unique industries was the cheese box factory founded by William Warren Cooley, who had come to Wisconsin from Michigan at the age of five with his parents. He enlisted in the Civil War in the famed Iron Brigade, and returned to Waubeka after the war to teach school. However, in 1867 he left the classroom forever to enter the lumber business, for the "inexhaustible" water power in Waubeka seemed to be the foundation of a large future city. Seeing a need, he turned to making cheese boxes and butter tubs. When railroads were being considered in the area, local Waubeka businessmen offered surveyors a bribe of several hundred dollars to run the line into their village, but the railroad men wanted $1400. That was too rich for the businessmen, they refused, and the railroad bypassed Waubeka, dooming its hopes of ever becoming an industrial and trade center. We must remember that graft was in vogue then, with many a town offering money to the surveyors.

This eventually worked to the advantage of West Bend, for after Cooley's son, Herbert E., joined the firm they bought land on Wisconsin Avenue in West Bend in 1910 to be near both the railroad and several cheese factories.

It was easy to find the raw material for the boxes because farmers were still clearing the land when the Cooley's started their company, and they were only too glad to have some place to take their trees. Later, the company went directly to the farms and removed the trees gratis, but eventually, of course, they had to buy the lumber when the local forests were depleted. Elm wood was perferred, both because there was plenty of it and because it had few other uses, so it was cheaper.

To make the boxes, the trees were cut into short lengths and soaked in water before being steamed for up to 24 hours to loosen the bark. Then they went to a veneer machine which peeled the logs apart, much like unrolling paper off a roll. Reheated for more flexibility, they were bent over a drum by a shaper; then a rim was nailed on, a bottom added, and a cover made. The last step was to dry the boxes under fans of hot air for up to five hours, after which they were ready for shipment. Several thousand could be made per day by this process.

In 1917 Herbert, his wife Philippine Cooley and E. J. Krieger incorporated, but Krieger bought the Cooleys out a year later. By 1925 the Cooleys regained possession, and over the years the three sons of Herbert joined their father in the company, adding the sale and servicing of International Harvester trucks and McCormick Deering farm equipment in 1936.

When cheese dropped to three cents a pound if bought by the box, the box cost six cents, so Herbert invented and patented a corrugated paper box with wood used only on the top and bottom. This took up less space in the freight cars and reduced the cost. Also, wood became more and more scarce, so the invention was a profitable one. By 1945 Herbert retired and the sons ran the box factory, which reached a peak in 1949. Today there are no more cheese boxes made, and the factory was razed in 1970, but the Cooleys still sell International trucks and Scout vehicles.

Aside from the furniture and Cooley's box factory, the other industry dealing exclusively with wood in the city was a local stave factory owned by Michael Ruplinger in 1878. Fire destroyed it but it was rebuilt and at one time produced a million and a half staves yearly, until barrels were no longer in demand. A related industry, that of making stave bolts, began operation in West Bend but moved to Hewitt, Wisconsin, when materials became scarce in this area.

Cannery

The first cannery appeared in 1912 south of Water Street, and was owned by Louis and Walter Ottmer, and Ed. J. Krieger. It was a shaky start for the young company as it was difficult to find seasonal help for the long hours. In the second year of its operation the peas were ready to can the week of the Homecoming celebration, and no help was to be found, but the farmers pitched in to save their crop and by the following year conditions were better. That first year they canned between 40 and 50 thousand cases of peas, and by 1950 they could produce up to 7,000 cases a day. The factory is no longer in operation.

West Bend Aluminum Company

Surely one of the best known manufacturing companies in the world is The West Bend Aluminum Company. The author, for instance, has yet to be in a foreign land where at least one person has not heard of West Bend coffee pots. This all began as the brain child of B. C. Ziegler after his father had asked him one day why he did not use his considerable talents to manufacture something that people needed every day. As he had been driving to Manitowoc and Two Rivers to sell insurance, he grew familiar with the aluminum industry there, and one day Edwin and Andrew J. Pick accompanied him to Two Rivers to visit B. C.'s jeweler friend. E. A. Meckelberg, who was most enthusiastic about the future of aluminum products. He recommended two brothers, Carl and Robert Wentorf,* who had come into the shop to buy records, as highly skilled men in the industry.

Consequently, on September 27, 1911, B. C. Ziegler, S. F. Mayer, Edwin and Andrew Pick, and Martin Walter formed the West Bend Aluminum Company and started manufacturing in that "Cradle of West Bend industry," the present West Bend

*Robert Wentorf developed the manufacturing techniques in the factory and by 1920 he had become a director in the company, a position he resigned in 1962. He had been active in Skat and Schafskopf groups, was a charter member of the West Bend Country Club, a Rotarian, Mason (Scottish Rites), and a member of the Milwaukee Tripoli Shrine Temple, among other organizations. He typified that West Bend spirit.

First West Bend Company, 1911, located in the "Cradle of West Bend Industry" building.

Plating Works, with the Wentorfs as the experts. Each one had put in $1000, except the Wentorfs, who did not have the cash at that time, so they were paid $100 a week, from which $25 was deducted until their thousand was paid off.

The company surely started in less than desirable quarters, for there was virtually no office space, just a file and a desk in the nearby malt house. When Armand Langenbach was appointed sales manager, he had only a rough table and revolving piano stool as his office furniture. Later they moved the office to the front room of Rolf's Cigar Factory at the corner of Highway 33 and Main Street.

Their ten employees started with a ton and a half of aluminum to make 15 different household products, among them an aluminum frying pan, a water dipper, and several sizes of sauce pans. Aluminum came to the plant in huge rolls, from which discs the size of the desired utensil were cut, pressed into shape, sent to the bending machine to have the edges curled, and then polished and buffed. A local editor who went to visit the plant in that first year discovered the buffers all covered with aluminum dust which blackened their faces, as well as a terrific din where the handles were riveted and the holes cut for the covers, but he concluded, "Unless the careful calculations of several of our far-sighted and influential business men go entirely astray,

West Bend will in the course of a few years have nurtured and developed a great factory." How prophetic was his insight.

To introduce the products to a larger market, A. J. Pick and B. C. Ziegler carried samples of their wares to the National Hardware Convention in 1912, and took turns exhibiting the products. This proved to be a show stopper, and soon huge orders began to roll in. One of their ace salesmen, "Carload Morgan" earned his title by bringing in orders from such firms as Gimbels, Lewis and Conger, and Wanamakers in New York. It did not take long to see that if they had larger quarters they could have a really thriving business, so they built on the present site, on land owned by Mayer and Pick. To do so, they had to re-route the Milwaukee River. This required a retaining wall, a costly venture for the city, so the company loaned the city the necessary $50,000 without interest. Thousands of yards of dirt were needed for the project, some of which came from the railroad company, in exchange for a right of way on their land.

When World War I broke out, the company was really just getting started, so they were not involved with government orders. They chose their employees from the West Bend High School, one of whom was Al Kieckhafer, who began as an office boy and rose to become company president. His career was interrupted by the war, and Norman Schowalter replaced him, but when Al returned he became Sales Manager and rose steadily from there. Soon the company was the largest employer in West Bend.

After World War I the business boomed, especially after the introduction of the Waterless Cooker, in which one could cook an entire meal on one burner. Kieckhafer was dubious about its acceptance by the public, so he worked out a careful sales pitch and sent salesmen out on the road; the results are history.

When the Great Depression neared, they were in the process of undergoing a big building program, but B. C. had been out on the road and noted disturbing signs of forthcoming financial disaster, so he ordered all building stopped, the cancellation of as many orders for material as possible, and a reduction of inventory. These measures enabled the company to weather the depression, and their employees did not lose their jobs in spite of hard times elsewhere. As early as 1933, at the depth of the depression, the company had "Help Wanted" signs out again. They began their aborted building program when labor and

The West Bend Company Today

materials were at their cheapest, so they were able to forge ahead of their competitors when the depression ended.

Again due to the business acumen of their founder, they were tooled for defense even before Pearl Harbor. Three weeks after December 7, 1941, they made their last aluminum utensils, and began to work for Uncle Sam, operating three shifts seven days a week. They turned out as many as 6,000,00 cartridge cases a month, along with at least 300 other items for war, and earned the coveted Navy E for excellence, which eventually had five stars added for their superb productive efforts. Later they bought out the Kissel Company of Hartford, but they have since sold the plant to Chrysler.

A list of their best selling products would include the automatic coffee pots, the portable humidifier, the popular Cook and Serve utensils, and several Teflon lined pots and pans. Under the popular presidency of J. R. Brown in the 1950's, the company grew dramatically; over the years they have built plants in Barrie, Ontario; Sheridan, Arkansas; Peoria, Illinois; Taunton, Massachusetts; and Toronto, Canada.

In 1968 the company passed completely out of local ownership when it became one part of the vast multi-national Dart Industries. Today their 3000 employees make more than a thousand products for the home, a tribute to the original founders who had both business foresight and faith in West Bend.

West Bend Equipment Company

Just before the outbreak of World War I the first West Bend Equipment Company was born in West Bend (1913) under the ownership of Mathias Lochen, N. N. Gehl and J. C. Fitzgerald, who owned a patent on automatic swinging barn stanchions. They operated out of the old Pearl Button factory until their new plant was built, but the post World War I depression was a difficult time for them, and they often had to take merchandise from the farmers in lieu of cash. A typical payment might be a half a steer. Their best selling item proved to be a lever operated swinging stanchion, by which a whole row of cows could be released by pulling one lever. Soon other companies imitated them, but they were the first to think of this.

By 1925 they sold the barn equipment part of the business and made Weld Bilt skids, portable elevators and stackers. The business prospered and during World War II they joined in the country's defense by manufacturing pallet lift trucks and power conveyances.

West Bend Plating Works

The most venerable factory building in West Bend is the current home of the West Bend Plating Works. That aged gray building which received its last coat of paint in 1950, was once the first sawmill in the village, and has served at various times as a button factory, knitting mill, Enger Kress factory, West Bend Aluminum Company, storage area, Helm Woodworking Company, and the Pick Manufacturing Company; it has earned the sobriquet of "Cradle of West Bend Industry." The firm began in Barton and moved to West Bend where owner Elmer Wentorf, who had formerly worked for William Kocher, plated items for the West Bend Aluminum Company.

The tin came from the Dutch East Indies via New York, and the three employees were busy all the year around. When items came to the plant to be plated, they were always encased in oil to prevent rust, and the oil had to removed. So the pieces were placed in a tumbling barrel which contained sawdust to remove the grease, oil, dirt, etc. Then they were placed into a dipping basket which was immersed in an alkali tank heated to

212 degrees for fifteen minutes, after which they were rinsed. The next step was a pickling tank where they were heated in a muriatic bath to remove the alkali so that the tin would adhere. After another rinsing in cold water, they were dipped into the tinning flux and then into the hot tin. For a hard finish they were chilled and rinsed in sawdust to dry.

During World War II the company was busy zinc plating and galvanizing parts for the army; some of the articles included magazine cases, mess kits, soup ladles, meat platters, bean kettles, and soup spoons. Tin was scarce during the war because the source of tin was cut off by the Japanese and every drop had to be accounted for. It takes a great deal of skill to plate goods without dropping beads of tin or having it run. At the present time much of their work is for the West Bend Company, as well as for food handling equipment firms.

Pick Manufacturing Company

The Carl Pick Manufacturing Company began life in the Plating Company building after Milwaukeean John Wittemann, a brother of Peter J. Wittemann of West Bend, invented universal joints and Carl Pick began to manufacture them for power machines and trucks. As the business grew, they added flexible couplings, replacement hub caps, radiator caps, and brake bands to their line so that by 1930 Pick's was the largest manufacturer of replacement brake shoes in the United States. They would buy a shoe from an auto company and then duplicate it.

During World War II Pick Industries became a separate company to meet the increasing needs of the military for its products. They worked around the clock for the government, making army cots, tent poles, etc., and had a spur directly from the railroad to ship out the ten carloads of merchandise they manufactured daily. To get wood, they purchased their own sawmill in Michigan and bought out Schmidt and Stork to provide the manufacturing space. A more complete account will be found in the chapter on the war.

Since World War II, they have continued to make brake shoes, but have branched out to manufacture water pumps, rebuilt shock absorbers, etc. Management passed from Carl to his sons, Robert and Alan, but in 1967 the EIS Company of Middleton, Connecticut, bought the Oak Street firm. Both Weasler Engineering Company and Kasten Manufacturing Corporation are offshoots of the company.

Whenever an automotive company designs a new brake system, Pick's redesigns the machinery to duplicate it. They can make ¼ of a million brake shoes a month, and are one of three in the United States to make disc and drum brakes. They employ approximately 150 workers, one of the major employers in West Bend.

Founder Carl Pick was a local high school graduate and attended Notre Dame, after which he worked as a brewery employee before founding the company that bears his name. He is one of the men who helped to industrialize West Bend. A sports enthusiast, he was always promoting West Bend High School and left money for an athletic award that is given annually on Awards Day. He was a hunter and a fisherman, belonged to the Milwaukee Athletic Club, the Wisconsin Club, Bluemound Country Club, West Bend Country Club, Loyal Order of Moose, etc. He served as Vice-President of the West Bend Lithia Company and published the *West Bend Pilot* at one time.

West Bend Concrete Products

After a course in a Milwaukee business school, young Leonard Yahr borrowed money from his father and began to build silos. After a year of service during World War I he returned and by 1923 was making the first concrete building blocks in the area. Before that, houses were built of field stone or poured concrete foundations. Now almost every home uses blocks. The 1923 blocks were square with a round hole in the middle, but by 1927 they were oblong, as they still are.

At various times they have made flower pots, septic tanks, chimney caps, etc. Mr. Yahr sent his crews all over Wisconsin and into Illinois to make silos and grain bins for elevators, and developed his own forms to cast the products. Ownership passed to Fred and Allen Yahr.

Wesbar

The Wesbar Corporation derives its name from the first three letters of West Bend and the first three letters of Barton, its home at one time. The company came into being in 1934 when C. I. Nielsen bought the Miller Spouting Company, which had its beginning in 1922 when tool and die makers William Griep and John Adler of Two Rivers began to manufacture aluminum hub caps. In 1929 they moved to Barton. Nielsen originally named it the Wesbar Stamping Company, but since 1970 it has been known as the Wesbar Corporation.

Nielsen manufactured hub caps, grease caps, and cartop carriers; in World War II he turned to hand tools for the military. When the war ended, the company manufactured wheels for small semi-pneumatic tires and a child's folding chair.

When C. I. Nielsen died in 1960 his son C. I. (Chet) took over the management, but he died tragically in a home fire in 1965 and active management passed to engineer Bernard Weber, who had been vice president of the Culton Company in West Allis. Mrs. C. I. Nielsen and her daughter-in-law and later C. I. Nielsen III retained control. By 1972 they were making lights for trailers and revolutionized the design, holding a patent on the connection part of the lights.

When they tried to locate on land east of the courthouse in West Bend, the county wanted as much for six acres of land as the town of Polk wanted for 76 acres, so since 1970 they have been located five miles south of West Bend on Highway 45, which makes it convenient for workers outside of West Bend. The growing business has undergone additions to its original 1970 building and is constantly growing and adding to its line such items as jacks for trailers, strong winch hooks and an electronic converter for connecting cars and trailers.

Others

In 1950 the Dyken Manufacturing Company on Indiana Avenue made rolling and wrapping machines but they sold out in 1956. In 1950 also A. Weasler, former Vice-President and General Manager of Pick's, formed Weasler Engineering, Inc., a still-flourishing firm. There have been other companies that operated for a brief time and then departed. The giants are left to supply West Bend with job opportunities for thousands of workers.

CHAPTER 4

B. C. Ziegler

Quite possibly the single most important individual to plot the fate of West Bend was Bernhardt C. Ziegler, a far sighted gentleman who had complete faith in both himself and the future of his hometown — West Bend. Born in 1884 to Jacob and Ernestine Ziegler of Trenton, he moved with his family to West Bend where his father was City Treasurer and saloon owner. By the time young Ben was a high school sophomore he was keeping the city books for his father.

In addition, his mother ran a boarding house in connection with the saloon and he rose between four and five o'clock in the morning to operate the hand-turned barrel type washing machine for his mother who had as many as 20 boarders to care for. Then it was his duty to churn the butter, milk the four cows, scrub the barroom and wash the glasses. After a hearty breakfast of ham, eggs and oatmeal, he was off to school. Even after he graduated from high school, he would come home every night to help his mother with her onerous tasks.

By 1902 his father was County Treasurer and young Ben kept those books, too. In addition, he helped the Register of Deeds and sold insurance on the side for Henry Opgenorth. That same year a local insurance agent, Henry Sievers, pleaded that he could not pay a note of $400 that Ben's father had co-signed, and it cost the senior Ziegler $400. The company then had to find a new agent — and they did — 18 year old Ben Ziegler. On the same day that he was appointed agent he made his first sale — a first insurance policy to Adam Kuehlthau, a friend of his father who owned the West Bend Heating and Lighting Company. The need for fire insurance was becoming obvious to a community that had watched so much of its industry burn at one time or another.

Nobody worked harder than young Ben. Early and late he could be seen on the street or in buggy on the rural roads preaching the wisdom of fire insurance, or lending money to the farmers. Owning a horse, which he named Bessie Le Croix, was his one luxury, and he used to talk out his thoughts to the horse as he traversed the country.

The so-called Roosevelt panic in 1907 closed all the banks, and there was now no one to lend any money. Here was his opportunity. The same day the banks closed he made three loans of $2,000, $4,000 and $7,000. His customers bought up the mortgages with cash as they had been foresighted enough to remove their money before the local banks fell.

An inner sense told him not to put his money into the banks when they re-opened, so he went to the County Treasurer, Anton Miller, to ask him to keep the money in the county vault. Soon he used up all the space in the county vault. When it would hold no more, be brought the extra money home to his bureau drawers. When they filled, too, his bookkeeper, Miss Handke, took large amounts of money home with her. Can the readers imagine such a procedure today? But everybody else was hoarding, too, so the only unusual thing about Ziegler's was the vast quantity.

By age 21 he had saved $6500 which he gave to his father to pay off the mortgage on his farm and his saloon. In return his father gave him a piece of property for his business. Always conscious of the hard work and the long, long hours his mother worked, he saved for another two years to buy his parents a home and "rescue" them from the hotel and saloon business. He had a plan to live on one third of his income and save two thirds.

His business grew. Farmers often came to him for loans, but he did not wait for them to come to him. Everyone who owned property was a prospect, and when the auto arrived, he bought a 1910 Maxwell and canvassed nearly every home in the vicinity. When he had done that, he went to nearly all the businesses to learn how they were run; stores, elevators, breweries — he became informed about them all while he was learning the role of loaning money and selling insurance. When he exhausted the business in West Bend, he went to Two Rivers and was soon as widely known there for the large business he generated.

He possessed an uncanny knack for selecting capable people to work for and with him. One of the most successful ones was D. J. Kenney, who in 1911, as Assistant Principal of the West Bend High School, rode with Ziegler on a train to Chicago to a convention; before the day was over D. J. had a job with the Ziegler Company. By the age of 45 he was company president.

Perhaps B. C.'s greatest opportunity came in 1929. He had been in Kansas and had known the farmers were in financial trouble even then. He smelled future misfortune for the country if farmers were plagued. In May of '29, he sold all the stock that he owned and took the cash. Then he told Norman Schowalter of the West Bend Aluminum Company to cancel as many commitments as possible and take on no more. He advised Oscar Klein to pay up all loans, which he did in 60 days. When the crash came in October B. C. was ready. He had no debts and almost no commitments, and all of his assets were in cash. As a Director of the First National Bank, he had tried to convince the directors to sell their bonds, but they hesitated. He finally convinced them to compromise and sell half of them, which they did. Had they taken his advice, they would have become rich and famous overnight, he always said. As it was, the half they did sell permitted them to be in the best financial state of any of the banks in the area.

When the local farmers began to go bankrupt he bought the

B. C. Ziegler Company

farms and managed them. This is also the source of the chief criticism against him — foreclosing when people could not pay. By the second year of the depression, he was loaning money to people to buy houses in town. He helped West Bend to weather the Great Depression.

Another financial institution he helped to organize was the First National Bank and in 1917 he became its first president. Two years later he married Edna Eickelburg, who had come to town to book a Chautauqua. They had three children, Bernard, Robert Douglas and Barbara. The year after his marriage, he founded and served as president of the B. C. Ziegler Company with O. J. Klein, D. J. Kenny and Walter P. Ziegler, his brother. Soon he was a director of the West Bend Mutual Insurance Company and a large stockholder in the Gehl Brothers Manufacturing Company.

During the depression, the only mortgages that people trusted were church mortgages. Churches needed to build or expand but seldom had the money, and few banks were willing to loan money to churches. He had had his first experience as a teenager when he loaned money to the local Holy Angels church and had been repaid. He took a mortgage on a second church and then sought out others. By 1922 the B. C. Ziegler Company had made its first big church loan to St. Sebastian of Milwaukee — $100,000 worth. Six years later he made a $485,000 deal outside of Wisconsin — to the Waukegan Hospital, and soon his name became the most trusted name in church and hospital loans.

In time the church loan business slowed, so he turned most of his attention to hospital and health care, and the company has become the number one securities underwriter of hospital bonds, as well as retaining its title as number one in the church bond business.

In 1971 the business went public and sold 483,000 shares; by 1978 there were 2½ million shares with 2200 stockholders in 33 states holding stock in the B. C. Ziegler Company and its subsidiaries. Some of their business involves leasing hospital equipment such as nuclear medicine devices, diagnostic laboratory X-ray machines, operating room equipment, intensive care units, and cardiac care systems. They have sold four billion dollars worth of bonds since the small start in 1913, and when they celebrated their 75th anniversary in 1977, they alone served one sixth of all United States non-profit hospitals.

Among the "firsts" of which the company is proud are the following:

1 — underwrote the first securities issued which were registered for sale under Wisconsin's first security laws; (in fact it was one of the first in the United States to do so)

2 — first in Wisconsin to be registered to sell securities

3 — first in Wisconsin to receive AAA rating for institutional issues

4 — first to pay graduated interest on corporation bonds

5 — first underwriter of real estate bond securities to be registered under the SEC — for the Leamington Hotel in Minneapolis

6 — issued the first FHA issued bond, underwriting the Presbyterian ministries in Seattle

7 — first to underwrite an international loan under AID to a Nicaraguan hotel company

8 — first to issue split coupon bonds, with one interest rate the first year and progressively higher until maturity.

B. C. gave advice freely to those who would listen, and those who did, profited. Over the years he condensed his personal wisdom to three points: Own your own home, stay out of debt, and save permanently. Is there any better wisdom today?

In addition to the financial institutions with which he was associated, he was the first president of the Country Club, was associated with both the Milwaukee Athletic Club and the one in Chicago, was a president of the West Bend Chamber of Commerce, served on the 1926 high school building committee, chaired five liberty loan drives in World War I, chaired the Washington County Council of Defense in World War II and was associated with the subdivisions of Decorah Lawns, Decorah Heights and Decorah Hills and almost every civic and social activity in the city. One is left with a question: Where would West Bend be today if it had not been for B. C. Ziegler?

CHAPTER 5

Labor

The history of labor, as such, in West Bend, goes back to the earliest years. Written records show that anyone who wanted labor could find it in the frontier community. The first record of any laborers uniting to protect themselves seems to be that of independent blacksmiths, who combined to raise their prices for horseshoeing after the price for the iron rose. Perhaps the first successful complainers were the retail clerks, for their hours were from sunup to midnight. When an editor suggested that their hours ought to be reduced for they were becoming cranky and out of sorts and had no time for their families, he was ahead of his time.

After the turn of the century there were some improvements. Meat markets closed at nine o'clock on Sundays, and barbershops led the others in closing their shops on Sundays to get some rest, but they were open on Friday nights until nine and on Saturdays until 11, although they closed "early" on other nights — at eight! A Mr. L. O'Rourke let his clerks go at 6:00 P.M. on weekdays so that they might get a few hours of recreation. "Modern skins are not as robust as those of our ancestors."

In 1902 the clerks were granted store closings on three nights a week.

The first recorded strike occurred in 1898 when the workers at the Pearl Button Factory voted to strike. They wanted 26 cents more per gross of buttons; the dispute was taken to a state arbitrator who awarded them one cent. Laws and governmental agencies were not noted for siding with laborers.

First Labor Organization

The first labor organization was probably that of the Washington County mail carriers who wanted better roads, improved working conditions, new and larger mailboxes, and enforced postal laws. Mr. M. N. Emery was their first president. While most of the country celebrated the new Labor Day in 1913, the Aluminum Company did not recognize it, although Enger Kress led the industries in giving the employees a full day off. Some others gave a half day, dismissing at noon. The local employees that did not have any holiday were "burned up," and urged the owners to join the rest of the country in providing a holiday.

Over the years there have been some bitter labor disputes and strikes. One of them concerned Pick's in the 1930's. Of their numerous difficulties, one concerned their discharging of 12 experienced men who had been labor organizers. The case dragged on through all the levels to the national level, and Pick's was given ten days to rehire 11 of the men. Other difficulties arose over wages and the right to organize. Fistfights, paint on the houses of non-union workers, roofing nails in the parking lot, and arguments with officers resulted in fines and arrests for harming the lawmen. In 1951 the AFL-CIO organized Picks by a vote of 85-44.

Other companies that had difficulty organizing were the West Bend Aluminum Company, Gehls, and the leather companies. The International Ladies Handbag, Pocketbook and Novelty Union tried to organize West Bend leather workers as early as 1937, but failed, possibly due to the disrespect the local people had for the union organizer, an ex-West Bend worker. They were eventually organized. All have had major strikes. One in 1948 hit the West Bend Aluminum Company for 8 weeks in both Hartford and West Bend. The company offered 10 cents an hour and the union wanted 20. The settlement was for 13 cents and some side benefits, and the company had to pay properly for overtime.

Enger-Kress survived a major strike in 1955 for eight weeks, the workers demanding a 15 cent an hour increase and a guaranteed base rate. They received 10½ cents, of which 3½ was in lieu of life insurance and other insurance which their union provided. By 1951 cost of living increases began to be written into the contracts. The last major strike was at Gehls in 1973.

Child labor was rife, but the Federal Labor Law of September 1, 1917, at least stopped youngsters under the age of 14 from working in factories. But unionization was slow in coming to the city. In 1937 there were only 37 union members in the entire county, one of the last northern bastians of paternalism. Gehl's was the first to organize in West Bend. Wages at that time were 35-40 cents an hour, with few or no vacations, little or no coverage for health or accidents, but some of the more skilled workmen fared a little better.

Home Owned Industries

One of the interesting points about West Bend has always been that the industry was home-owned. The first recorded instance of an "outside company" asking to come in occurred in 1933 when the Nunn-Bush Shoe Company and the Weldon Shoe Company offered to employ at least 400 people, besides paying taxes, if the city would build them a plant and eventually deed it to the company. This might upset the wage pattern, and a speech by a prominent businessman at a Chamber of Commerce meeting stopped the idea. In spite of past resistance to outside companies, West Bend has lost much of its home-owned industry reputation and is heavily controlled by outside firms, the effect of which has yet to be determined.

The Chamber of Commerce praises the labor force as rural-oriented, conscientious and hard working, taking pride in their products — a "crafter's attitude" — and stable, with a low turnover. When the West Bend School District surveyed all the pupils in 1978, it was found that only half of the fathers worked in the city, another 10% worked in the county, 22% went to Milwaukee for employment, and the rest were scattered. On the other hand, three-fourths of the mothers who worked stayed in the city. Incidentally, 60% of the mothers of school age children work.

The Washington County Central Labor Council reports that

bricklayers, printers, masons, postal workers, firefighters, plumbers, carpenters, the workers at the West Bend Equipment Company and those of the telephone company all belong to the AFL-CIO while workers at Weasler, Picks, Gehl's, Wesbar, Amity, Enger-Kress and the West Bend Company are Allied Industrial Workers members. Some of the unions in the city are not a part of the Washington County Labor Council and they include the retail clerks, butchers, construction workers and municipal employees. Generally speaking, the workers in the city are organized.

The most salient negative factor about West Bend's labor history would seem to be the relatively low wages paid in industries dominated by women workers and in other employment where women are the largest number of workers, such as in office work and in nursing and many are bitter about the situation. The full history of labor in West Bend requires a more thorough investigation.

SECTION X
BANKS AND POST OFFICES

CHAPTER 1
Banks and Other Financial Institutions

Wisconsin was in a peculiar financial position in its early years as a state, for the voters had a general distrust of banks, and they had mandated that there were to be no banks in the state for five years after the Constitution was written, and then only after a statewide referendum. So ready cash was always a problem, and business was often carried on by simple barter. The only "ready money" for a while was that which the early settlers had brought with them, for they had no place to borrow money. This lack of cash also meant that merchants often had to take a cow, for instance, in lieu of a cash payment.

When banks became legal, the law stated that the banker had to deposit $25,000 with the State Bank Comptroller, and with that money the state bought United States bonds, Wisconsin bonds, or railroad bonds. Then the Comptroller issued paper money that the banker could lend in turn at 10% interest. Meanwhile the state paid the banker an interest rate of 6% on the $25,000 they were keeping for him. A little arithmetic shows that a banker could thus make up to 16% on his money. Bankers were also supposed to have another $25,000 in cash in their local bank, but that law was not enforced.

The early West Bend papers are filled with nineteenth century tragedies about people who could not meet their mortgages, declared bankruptcy, and then left to start life again elsewhere. Most mortgages were held by Eastern banks, who demanded their money or they foreclosed. Such tales were weekly occurrences in West Bend in 1865. The village did not get a bank until 1867 when C. Eckstein established the Bank of West Bend, the only one in the county. C. H. Miller managed it, and it prospered. Two years later Maxon Hirsch bought it and held it until 1875 when Ernst Franckenberg acquired it. A remarkable man, he was active in the banking business unto his 90th year. The bank grew over the years and when Franckenberg installed a time lock and a safe, his bank became a real village curiosity. The bank eventually failed, but the investors were paid.

S. F. Mayer

Shortly after the turn of the century C. C. Henry became president of the First State Bank, another flourishing institution, and served in that capacity until 1920 when S. F. Mayer assumed the role and remained until 1935, at which time Ed Altendorf, who had started out as a cashier in 1916, became president. In 1936 they absorbed the failing Barton bank. The bank is now the Marine Bank in a new location on West Washington Avenue in a handsome modern building.

In 1917 the largest bank in the city, The First National Bank, was formed with 140 stockholders, primarily local businessmen and substantial farmers. It was the brainchild of B. C. Ziegler and became an immediate success. On grand opening day they were surprised to have attracted more than 200 depositors who put in over $200,000. The newest bank in West Bend is the Heritage Bank on the south side of the city.

Savings and Loans

Another financial institution in the city is the West Bend Savings and Loan Association, formed in 1913 with C. H. Wallau as President, C. F. Leins as Vice President, B. C. Ziegler as Secretary, Ernst Franckenberg as Treasurer, and F. Bucklin, Counsel. The business of lending money to home buyers was taken over by the West Bend Building and Loan Company in 1926. Robert Rolfs was the President, W. C. Eickelberger the Vice President, August Moths the Secretary and H. A. Fuge the Treasurer. It was a novel idea in 1926 to help people own their own homes; usually one waited for years to save the money and few young couples could imagine owning property for many years. This company allowed them to make monthly payments that reduced the premium, and so permitted a whole new group of citizens to own homes. They started out slowly, making their first loan in July of 1926, and four more later that year. In 1951 the West Bend Savings and Loan Association had taken over the home loaning business with Albert Larson, Executive Secretary, Henry Peters as Vice President, and E. W. Eberhardt as President.

They operated over the Men's Apparel Store, went to 126 North Main, and finally moved to Fifth Avenue and Walnut Streets. They prospered and expanded in 1966, and are currently in the midst of a large project which will front on Main Street. These men had faith in the future of West Bend and they still do, and are of the sort to typify that West Bend spirit.

Two other savings and loan companies also serve the city: Guaranty Savings and Loan on South Main Street and First American on West Washington.

West Bend Mutual

A large insurance company, the West Bend Mutual, began life in 1894 as the home office of a prosperous firm and is located on South Highway 45. It was chartered in 1894 by Mayor Patrick O'Meara, First Ward Alderman John Lohr, Math Regner, First Ward Supervisor S. F. Mayer, A. C. Fuge, Chas. F. Leins, and Arthur Franckenberg.

Taken all together, West Bend is well served by financial

and insurance institutions. In 1978 the average total deposits in West Bend were as follows:

West Bend Savings and Loan	$66,000,000
First National Bank	62,300,000
West Bend Marine Bank	35,700,000
Heritage Bank	13,400,000
Guaranty Savings and Loan	9,500,000

West Bend Savings & Loan Association, Fifth and Walnut office.

D. J. Kenny

There is one other name in West Bend in connection with financial institutions that merits recognition — that of D. J. Kenny. While the account of the B. C. Ziegler Company is recorded in the chapter on B. C. Ziegler, one of the company's leading lights was Mr. Kenny. Born in 1896 he graduated from Platteville with a B.Ed. degree in 1913, came to West Bend as an Assistant Principal in the High School in 1914 and served in that capacity for three years. He entered the army in 1917 as a private and emerged as a 2nd Lieutenant in Motor Transport, being discharged in 1919. He became an assistant to Mr. Ziegler and served as secretary until he was tapped for the presidency in 1940 and served until 1965 at which time he became Chairman of the Board. His son Thomas became the president at that time.

Prior to his death in 1966 he had belonged to the Elks, Knights of Columbus, the Milwaukee Club, had been on the School Board for 17 years, was a President and District Governor of Rotary, helped establish the local American Legion and was its first Commander. He went on to become Commander of the Wisconsin American Legion.

D. J. Kenney — seated at left.

In World War II he received a personal Navy E for excellence. Active in politics, he was a life-long Republican, served as Chairman of the 6th Congressional District Republican Party, was on the Republican National Executive Committee in 1926-29 and ran for governor on the Republican ticket in 1946 and 1948. One of his major contributions to West Bend finance was the introduction of church financing, at which the B. C. Ziegler Company led the United States.

CHAPTER 2

The Post Office

When we consider the large part the Post Office plays in our lives today, it is difficult to imagine a time when there was only sporadic delivery from Milwaukee, the nearest Post Office. Of course, letter writing was a rarity, and the phrase "junk mail" had not yet appeared in our lexicon. To receive a letter was a high moment in one's life, especially if it came from home folks overseas.

The first mail came to West Bend via horseback from Cedar Creek, an established community before West Bend was even settled. In 1861 a hapless carrier stopped at Cedar Creek one day to sort the mail, neglecting to tie his oxen. They immediately started off for West Bend, and the mailman had no choice later but to walk all the way to West Bend, for the mail must go through. Then followed a brief period of the pony express, after which a stage coach began a regular route in 1848 to the 30 families settled here. By the 1850's a small Post Office was located in various downtown stores, with the storekeepers serving as Postmaster when it was their turn to have the honor. By 1880, however, there was enough business generated to warrant a full-time regular Postmistress, Mrs. Abigail Johann, who worked out of the Pautsch and Wolf store.

What a different system that was! Envelopes as we know them did not exist; letters were sealed with sealing wax for privacy. It was up to the recipient, not the sender, to pay the postage, usually 25 cents a letter. But the local business men needed a more efficient service than the local office could provide, so they hired a private delivery service, run by Ed. Riebe, for the Main Street stores.

When the railroad came to West Bend service improved immeasurably, and the private service was disbanded. With four trains going north and another four traveling south, it was pos-

First Rural Mail Delivery — Ben Rusco.

sible in 1877 to receive a letter from Milwaukee and get an answer back to Milwaukee the same day.

What a rivalry there often was for the job of Postmaster. In 1876 there was a "war" of sorts between Dr. Hunt and John Reisse. "If not as bloody as the European struggle, it is about as lasting." Dr. Hunt had had the honor, which paid $700, for eight years, and the matter was finally settled in favor of John Reisse, so that the doctor could devote full time to his medical practice. There is probably a great story there about the financial status of doctors back then, too. Other early postmasters included Byron Fairbanks, Henry Lemke, Dr. Hausmann, Sr., Henry Kaempfer and Jos. Huber, Sr.

By 1898 the Post Office also had the village telegraph, which was used to warn of impending unusual weather conditions, and then it was up to the Postmaster to warn the residents. Rural free delivery reached West Bend in 1900.

Free Home Delivery

The major improvement came in 1913 with free mail delivery to the homes. There were two routes, with Hickory Street being the dividing line; each home had two daily deliveries, while the businesses had three, at 8 A.M., 1 P.M. and 4 P.M. Frank P. O'Meara and Frank Petzold, Jr., were the local carriers. That was still the time when service as the motto took precedence over postal efficiency and profit. The home delivery generated another change, too, the need for street names, signs and numbers, and two local companies vied for the business of street signs. That year the Post Office reported that during the Christmas rush they had sold over 12,000 one cent stamps for Christmas cards, and had gone into the business of parcel post. This angered the local Express agent who feared he would lose customers, but he found that he had an increase in his business, too. Miss Ada Maxim mailed the first package from the West Bend Post Office.

By 1917 the Post Office was open on Sundays from 10-12 and 1-2 before Christmas and residents were warned that there would be "only" one delivery on Christmas Day. The Post Office was now located "permanently" in J. Reisse's store and "there would be plenty of room there for the army of loiterers who come when the mail arrives."

How the city rejoiced when in 1936 it received a "real" Post Office. At first the federal government planned a simpler, more inexpensive building for West Bend, but the local service clubs, among others, complained so effectively through a letter writing campaign to their Congressman, that a fine light gray Bedford stone and russet brick building was erected instead. The Elm Street structure has been one of West Bend's more imposing structures.

SECTION XI

RECREATION, CULTURE, CLUBS, AND WOMEN

CHAPTER 1

Recreation

Lest the reader think that life in West Bend was all work, the record shows that there was a time for fun, too. In the very earliest years there were fox hunts as well as other hunting and fishing, as much for food as recreation. In the summer swimming headed the list of outdoor fun, but in addition to the sport, it served the dual purpose of a bath. All sorts of competitive contests were sure to draw an appreciative crowd; one of the more unusual was the butchering contest to see who could slaughter an animal the fastest. When the West Bend Schuetzenverein was formed in 1868 outdoor bowling became popular.

Holidays were important and among the most important were Thanksgiving and Christmas. Mrs. Izena Gonnering left a written account of an 1885 Thanksgiving dinner, with chicken, turkey, pies and cakes, homemade butter and cheese (most of the families in town kept a cow). She preferred the good old wood stove to the modern ranges. Everybody in town knew everybody else and holidays were a time for visiting, so the housewives kept extra food on hand for unexpected guests.

The biggest celebration was Christmas, brought to America by the Germans. In the earliest years paper was scarce, so every scrap was hoarded from which ornaments were made. They also used nuts, berries and other natural materials. Most of the churches held Christmas eve services and they tried to attract the un-affiliated with the prospect of seeing a lighted tree. Inasmuch as fire was ever a possibility, a bucket of water or sand was kept handy to douse any possible flames from the candles. Generally there was a goose for Christmas dinner; most of the gifts were homemade, with sleds, dolls, skates, etc., heading the list for children. The Catholics had an extra December holiday on St. Nicholas Day, when the good children were rewarded with a sweet in the shoe while the "bad" ones were given a switch. Supposedly, this shaped up the miscreants in time to receive gifts at Christmas.

Weddings, baptisms and funerals were occasions to join families and friends for eating and drinking. The bride's home was usually the scene of the reception where the family provided ample food and beverage and everybody brought a gift so the couple could set up housekeeping. It was considered correct for the newly married couple to leave the reception at midnight and head for the honeymoon destination. When they returned, friends and neighbors greeted them with a "shivaree," a noisy party that ended with the newlyweds providing food and drink, a way of repaying those who had brought them gifts.

Fourth of July

Other holidays were important, too, and chief among them was the Fourth of July. The one in 1860 was so graphically described in the newspaper and reprinted in the July 5, 1960, *West Bend News* that it bears repeating. The celebrations were in two distinct parts. The first began at nine o'clock in the morning with the "Invincible, Unconquerable, Unquenchable, Unterrified Never Say Die Brigade," masked and uniformed in parade through town and into Barton. A drum and fife led the motley group and an enormous hoop skirt represented the flag, attached to a hickory pole and "appropriately ornamented with garlands of pigweed and tickle grass." They were received by the "largest concourse of spectators ever assembled in West Bend who voiciferously manifested their appreciation of the ridiculous."

After parading in Barton and Young America they were treated to two or three kegs of beer imbibed "through conduits of wooden and clay pipe stems" after which they marched back to West Bend and gathered around a woodpile to hear a mock imitation of the Declaration of Independence and an address by H. L. Palmer "16 rods long;" then the assemblage moved to Ewe's park for a splendid dinner. A brass band from Milwaukee played till dawn for the lively dancing. In the meantime others were having more restrained fun on the "island." The Turners met there at ten o'clock and heard Charley Miller read the Declaration of Independence in German. Professor Regenfuss spoke

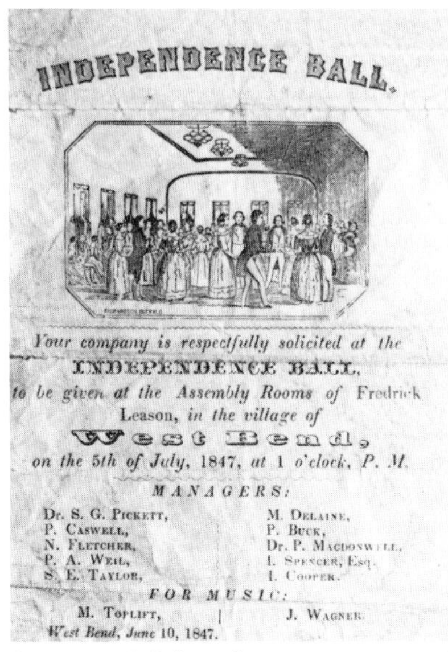

INDEPENDENCE BALL.

Your company is respectfully solicited at the
INDEPENDENCE BALL,
to be given at the Assembly Rooms of Fredrick Leason, *in the village of*
West Bend,
on the 5th of July, 1847, *at* 1 *o'clock, P. M.*

MANAGERS:

Dr. S. G. Pickett, P. Caswell, N. Fletcher, P. A. Weil, S. E. Taylor,
M. Delaine, P. Buck, Dr. P. Macdonwell, I. Spencer, Esq. I. Cooper.

FOR MUSIC:

M. Toplift, | J. Wagner.

West Bend, June 10, 1847.

An 1847 Celebration.

4. und 5. Juli, 1886.

JOHN BURCKARDT

An beiden Tagen Concert u. Ball.

Prof. Hensler's Jugend-Kapelle von Milwaukee

beide Tage Gesangs-Vorträge des West Bend Liederkranz

Für die Beleuchtung des Parks, Feuerwerk, etc.,

Grand CELEBRATION!

SPECIAL ATTRACTIONS for JULY 4th and 5th, at Schlitz's Grove.

Pferde-Rennen HORSE RACES.

1886, Fourth and Fifth of July Celebration.

A 1920 4th of July Celebration.

Band of 1885.

in German and F. O. Thorpe gave an address in English — something for everybody. After a bounteous dinner a German couple named Bingenheimer celebrated their golden wedding anniversary and the merry crowd danced til dark, after which they formed a torchlight parade back to town and joined the others there for the rest of the night in lively dance. There were fireworks, too, although the editor concluded that they were "on a small scale we must confess."

Celebration continued into the next day, and on the Fifth there was a successful balloon ascension "got up by Goetter and Vieth" and more dancing. "Our people have too much money and patriotism to spend it all in one day. Altogether we are not ashamed to hold up our heads with our neighbors when they speak of a Fourth of July splurge." West Bend may have been the first town to celebrate the Fourth AND the Fifth of July.

Another favorite holiday was Memorial Day, for it meant a parade, too. As a typical example: in 1885 Luckow's band, 40 members of the Civil War Veterans Association under Captain George Jones, two fire companies, the Germania Lodge, school children and veteran's daughters with flowers all paraded to the cemetery on Tenth Avenue and decorated the graves of the veterans; then they paraded back to the Court House Square to hear a speaker say that this sort of celebration was peculiar to our country and time, for nowhere else did men stop work and lay aside the tools of their trade or industry to remember the soldiers who had given their lives for freedom.

There have been many unusual kinds of entertainment, too.

At some time in the 1870's or 1880's frog parties were held on the "Island" when Mrs. Horstman would cook them by the hundreds for an appreciative crowd. When the frogs were gone, the parties stopped. An editor wrote that the marsh was silent and a lone frog seemed to be saying, "all gone."

German Gemutlichkeit, 1870. Left to right: (1) Wm. Blick, (2) F. W. Nolting, (3) Emil Franckenberg, (4) C. H. Miller, (5) Ed. Miller, (6) unknown, (7) Chas. Broich, (8) Wm. Miller, (9) A. D. Artzbacher, (10) Henry Weil, (11) James Vollmar, (12) George Kleffler.

Indoor Recreation

Two indoor sports were always popular, dancing and card playing. New barns meant a barn dance, with cornstarch, soap chips and wax to make the floor slippery enough to dance on, and what fun they had. It was not uncommon to dance until the hour of 3 A.M. Sometimes there was a full band from West Bend or a neighboring town; at other times there was only a single instrument such as a cornet or concertina, but it made no difference to the fun. Polkas and schottisches were the most common dances, but the rye waltz, Herrschmidt, two steps, square dances, waltzes, and quadrilles were also popular. For a time the Germans had separate parties from the Yankees, and one editor felt that the Germans had much more fun at their dances than did the more staid "Americans." If there was no one at home to teach one to dance, Professor Borchert was among the many who taught dancing school, which was usually held between 7:30 and 8:30 on the evening before an adult dance. Among the niceties of etiquette taught was that a girl must never, never cross a

West Bend Tennis Club Court, 1899, at Shooting Park. Left to right: Lulu Rix Kuehlthau, Cora Wilfrum Stubbs.

dance floor alone; bashful boys learned how to hold a girl and how to ask a girl for a dance. Over the years there were many others who taught dancing, among them Professor Vizay who taught at Glantz's Hall and Professor Severenz in Hangartner Hall, while Avis McHenry taught the art of barefoot dancing. Among the dancing parties that are remembered are the masquerade balls and an annual Harvest Dance.

Later it became fashionable to go to the nearby lakes to dance, and Big Cedar Lake was a popular place. Celebrants rode a buggy to the lake and then took a launch across the lake for the dance. Other dances were held in local hotels, and one of the nicer places was the Mermac (the old Washington House) where Charles Raloff, violinist and conductor, Alex Yahr, flutist and manager, Arthur Franckenberg on the piano, and Henry and Jake Kaempfer on the brass were the regularly featured intertainers.

In the saloons and in the homes, especially in the winter, skat and schafskopf were the popular games. Skat clubs were common and weekly scores were printed in the newspaper. Tournaments for schafskopf players attracted the best, and over the years that meant John Schroeder, N. N. Gehl, Fred Schultz, John Knapp, Henry Lemke, Wm. Eickstedt, Fred Klemke, G. Schlegel, Wm. Weber and Matt Goeden.

West Bend High School Girls' Basketball Team. Left to right, top row: Dorchen Pick Ottmer, Florence Stork, Clarinda Sievers, Marion Moores Kuechenmeister, Millie O'Meara Noelke, Millie Thoma, Clara Lau, Rachel Lynch, Madge McCormick, Irene Bennet Sparling, Abbie Meyer. Bottom row: Flora Wagner Hanseyr, Olive Flaherty, Minnie Weinand Hausmann, Georgia Maxon, Edna Klumb.

Other Celebrations

There were other celebrations, also. When the circus came to town it was a big day. The first ones set up their tents where the Union Cemetery is now and included such big names as Barnum & Bailey. Another was the arrival of the Chautauqua for the adults and children. Musicians, actors, artists, cartoonists, comedians, and lecturers came to town, usually for a stay of a week, and there was a performance in their tent morning, noon and night. Often families shared tickets so that someone could always be there to use them. Another fine time was New Year's Eve, often a noisy affair: in 1900 the new century was ushered in in grand style with the boom of a cannon, the blowing of all the factory whistles, the shooting of firearms, ringing of church bells and general hilarity down town.

Other entertainments drew large crowds; a balloon ascension in 1884 featured a lady aeronaut, Miss Lottie St. Claire, who rose a mile up in the air and then landed ignominiously in the river. Sports gripped the attention of most of the males, especially baseball. Tennis clubs were popular; in 1900 a team of Patrick Lynch, Rose Kuehlthau, Martha Kuchenmeister, W. Friedlander, Webster Lynch and John Barney were ready to challenge teams from neighboring towns. At other times it was basketball that was the attraction and the city has had some fine teams. Not to be outdone by their male counterparts, the ladies had fine teams, too. In 1901 Dorchen Pick, Marion Mooers, Minnie Weinand, Mary Thomas, Abbie Meyer, Millie O'Meara, Clarinda Sievers, Florence Stork, Irene Bennett and Georgia Maxon were formidable basketball foes for other girls' teams from the area. That same year the boys had an unbroken record of victories in basketball and the roster included the names of Ziegler, Schloemer, Krieger, Leinberger, Salter, Opgenorth, Kuechenmeister, Hendricks, O'Meara and Stafford.

Private Parks

West Bend was fortunate to have private parks for its gala celebrations. There was supposed to be a public park, as Jasper Vliet had platted one along the river, but it never materialized for the land was sold to William Wightman. The next mention of a village park is on land owned by Wightman, but that never came into being either, except for the land on Court House Square, which was often used for park purposes. Mann's Woods had a creek and a forest, the village was full of vacant lots, wooded areas were everywhere, and there was the river for swimming, so there was no public clamor for a village park; West Bend had to wait for Regner Park in the thirties for a public park. But the Germans were fond of parks, so private ones came to the rescue.

Over the years West Bend has had some memorable private parks. The first of these was opened in 1868, Schuetzenverein or Shooting Park, the name deriving from the practice of throwing small brown glass balls into the air for target practice with guns. In 1876 it was purchased by Charles Hoppe and his sister Mrs. Charles Richter, grandmother of Miss Thecla Richter. It was not common for women to be engaged in business ventures, but Mrs. Richter's husband had been seriously hurt in a sawmill accident and the only means of bringing him into West Bend to a doctor was by oxen; he did not survive the slow trip to town. Mrs. Richter (Sophie) and her brother had a dance hall (60x72 feet), a dining hall, bandstand, and an outdoor bowling alley; the park became a popular site for church picnics, too. On a typical summer day, Thecla remembers, her grandmother would make barrels of homemade lemonade, for there was no liquor served there. Later the site became West Park and now is the site of the YMCA.

The second popular park in the city was known as Schlitz Grove and Summer Resort, located where the Enger-Kress factory is now. The daughter of Stephen Mayer married a Schlitz of the Milwaukee brewer family, who owned the park. On 65 acres of prime forest land they built a 75x38 foot dance hall that could accommodate 100 couples (if they were friendly!). Inside the large 200x100 foot building was a stage with three changes of scenery and dressing rooms. In addition there were three bowling alleys, a bar, billiard room, refreshment stands, a band stand and gym equipment for the Turners. It was considered "elegant." When excursions came in from Milwaukee — up to ten train carloads — it took three "busses" to keep transporting people from Shooting Park to Schlitz Grove. When the special trains pulled into the depot, a civic band greeted them and drove them through town, every hitching post therein having been decorated with green saplings to welcome the guests. The parks made a great deal of money in those days, for they were renowned for their bounteous meals.

Earlier a Mr. Ewe had a park called the Retreat east of the Milwaukee River. Little is known of it except that it had a roofless dance floor and illumination was provided by fastening candles to nearby trees. Another park was called Homrighausen's which later developed into Strube's. But the private park became the victim of "progress," as did the lovely spots in which they were located. They served their function and disappeared into the pages of history, but everyone who lived in their era remembers them with fondness and longing for the great times they had there.

Regner Park

The real prize, though, is Regner Park, the public park dedicated in honor of West Bend's mayor (during 1926-1930). At the ceremony Judge F. W. Bucklin said, "To be great it is not necessary to startle the world but to render a service to your fellow man. Henry O. Regner, in this sense, was a great man." Dr. W. J. Wehle began to spark interest in a public park and together with Mayor Regner, Jos. Huber, John Schroeder, H. W. Schoofs, Jos. M. Knippel, A. O. Stautz and Otto Weber were able to convince the city to purchase the land formerly known as Goebel's Woods for $3000.

Actual construction began in 1933 under the New Deal's CWA which allotted $29,000 for labor. The lagoon was dug, hills graded, and trees removed. Then the government funds were cut off. Meantime the city had spent $7000 for materials, machines and supervision. Later that year a $10,000 bond made it possible to build the bandstand, refreshment stand and restrooms. Eventually other federal programs (FERA and WPA) helped to finance the propect and altogether a total of $62,000 was spent, of which the city paid $22,000 and the federal government the rest, enabling the city to complete the project 20 years earlier than originally estimated. Today it encompasses 75 acres.

Now there are also 5 neighborhood parks: Barton, Decorah, Riverside, Ziegler, and Sunset, three play lots at Deerfield, Maplewynde, and Muenck park, plus the small triangular Settler's Park downtown and the Silverbrook parkway. One of the finest and most recent is Ridge Run Park, with its hiking trails, hardwood forests, flowers, picnic and camping areas and its three small lakes.

The Recreation Department and the YMCA provide year round swimming and league sports of all kinds. There is a full program of summer baseball as well as the city Lithia team. Gliding has become popular with some people while others prefer to bowl, fish, ski, snowmobile, etc. The many tennis courts are busy and a full program of high school sports attracts many spectators. Numerous card clubs keep others happily occupied, so there are many activities in West Bend in the 1970's.

Motion Pictures

Eventually the movies came to West Bend, and West Bend has had two theaters: the Mermac and the West Bend Theater. In 1929 Matt Regner managed the West Bend Theater; this was before the age of talkies, and Ronald Everton played the "golden voiced Barton organ" to provide background for the films. There one could view the latest Hearst news or laugh at Laurel and Hardy. Every Sunday there was vaudeville on the theater stage, while the rest of the week there were forty-cent movies. Many senior citizens remember the weekly dime handed to them by their parents for the Saturday visit to the movies, something most city children considered a sacred right! In 1979 there is one theater, the West Bend Theater, with two separate screens.

CHAPTER 2

Culture

Music and Drama

The subject of the past culture of West Bend is a vast one. Many long-time residents feel the city was more "cultured" years ago, when the city had fine musical groups and entertained the best of visiting drama organizations, dance organizations, and musicals. The cultural center was the Hangartner Opera House, originally a three story building, but now only two. It was known as the nicest place in town and the scene of varied activities in addition to music and plays, lyceums, masked balls, meeting place for such groups as Old Settlers, and a stage for local talent.

West Bend had a genuine interest in music in the nineteenth century. Early settlers often brought a musical instrument with them, as Germans are noted for their culture. The first band of which there is any record was led by violinist August Luckow in 1861. Band members were Oscar Selinger, E flat alto horn; Wenzel Brown, cymbals, drums, and double bass; Emil Lummer, B flat clarinet and snare drum; and Frank Brown, bass tuba. The popular group was in high demand for all manner of celebrations, parades, and dances as they were exceptionally good for a tiny community. Luckow retired in 1888 and Selinger took over the leadership. There was a Geier's band in the 1870's, too, but little is known of it.

In the early 1900's, Charles Raloff led the Harmony Orchestra and played first violin; Alex Yahr, flute; Arthur Franckenberg, piano; Henry and Jake Kaempfer, brass. They played for private and public dances, and gave concerts in such places as the Mermac Theater on Sundays. They were all fine musicians, according to Alex Yahr's daughter, Miss Evelyn Yahr, and played "sweet" music.

In 1921 Raloff led a symphony orchestra with Leroy Weber and Lester Franckenberg, violins; W. Hackbarth and Al Hron, cornets; C. Weber and Fred Buss, trombones; Leopold Meyer, base viol; and Eugene Lucas, percussion.

There had always been interest in vocal music, too, but it was not until Mrs. C. C. Henry organized the Mendelsohn Choral Club in 1900 that any vocal group rated much news space. Olive

Stork accompanied the singers which included: Sarah Barney, Cora Wolfrum, Harriet Harns, Elizabeth Ott, Thecla Pick, Nellie Husting, Rose Kuehlthau, Alvina Heipp, Florence Krueger, Hulda Stork, Rose Klumb, Emma Pick, Libbie Treveronis, Anna Klumb and Louisa Silberzahn. They sang the best of the classics as well as popular music and were in great demand. Mrs. Henry was a noted singer, performing at many private and public functions.

By 1927 the most popular music group in town was Heinie's Foot Warmers, led by accordionist Henry Dean and including Lavern Rosenthal, drums; Melvin Stautz, sax and clarinet; Clarence Kluever, sax and violin; and Orville Potter, banjo.

In the 1930's Dr. A. Carl Marth was president of a community chorus directed by Mrs. George Kessel, with Francis Flaherty at the piano.

Another West Bend musician who was important to West Bend's musical history was Leonard Oelhafen who played every instrument in the band, gave music lessons, and directed the Civic Concert Band. Young William Friedlander, who moved to West Bend at the age of 12, wrote musical plays for the high school and St. James Episcopal Church, although he was not a member. His plays were performed in the Hangartner Opera House. He eventually journeyed to New York where he had success as a writer and producer. One of his productions was the popular "Separate Rooms." Eventually he was converted to Christianity and wrote a book of hymns entitled, "Hymns to My Savior."

Over the years there were other community ventures, often directed by capable Roy Christiansen. In the 1970's the Musical Masquers provided entertainment and the University Center often presents fine talent. A local drama group recently initiated dinner theater at the Linden Inn.

Washington County Museum

West Bend is fortunate to be the home of the Washington County Museum. What treasures await the researcher there! It all began in 1937 when Miss Edith Heidner, who was teaching history in West Bend High School, became worried that people were throwing out priceless family records and other items of historical value; in their haste for everything "new" they were in effect destroying their heritage. So she began to gather material. At first it was all contained in a showcase in her room, but it outgrew its humble beginnings and moved to the high school library in a space eventually labeled "The Museum." It continued to grow.

Up to 1946 it was largely the result of Miss Heidner's labor of love, but in 1946 the Washington County Historical Society was born, an outgrowth of the former Old Settler's Association. It was incorporated under the leadership of Judge Bucklin, Edwin Pick, Mrs. Charlotte Muth, Miss Martha Kuechenmeister and, of course, Miss Heidner. Since 1962 the museum has been at home in the old Washington County Jail on Sixth Avenue, with the luxury of having an entire building to display its ever-growing collection. The museum is on land deeded to the county "forever" by the Wightmans, Kilbourns, Kneelands and Wolcotts.

Edith Heidner

Miss Edith Heidner

West Bend owes an incalculable debt of gratitude to Miss Heidner, the founder, and is the richer for her hobby and lifelong interest. Hundreds of school children have been treated to her expertise on the subject of local history and many of them tried their hand at writing about some phase of the county's story, their efforts reposing in the museum to guide future researchers. She received the Award of Merit from the State Historical Society in 1965.

1937 High School Museum — Seed of County Museum. Left to right: Paul Klingbiel, Edith Heidner, Ralph Hansen, Dolores Schneider, Eugene Hirschboeck, Cora Wegner, Florence Braasch, Dolores Van Beek.

When the elected officials of the city wanted to purchase the land on which the museum sits and convert it into a parking lot, which would have been a depredation, to say the least, Miss Heidner spearheaded the drive that saved it by proving that the land was indeed deeded to the county "forever." Similarly, when the County Board wanted to tear down the steeple on the old courthouse because of the pigeons and their dirt, she again led the drive to save it by enlisting the services of famed architect Richard Perrin and many townspeople. She succeeded. Elected officials rarely have a sense of history, and it is up to such as she to be vigilant.

She retains her active interest in the museum and is often to be found there busily at work, along with Miss Zella Loomer, preserving the heritage of the city and county for which she has so much affection.

Gallery of Fine Arts

A recent source of pride for West Bend is the Gallery of Fine Arts, founded in 1961 with Miss Joan Pick as the first President. Her co-founders were her sister Melitta and her mother, Mrs. Andrew Pick, Sr. One of their intentions was to provide a home for the paintings of Mrs. Pick's uncle, Carl Von Marr, and to make West Bend the center for his works. Joan and Melitta's great uncle was S. F. Mayer, one of the early founders cited previously. While Joan and Melitta made the down payment, there is now a West Bend Memorial Foundation to maintain the gallery in its home at 300 South Sixth Avenue in the former West Bend Mutual building.

What a proud day it was in 1975 when the *Flagellants* came into the possession of the local gallery. After winning First Prize at the World's Fair in St. Louis in 1904, the Pabst family bought it for the Milwaukee Public Library, and from there it passed to the Milwaukee Auditorium where it adorned the Plankinton Room. Allowed to deteriorate, it was all dirty and torn when gallery President Edward Kocher bid for it and received it as a gift. To restore it, skilled workmen constructed a bridge on wheels to fit over the large (14x24 feet) painting which was laid on the floor of the gallery. Wearing white gloves, and crouched on their knees, they skillfully restored it to its former glory and now it proudly occupies an entire wall in the gallery, and is its most prized possession.

The remarkable masterpiece is a visual representation of the heretical sect which existed in the 13th century. They would strip to the waist and scourge themselves with leather thongs until they drew blood on their backs. Then they would sing hymns and prostrate themselves before an altar. Von Marr's painting shows at least 100 separate figures, of which ten are life size, faithfully capturing all the horror and the beauty of the scene.

Carl Von Marr came into Milwaukee from Germany in 1858 at the age of 16. As his talent grew, he realized that Milwaukee was not interested in the Fine Arts to the degree that he had hoped, so he returned to his native country in 1882 and died there in 1936. His works won him a seat in the Royal Academy of Fine Arts in both Berlin and Munich, and the Milwaukee Art Center as well as the Metropolitan Museum in New York have examples of his work. In 1929 the University of Wisconsin in Madison conferred an honorary degree on him; he had also won countless gold medals in exhibitions all over the world, was knighted in Bavaria, and honored by an Italian king. West Bend is indeed fortunate to possess the masterwork of so fine an artist.

The gallery sponsors receptions for its visiting artists on a regular basis and offers free travelogues during the winter. It is truly representative of the finest spirit of West Bend.

Library

Books in early West Bend were a rarity. Outside of the family Bible, few homes had any books at all. Yet the immigrants brought with them a desire to read, and as more of their children learned English at school, the need for a public supply of books increased. So in the early 1880's a "collection of young ladies canvassed the town for funds to purchase a certain collection of books to be kept in a convenient place for the free use of the public." Accordingly a few books were purchased with the meager funds, and Fred Wolfrum volunteered to serve as the librarian in his drug store. But there were no funds for subsequent purchases or for repairs; hence the project died a-borning.

West Bend Library Board, 1913. Top row: Mrs. G. A. Kuechenmeister, Frank Petzold, Mrs. Anna Keeley. Bottom row: Mr. C. A. Moores, S. F. Mayer, Mrs. Edwin Pick, Mr. Wallau.

Cora Wolfrum Stubbs, First Librarian, 1898.

Interest in a public library persisted, so in 1884 a West Bend Library Association was formed with E. Franckenberg as the first president. A committee was appointed to select 100 books, and space for them was donated by Drs. Campbell and Hillweg in their professional suite. The well-chosen committee concentrated on selecting fine literature, and one could borrow such books as those by Dickens and Cooper, Scott's *Ivanhoe,* or Grimm's *Fairy Tales.* To stimulate the new citizens to read, there were histories and biographies, and American success stories to inspire them; within a year up to 30 books were being withdrawn each day. The library was open five hours daily on Monday through Saturday, and occasionally for a time on Sundays to accommodate those who could not come in otherwise, for the six day work week was still standard. To augment the collection, the high school library of another 343 volumes was made available every summer when school closed in July.

But all this was insufficient for a growing community, so the enterprising women of the Woman's Club began to consider what they might do. When Mmes. Flaherty and Moser were delegates to the Wisconsin Federation of Women's Clubs' state convention in Racine in 1900, they arranged for Miss Lutie Stearn of the Wisconsin Library Association to come to West Bend to plead the cause of a Public Library at a public meeting.

However, she was considered a "radical," and only nine voters showed up for her presentation. Disappointment.

But it did not discourage the determined ladies. They placed a mite box in their Club Room and collected $15. Dr. Lynch donated 10 books. The Woman's Club gave a public entertainment and netted $115, while downtown stores and industries anted another $500. A public ball cleared $40 and several of the ladies presented books from their own libraries until they possessed 730 books, and a real library could be opened. Cora Wolfrum served as the first librarian for ten dollars a month. Because so many of the residents spoke and read only German, another sum of $43.75 was solicited to buy books in that language and German borrowers were allowed to keep a book up to five months.

But the burden of the upkeep was too great for a single club, so in 1901 they gave the collection to the city in exchange for the city's pledge to run the library, provide for all the expenses, and purchase new books periodically. The library was located up a steep stairway on the second floor of the City Hall where the patrons were greeted with the "odiferous fumes of stable fragrance," for the city stabled its horses in the room directly below the Library. Horses were used for both road work and to drive the fire engine, and a vent in the floor sent the heat and fumes directly above into the Library. A local druggist deplored the stench, but felt that at least it was not unhealthy, for in Germany TB patients were treated with these fumes as a health measure!

Anna Klumb served as the second librarian and someone from Madison came to classify the books properly. Soon a rental library was added and for five cents a week a patron could read the more recent books. The librarian's wages were subsequently doubled. Among the local citizens deserving credit for the first public library were: Mrs. G. A. Kuechenmeister, who served as president of the library board for 17 years, Mrs. G. A. Heidner, and the Messrs. Fahn, Wm. Peters, S. F. Mayer, D. E. McLane, F. Petzold, C. Moser and John Boerens.

On his way to making millions, industrialist Andrew Carnegie had used the public library to get his education, as he lacked any formal education. Realizing the value of such, he agreed to give $10,000 to any community that would raise the rest of the money for a proper library building. In 1917 West Bend purchased land on 6th and Elm for a library but the City Council felt they should ask for $15,000 instead of Carnegie's proffered

$10,000, because they did not think they could raise the rest locally. The request was denied as it flew against the established criteria, and West Bend collected — nothing.

To increase readership, the city had five substations in local factories by 1921, but continued to use the inadequate space over the City Hall. In 1940 they made the move to the old school on Eighth and Elm, the present site of the Recreation Building, but by the 1960's that, too, was plainly inadequate. Civic minded private citizens donated $100,000 for the land on Sixth Avenue, and a Friends of the Library Committee was chaired by Norman A. Schowalter, who organized 104 volunteers to collect a quarter of a million dollars in 1966. Six months later, co-chairmen Mrs. Irving Johnson and Stanley Hetland proudly announced that they had gone "over the top." A year later the city received a Federal grant of $125,000 and the Common Council added $235,-000. Altogether the building cost $534,613.93, of which the city taxes contributed less than forty percent.

In 1969 the fine ediface was dedicated. Anonymous donors contributed the money for the flagpole and the landscaping. It houses 31,000 volumes with space for more than double that number of volumes, and is one of the buildings that West Bend shows off with pride.

CHAPTER 3

Clubs

Humane Society

One of the organizations in the city which had a far-reaching effect was the Humane Society. As was generally true elsewhere, animals were often sorely mistreated in early West Bend, and horses bore the brunt of man's inhumanity. Some drove horses when they were lame; some men nearly starved the faithful beasts; others beat them mercilessly. In the winter they were often tied outdoors to one spot for long hours without any blankets or other shelter.

Dogs, too, were maltreated, often being turned loose to fend for themselves. Vicious dog fights in the streets were common. There were also reports of clandestine illegal cock fights.

And more unfortunately, perhaps, humans were abused, too. Before America developed a social conscience, many people were without food, fuel, or warm clothes. Beatings were common, especially among the poorest. But it was difficult to arouse citizens to become concerned over the misfortunes of human beings, and especially difficult about animals.

Patient men tried for years to establish a Humane Society in West Bend, with the power to act against mistreatment. Hartford founded one in the early 1880's, but it was not until 1913 that one was organized in West Bend. Dr. W. J. Wehle is given credit in the *West Bend News* for convincing West Bend to have its own Humane Society. The paper reported that Wehle did more for the city of West Bend to clean out cruelty and immorality than any other man. Several local citizens were responsible for the eventual founding, among them C. F. Leins, G. A. Kuechenmeister and Mrs. Charles Schlegel.

The local society dealt with hundreds of cases. Some of the goriest involved men who put hogs into boiling water before the animals were dead; one hung a calf alive on an iron hook and another nailed a cat between barn walls. There were indictments against people who drowned crippled horses and those who left them unblanketed in cold weather. People who left sheared sheep without shelter in the spring, or chickens without winter shelter so that their combs and feet froze, or, worse, the birds themselves froze to death, were among the culprits brought to court by the members of the Society.

In the human realm, one boy was made to work 20 out of 24 hours, and another was driven from his home nights to sleep in the woods. There was wife beating, even when women were in a "delicate condition." One mother had 6 children and no food in the house. This was the United States of America, within the memory of many local citizens.

While the worst culprits might be discovered and fined or sentenced, the important thing was to try to stop future cruelties, so the local schools taught the basic rules of kindness to man and animal and read stories about humane treatment. Rules were promulgated and published, advising people not to work sick or lame animals, nor to abandon, beat or tease them. People were advised, further, to extend kindness to our feathered friends and feed the birds during particularly heavy snows. Some churches preached of the need for compassion.

Whether all this teaching and advice had its affect is not substantiated, but as the city grew, fewer people in town kept chickens, cows or other animals. Automobiles replaced horses, and the trigger-tempered could take out their anger on an inanimate motor instead of a living creature. Local licensing laws for dogs helped to keep the mistreatment down. Today it is a rare human who mistreats an animal severely enough to warrant public notice, although there are infrequent reports of horses in the area that are either overworked or underfed, or both. Sadly, man has not yet learned to treat his own species any more kindly than ever, and wife beatings and human neglect continue.

Clubs

It is beyond the province of this paper to cover all the myriad clubs that exist or have existed in West Bend. The following represent some of the most influential in the past:

1858 Turnverein under the leadership of Jos. Hermitz, President, and Robert George, Secretary.

1863 West Bend Lodge #138 F & AM (Masons). Laid large cornerstone in 1922. Actually began in 1862. Albert Coe, first Worthy Master, and other officers: Joe Fishbein, Chauncey Gray, G. Elliot, F. O. Thorp, L. F. Frisby, N. Reynolds, D. Bullen.

1875 Old Settlers Club. Open to those of good moral character who had settled prior to January 1, 1856, would sign the constitution, and pay the one dollar fee. Favorite meeting place — the Washington House. "Grandma" Wightman, S. S. Barney, Balthazar Goetter, Maxon Hirsch, L. F. Frisby and a few others started the organization which lasted through 1942. Always met on Washington's birthday. In 1874 Maxon Hirsch gave a dinner for the Old Settlers and they liked it so well they continued it. Nearly impossible to get names of just the West Bend settlers, for they are listed by date of settlement and place of birth, not by town.

1880 Germania Lodge #426 with officers Wm. Franckenberg, Jacob Young, Joe Zettel, Jacob Heipp, John Eckstein, August Bastian.

1885 Grand Army of the Republic.

1894 West Bend High School Alumni Association.
1895 Order of the Eastern Star; Cora Wolfrum, first Worthy Matron and Emilie Franckenberg, Associate Matron.
1898 Cedar Lake Yacht Club.
1900 Woman's Club (see separate article).
1903 Washington County Medical Society.
1906 Royal Neighbors.
1912 Chamber of Commerce (has had other names — WBBA, etc.). During World War I it backed the drives for funds, has aroused interest in the hospital, community chest, a retailers organization, among other community projects.
1913 Town and Country Club organized by Mrs. Charlotte Schroeder Muth, Miss Clara Jones, Mrs. G. A. Kuechenmeister. Some rural husbands would not let their wives join. Their first project was to acquire Lizard Mound State Park. During World War I they knitted, made ditty bags, and donated to all worthy causes.
1913 Loyal Order of Moose, with J. S. Peters as first Worthy Dictator. They had their own band in the 1920's with Charles Raloff as conductor. Their watchword: purity, aid, progress. "One for all and all for one and all together."
1914 Red Cross. Florence Kuechenmeister Thomas took six weeks of training at her own expense to get the necessary background to start it.
1915 First Boy Scout troop.
1918 Camp Fire Girls.
1919 Knights of Columbus.
1919 American Legion Ray Dickop Post #36.
1920 Girl Scouts under the leadership of Mrs. B. C. Ziegler. Built the cabin in 1922.
1923 Veterans of Foreign Wars Fred A. Schaefer Post #1393.
1923 Women of the Moose.
1925 Rotary Club, with 19 charter members; met at Washington House. Frank Bucklin, first president; B. C. Ziegler, first vice president; Henry Regner, secretary; and L. Kuehlthau, treasurer. Art Klumb, Martin Walter, and R. Rolfs the first directors. Supported all the community drives, including the hospital, community chest, Boy Scouts, suitable PO, etc. Differs from other service clubs in that it takes in only one member from each specific business, profession or manufacturing plant. Conducts an

annual fish boil to raise money for scholarships. D. J. Kenny was a District Governor.

1926 American Legion Auxiliary.

1927 Order of DeMolay.

1927 Kiwanis with 44 members and Stan Hetland as first president and Norman Schowalter as first vice president, Ray Boldt, Treasurer and E. W. Eberhardt as trustee. Three of West Bend's mayors have been members while active in the club: J. Knippel, C. Schloemer, M. Gehl.

1928 Veterans of Foreign Wars Auxiliary.

1928 West Bend Country Club.

1930 Business and Professional Women.

1930 Columbian Squires.

1932 Cub Scouts.

1934 PTA

1937 West Bend Garden Club.

1949 Junior Chamber of Commerce—28 men—with Alan Pick, president, and Tom Merriam, vice president. Worked for better traffic laws and health regulations. Made Don Ripple an honorary life member for he was instrumental in founding the organization. In later years they have sponsored the Teen Age Road-E-O, the outstanding young farmer award, helped get wig-wags for Decorah train crossing, served food at the post-prom parties, sponsored the Alice contest, helped to get West Bend immunized with polio vaccine.

1960 Jaycettes — involved in many campaigns such as Mental Health, Cystic Fibrosis, Cerebral Palsy, etc.

1970 Chamber of Commerce replaced West Bend Business Men's Association (WBBA). Diane Bliss, energetic leader.

CHAPTER 4

The Contribution of Women

Surely a substantial factor in West Bend's culture and progress has been the caliber of its women. Starting with the earliest pioneers, women's adjustment to the wilderness was difficult.

They bore the children and all too often wept over their tiny graves. They helped the men to clear the homesite while they prepared the meals, sewed the clothes, nursed the sick, and yes, even in town, fed the poultry, gathered the eggs, tended the pigs, often milked the family cow, and made the butter and cheese and almost everything else, for there was no nearby convenience store. Oil lamps, and later those of kerosene, had to be cleaned daily. Most women made their own "spook yeast" from potato water. They soaked corn in lye to obtain hominy, made their own baking soda, and even had to prepare their own vinegar, one recipe calling for 40 gallons of rain water, one gallon of molasses and four pounds of acetic acid.

Butter and cheesemaking were time consuming chores but not to be compared to the ordeal of washing the clothes. First, women had to make the soap. Then someone had to bring in the buckets of water from the well so they could wash in the kitchen or the back room; in the summer they often washed outdoors in the backyard. If the women were especially blessed, the man would carry the water for them. Most houses had rainbarrels placed under the corner eaves to catch the precious soft rain water; later, dug cisterns with a pump in the kitchen were a real convenience. A dry summer, though, spelled trouble.

After heating the water and transferring it to the wash tub, the housewife scrubbed the clothes vigorously to dislodge the dirt; at times she whacked them with a stick to dislodge the stubborn dirt, for clothes were changed infrequently and required a great deal of elbow grease to cleanse them. Then the white clothes were transferred to a copper wash boiler for boiling, after which they were wrung by hand and either placed on the grass to dry or hung on the limbs of trees until they could have a regular clothes line. Ironing was no simple chore, either, with frequent trips from the stove to the ironing board to keep the sadirons at the proper temperature to remove the wrinkles. And wrinkles there were, for drip dry fabrics were a century in the future. Their starch was potato water.

Another chore was the daily emptying of the slop jars and cleaning and trimming the lamps. Sweeping was no problem at first for the floors were often of dirt and one merely tramped the debris into the floor. Sanitation as we think of it today did not exist; all the kitchen scraps were thrown out into the yard, and in the homes with wooden floors the dirt was merely swept out into the street. Part of the scraps became food for the pigs and those who did not own the animals themselves trusted their neighbor's swine to serve as scavengers. But the beasts were also a plague to gardens, and many a wary housewife had to spend an inordinate amount of time shooing the pigs or chickens out of her garden. When family finances improved, one of the first additions to their yards was a picket fence, and pictures of early West Bend show many of them.

If a woman wanted to walk to the store she had to watch for filth in the street. Horse dumplings were a hazard both to the shoes and to the health, for they provided perfect breeding grounds for flies and mosquitoes. Insects had free range in the houses at first; there were no screens as Europeans were not familiar with them because large areas of their continent are flying-insect free. They dyed their own cloth with walnut shucks for the color brown and with sumac berries for black.

On top of all this, men preferred their women to have wasp waists, with 18 inches considered the ideal. To accomplish this, fashionable ladies had to strap themselves into corsets which were as hazardous to their cramped inner organs as they were uncomfortable to wear. Faintings were common after the ladies laced themselves into the torturous things and the local druggist made money from the various medicines to relieve "female complaints." Smelling salts were as common as today's tranquilizers. Older women, though, cared little for fashion and wore their hair parted in the middle and severly drawn straight back into a bun. Most of them wore bonnets. Families were larger then, for children were considered a financial asset and an insurance policy against committment to the county poor farm in their old age. Today's generation, confronted with the problem of worldwide over-population, often forgets that developing areas still breed children for the same reasons as did early West Bend families.

As the years passed, most women wanted carpets on the floor and they were often gaudy ones with flowers. The "front room" was kept strictly for company and usually had a library table with the family Bible and family pictures on it. By 1880 black horsehair upholstery was the style and the stiff prickly hair kept working through the upholstery to attack the unwary who sat down on it. Antimacassars covered the backs and arms of sofas and chairs and were more commonly called "tidies." Twice a year this room, as well as the rest of the house, underwent a drastic housecleaning when the carpets were taken outdoors and thoroughly whacked to remove the accumulated dirt and every inch of the house was scrubbed. It was difficult to keep dust out of a house in town, for the roads were of dirt and any traffic kicked up a swirl of the pesky stuff. On top of all this was the weekly baking session every Saturday until bakeries began to take some of that chore off their hands. Women read the Sears Roebuck catalogs avidly and when the catalog was replaced twice a year the old one served admirably for toilet paper. No one was concerned with softness then!

But even then women's rights were debated in West Bend. A lady lecturer arrived as early as 1862 to urge equality; over the years other speakers came with regularity. By 1923 the *West Bend News* editorialized for the rights of women, declaring that it took a constitutional amendment to secure the rights to vote and now "let's finish it." Let the reader note that more than a half century later justice still awaits.

Women Begin to Organize

While West Bend owes an incalculable debt of gratitude to the early pioneer women, it was not until they organized formally that their causes were adopted. This came about when the first Woman's Club was founded in 1900 with Mrs. S. S. Barney as the President, and while there are other women's organizations in the city, this one has an enviable record. When Mrs. Joseph Ott gave her farewell presidential address she reminisced that the men were skeptical at first and even accused the women of neglecting their homes, but she related how this was untrue as their homes were neat and orderly, their husbands in good humor, and their children were reared to be an honor to the community. She added that it was only when the Federated Women's Club of the nation began to study the nation's abuses, such as child labor, children's courts and sweat shops and then to air their findings that mistreatments really began to diminish.

The first Woman's Club organized as study groups in West Bend; in 1902 they studied Greece, for example, and read the great authors; later they researched France and Germany and compared the two. They studied Germany's great poets, writers, educators, painters, etc. By 1908 they could claim that they had met with both "kindness and rebuff," but they "courageously persevered."

Their local triumphs are legion. They sponsored public forums, lectures and music programs, petitioned the railroad for a depot to replace the old eyesore, succeeded in getting a curfew law to "give the children back to the home," sponsored garbage collection, and in 1915 under the leadership of Mrs. D. T. Keeley, successfully urged the city fathers to have the city undergo a massive cleanup.

One of their greatest successes is the public library, which they began or as one said, they "nurtured a baby library and when it grew up they gave it to the city." When the School Board was not inclined to add Manual Training to the high school, they paid for the equipment to get it started, and did the same thing with Domestic Science. To raise money for their projects they presented plays, which developed into a full fledged Children's Theatre in 1942. In 1955 they started the American Field Services in West Bend while Mrs. Jac Anderson was president. Today they sponsor scholarships, a Bridge Marathon, Meals on Wheels, continue the delightful Children's Theatre and and whenever there is a cause for the improvement of West Bend, you may be certain that the Woman's Club of West Bend will be urging its adoption.

To list individual women who have contributed to the spirit of West Bend would be a formidable task, but in addition to those whose names appear throughout this book there should be added Mrs. George Kuehlthau. Among her contributions to the city was her service on the school board which lasted for 16 years during a time of the great forward progress in the schools. Gifted with foresight, she used it for the advancement of West Bend's schools.

Collectively, women are responsible for supporting every cultural event in the city. In addition, they are the major fund raisers for many of the churches. One of the more lucrative and far-reaching projects by a group of women is the cookbook, "Our Favorite Recipes," first published in 1959 by the Ladies' Guild of St. John's Lutheran Church. To date they have sold over 112,000 copies, some to every state in the United States and to several foreign countries. The book is illustrated by the delightful drawings of Miss Joan Pick.

Women organized a much-needed League of Women Voters and belong to other worthwhile organizations in addition to those highlighted herein. If there is such a thing as a West Bend spirit, surely a large share of it belongs to the women.

A German Society — 12te Fahressitzung der G U G Germania 19 bis 21 Juli 1900. In front of entrance to court house.

West Bend Baseball Team, 1904. Top row, left to right: Walter Dean, Art Hendricks, Walter Kuehlthau, George Lemke, Hugo Sievers, Louis Kuehlthau, Oscar Burckhardt. Middle row: Wm. Leins, John Regner, Horace Barnes. Front row: Jack Taylor, Gus Zettel, Art Wiskerchen.

Girls' Glee Club — early 1900's. Back row, left to right: Hattie Harnes Biederman, Dimple Ott Kissel, Emma Pick O'Meara, Sarah Barney Rix, Cora Wolfrum Stubbs, Mrs. C. C. Henry (Director). Middle row: Florence Krieger Schellenberg, Rose Kuehlthau Bucklin, Marie Pick Husting, Anna Klumb Reisland, Thecla Pick. Front row: Olive Stork, Libbie Treveranus Yahr, Hulda Stork Russel, Rosa Klumb, Louisa Silberzahn Proevost.

Shooting Park, 1868

Strube's Hall

SECTION XII
NEWSPAPERS

No town's story would be complete without an accounting of its newspapers. One of the rewards of reading the early ones is their complete candor, as no reader needed to guess, for example, of what malady a person died; the papers were very explicit. If there were an illness the paper might state frankly, "He will probably die," or "There is no visible change for the better." When one young lady came in from Jackson to buy a pair of shoes, an editor wrote "No store in town has them big enough." If a fire destroyed a barn or house, the amount of the loss was habitually given together with the amount of the insurance; usually there was a financial loss, for people were not particularly insurance minded yet, even though disasters were weekly occurrences. When there was an adult birthday party, the age of the celebrant was often given. One item spoke of a "weak minded old lady." Today's editors would be sued for such a statement.

The first newspaper in West Bend was the *Washington County Organ*, begun in 1855, just one decade after the town was founded. R. B. Wentworth was the publisher, editor, and printer of the paper, just a four page folio one quarter the size of today's papers. He claimed to have bad luck, while an observer called him "shiftless." His printer's devil, the one-armed N. N. Emery, later called him "rattleheaded." Anyway, he sold the paper within a year to the witty Josiah T. Ferrar. Exactly where the press was located is a matter of conjecture but it was on "River Street in a straggling low frame building amidst the log cabins." It was touted as a "family journal, devoted to literature, the arts and sciences, general intelligence, etc." No copies of that paper exist today, unfortunately.

When the aforementioned Nathaniel Emery recalled his days with the paper, he remembered that he was merely the one who turned the hand crank, carried the two or three hundred copies to the Post Office, ran errands and made some of the type cases, for most of the equipment used for producing newspapers was hand made. Emery had come to West Bend from Canada in 1848, married Eliza McQueen, served in the Civil War and was present at Lee's surrender. He worked on a 33 mile a day mail

Mr. and Mrs. N. N. Emery at their golden wedding celebration, February 5, 1902. Mr. Emery — born 1829, died 1923; Mrs. Emery — born 1836, died 1927.

route in Sheboygan (walking), served as a waiter in Wightman's Hotel, owned a butcher shop, worked as a millwright, and eventually became a farmer.

In 1856, the Organ changed its name to the *West Bend Post* and was owned by Charles Waldo and edited by P. Kellogg. From then on there was a succession of editors, one of the more popular being Jacob McMann, but he left for the Civil War, at least briefly, and his wife ran the paper during his absence. Most of the files in their era are missing, too. The next major change occurred in 1875 when Ernst Franckenberg and William Walters bought the Post and changed the name to the *West Bend Democrat.* The paper had always had a Democratic party philosophy and minced no words while deprecating the actions of the opposition, as well as praising every action of the Democrats. A short-lived rival paper, the *West Bend Times,* united with the *Democrat* in 1887.

German Newspapers

Probably the most widely read newspapers in the community, though, were the ones printed in German, of which the *Beobachter* was the most remembered. Its chief editor was the famous Carl Quickert, of which there will be more said later.

Democrat-Beobachter Office. Taken around the turn of the century. Left to right: (1) Leopold Meyer, (2) Arthur Franckenberg, (5) Mr. Mayer, Sr., (6) Joe Huber, Sr., (others unknown).

One rival German paper, the *Banner*, had an editor who wrote that it took him only three days of the week to put out the paper, but it took him the rest of the week to hunt subscriptions, and then all too often he was paid in vegetables. For a time he resorted to catching turtles in the river for meat because he was so poor, but he complained that people kept coming to the river to bathe, which scared the turtles away. One winter when the snowdrifts were up to 14 feet high, the farmers grumbled that they were not getting the paper on time, so he quit in utter disgust.

His troubles were all too typical of other early editors, too. At first subscriptions were paid in the form of barter — goods for the paper. But some people either could not — or would not — pay at all. In 1860 the editor of the *Post* wrote: "Won't some of our numerous friends bring us some butter? We have been without so long that the hinges of our jaws squeak like a dry grindstone." One editor begged for wood: "If you haven't got a cord, bring an armful." He was cold! Others asked for garden produce so they could eat. One editor wrote rather cleverly: "Please pay promptly for the pecuniary prosperity of the paper has a peculiar power in pushing public prosperity." Often the editor was the most educated person in town, and some of them were gifted writers.

Owning a paper was such a precarious business that editors came and went with regularity. Sometimes the local citizenry was accused of taking an out-of-town newspaper. "Stick to your hometown paper, no matter how poor. None are so poor as the ignorant, unless it be the depraved." Another paper said, "The local paper is the only one associated with the interests of your home . . . in its prosperity you have a vital interest."

To encourage sales, the *Democrat* once listed the numerous practical uses to which newspapers could be used after they had been read: cleaning a lamp chimney, polishing window glass, testing and cleaning a flatiron, packing winter clothes to keep them safe from moths (who do not like the smell and taste of ink), storing seeds and herbs, etc. What a useful list!

West Bend News

In 1894 the capable Joseph Huber joined Ernst and Art Franckenberg in the Washington County Publishing Company, located where the Rainbow Restaurant is now, and under his

West Bend News Office, 1979.

editorship the *Democrat* became the *West Bend News* on January 7, 1903. When the voters switched their loyalties to the Republican Party, the name of "Democrat" was appalling to the more rabid converts, so the name change helped to save readership. The paper has remained predominantly Republican to this day. In 1925 it moved to its present location on Sixth Avenue and Hickory in a "substantial modified Gothic building of russet face brick and sand lime brick with stone copings." After his father's death, Joseph Huber, Jr., assumed editorship. Huber had been a delivery boy for a Milwaukee grocer, a printer's devil in the *Democrat* office, became City Clerk, Alderman, Mayor, served as an Acting Postmaster, and was an untiring champion of the Republican Party who helped reduce the West Bend Democratic majority with the power of his pen.

When Joseph Huber, Jr., died in 1937, Mrs. Huber and her sons Mark and Joseph F. published the paper. Two of their managing editors were Arthur Kuehlthau (1937-49) followed by William Steiner, who still serves on the staff. Of Joseph, Jr., his business manager said, "If he could only be made to chase the political bee from under his bonnet and devote himself to his print shop, he could make a fortune in a few years."

Washington County Pilot

The major rival newspaper was the bright, newsy *Washington County Pilot* whose 1892 lawyer-owner was Charles S. Robin-

West Bend Pilot

son, but he did not like the job of managing a paper so he sold it in 1893 to D. T. Keeley, who later became Superintendent of Schools in West Bend. By the late 1890's the paper was in the capable hands of Henry B. Kaempfer, who had left school at the age of twelve to learn the printing business, and had worked around the *West Bend Times* — until it became the *Democrat* in 1875. Working together with his brother Jacob as shop foreman, he became the editor in 1892; he purchased the paper and in 1907 changed its name to the *West Bend Pilot.* Kaempfer died at the age of 45, and his son, Henry, Jr., stepped into the editorship. In 1949 a group formed the Pilot Press and bought him out.

The *Pilot* has had five different locations, one of them the gray concrete building at the foot of Hickory Street which still bears the name "The Pilot" on the front. Its last move was to Highway 33 where they published the paper and its companion *Shoppers Guide* until it and the *West Bend News* joined in 1954 in West Bend Newspapers, Inc.

The sole surviving paper in the city is the daily *West Bend News,* with John Torinus, Jr., as Editor and General Manager. It went daily in the 1970's. Of the past, one can say with certainty that the newspapers of West Bend played a role in creating the spirit that is West Bend.

Carl Quickert

Surely the most famous editor in West Bend was Carl Quickert, who lived alone in the Washington House for 40 years. Living in single blessedness it was said of him, "What his fellowmen miss in his companionship, they will in greater measure find in his writing." He had been a printer's devil in Milwaukee before coming to West Bend to work at the *Democrat* in 1899. He also edited the German paper the *Boebachter* until 1919 when it was forced to cease publication, a victim of the times. During his editorship he had "imbued the readers with noble American ideals, and kept awake the German ideas which deserve to be incorporated in the character of the American people." When he took over, there were about as many German as there were American papers sold in West Bend. Altogether there had been four other German papers at various times, but it was Quickert's which lasted until it outlived its purpose.

Quickert was a brilliant man, and an acute observer of both the natural world and of human nature. He was a constant reader of everything he could find, and was always urging his readers to do likewise. He authored several books which contain almost the only printed record of some aspects of early West Bend. He died in West Bend at the age of 82, widely beloved.

Reading the old nineteenth century newspapers is an exercise in both patience and frustration. Headlines were few. News and ads were intermixed and it was often impossible to tell whether one was reading an ad or a news item until the end of the article. But the one thing that strikes the reader forcibly is their unabashed civic spirit. Always the editors campaigned for better teachers, better schools, better civic buildings, better lighting, better streets, and all the rest. If there were a desired improvement, one could count upon the newspaper to be in the vanguard. They acted instead of reacting. They touted all the coming entertainments, and praised the most puerile of school children's efforts in their school and community programs. Always first and foremost they were for West Bend, and this author feels that they were a powerful force for good, and one of the motivators of West Bend's progress.

Printers' Picnic, 1915. Taken in park along Milwaukee River (now part of West Bend Company).

SECTION XIII

THE 1880'S AND 1890'S

CHAPTER 1

Life in the 1880's

Domestic Life

By the 1880's war was only a memory, and the burden of reconstruction was on the land. West Bend had survived the panic of 1873 although there had been some lean pocketbooks. Garfield had been elected President, but he was to join Lincoln in the martyr's fold and it was Chester A. Arthur who succeeded him. Barbed wire was the new-fangled device, and local farmers were tentatively experimenting with it. Custer was defeated at the battle of Little Big Horn and news of Edison's phonograph had set people dreaming. IMAGINE! Having OPERA in your own home! Trains were a lot safer after Westinghouse's air brake proved a success and Chicago's medical schools were growing in both number and quality, assuring the area of more qualified doctors.

Vast changes were occurring in West Bend, too. The seemingly inexhaustible forests were depleted. All around the city neat farms arose, with diversified crops instead of the once ubiquitous wheat. Most farmers were converting to dairy cattle since it had become profitable in the county. The village now had 7 churches, 5 stores, 1 bank, 2 shoe stores, a book store, 5 hotels, 1 doctor, 1 lawyer, and, oh, yes, 13 licensed saloons by 1884! A dentist was due to arrive.

Laws were constantly being enacted to improve the city. Butchers now had to move all slaughterhouses outside the city, putting an end to the days when the river ran red with blood on butchering days. The Village Board was concerned with the lack of firemen and agreed to dismiss their poll tax if men would only volunteer. (Yes, West Bend had a poll tax.) They were also concerned with "incorrigible" youngsters who dared to play ball in the streets or on the sidewalks and a fine was fixed at from one to five dollars for such play. A new officer, the Street Commissioner, had to report to a trustee EVERY DAY, as to where he had been working. They were taking no chances with possible laxity. In the summer the City Marshall took his hoe in hand and attacked the noxious weeds in the public streets.

Geese were the biggest street offenders now and fouled the sidewalks worse than cattle. 'Something ought to be done about it," everyone agreed. It gave a bad impression to visitors, too. The townspeople were all set to bear the indignation of dogs, cats, and cattle but NOT geese. The messy things had to go. The other offenders on the wooden sidewalks were nails, which kept popping up and catching the unwary. Businessmen were admonished to take a hammer and nail them down.

For years the editors had railed at the poor streets and sidewalks in West Bend. Villages "half our size" had better ones. The council was urged to get busy and DO something. So the council authorized a new set of walks with 12 inch planks two inches thick to be laid the long way at a total width of five feet four inches. The current sidewalks were all widths and of all heights from the ground. What became of that law is not recorded, for the diversity remained.

Another city concern was speeding. No one was to drive a

Home Funeral, Schueler Family — turn of the century.

Dr. D. W. Lynch and Joseph Finnegan (Supt. of Schools) Families, 1880.

Warnkey house,
419 Sixth Avenue.

Wightman house,
Hickory and Main.

West Bend looking west across Water Street Bridge.

Nineteenth Century view of the Milwaukee River.

Dr. Gustave Artzbacher family — Elm Street (razed 1972).

horse faster than a walk over the bridges, for they were made of easily dislodged boards. The problem was so serious that the fines were $500 or 20 days in jail.

In 1884 there was only a brewery, a malt house, and one small foundry — that was all the manufacturing that existed. With all the natural potential of the town, the logical question was "Why isn't there more industry?" The accusation was that a wealthy non-resident syndicate owned the land along the river and could afford to hang on to it.

New Jail and Court House

Perhaps the most visible change in the 1880's was the new jail and court house. The old ones were both plainly inadequate and had been almost since inception. So in 1886 a new brick jail was built, with the jailor's quarters in front. The building still stands on the Court House Square and houses the Washington County Historical Society. Mrs. Edward DeTuncq's father, Adam Held, was Sheriff at one time, and the family lived in the jail. Mrs. DeTuncq recalls the frightful amount of work her mother had to do in caring for the inmates while her father was out on the road. One of her vivid memories is of the man who had

Washington County Jail (now Washington County Museum) Court House in background.

Washington County Court House

walked from Milwaukee to West Bend, slept in a nearby farmer's barn one cold winter night, froze his legs and had to be brought to the jail for the amputation. Dr. Heidner sawed the legs off and the poor fellow yelled and yelled. No anesthetic, but it was not so much the pain that hurt — it was the thought of being legless. Someone made him a platform on wheels, similar to roller skates, and he maneuvered around on those until he was well enough to return to Milwaukee.

When the new jail was first built the heating system would not work properly, and the *Democrat* reported that "the prisoners had to rub themselves against the iron bars to keep warm." It was eventually repaired.

The new court house was ready by 1889, a shining Gothic Cream City brick and cut limestone building with a tower and four turrets and a marvelous red roof that is still easily visible from most parts of the city. On the north wall is a terra cotta relief panel at the spot where the circuit court justice's seat was located inside the Court House. The panel depicts the proverbial goddess of justice with her scales and her sword.

First Mayors

By this time, too, the village had become a city with two wards. The first city mayor was John Potter, a Yankee from New York who served in 1885-6. (Terms were for only one year then.) He was a man of many talents, as were the rest of the mayors of this decade. He was a money lender (many people still did not trust banks), a postmaster, store owner, and had been a village supervisor, Justice of the Peace and Superintendent of Schools. For the honor of being mayor, he was rewarded with a handsome yearly salary of $50.

Henry Lemke, a German from Wittenburg, was the second mayor and he, too, had a varied career. He was a first class mason and helped build the local Catholic Church. In 1871 he went to Chicago to assist that city after the disastrous fire. He had served as village treasurer and on the County Board, operated a saloon, and later became the postmaster.

Mayor number three was Barnabus Potter, John's brother. He was a storekeeper, real estate salesman, a miller, and later a member of the State Assembly. He was followed by Patrick O'Meara, an Irishman from Dodge County, and a graduate of the second law class of the University of Wisconsin, the first college educated mayor. He had been Washington County District Attorney, and later became County Judge for 24 years. Then came Charles Miller, the German born law partner of Patrick O'Meara (and son-in-law of William Wightman) who had been Register of Deeds and sent to the Wisconsin Legislature. At one time he had been clerk in the office of the Bank Comptroller in Madison. The last mayor of the decade was Joseph Ott, an Ohio Yankee, a hardware store dealer who had married Miller's daughter, and had been County Clerk, County Board Chairman, and founder of the Ott Coal Company. So one can see that the mayors of the 1880's were men of experience and talents, and a mixture of Yankee, German and an Irishman. West Bend had chosen its first mayors wisely.

At first the City Council met in Mr. Frisby's law office, but later they rented office space. A new City Hall was not to be a reality for another decade.

CHAPTER 2

The Spanish-American War

West Bend has an interesting and varied story to tell about its part in the nation's wars. The first one after its founding had been the Mexican-American War, but inasmuch as the war ended the year Wisconsin became a state (1848), it is doubtful if any young men from West Bend served in it. To complicate matters, the United States government would not accept any recruits from Wisconsin Territory, nor any of the German Riflemen from Milwaukee, so a patriotic youth would have had to go to a neighboring state to enlist. The next was, of course, the dreadful Civil War, which has been duly recorded in Section II.

But by 1898 enthusiasm ran high for the Spanish-American War. After the blowing up of the Maine, the *Democrat* reflected the sentiments of the community and the nation when it wrote on May 18, 1898: "Our nation is fighting a righteous war in behalf of humanity and to avenge the death of 266 Americans who were murdered by the treachery of Spanish officers." Inasmuch as the nation was not informed of the facts because the pace setting New York press was more interested in selling sensational stories than in printing the truth, the local paper was as ill-informed as the rest of the United States. To be fair, the cause of the blowing up of the Maine has never been honestly assessed to this day.

Young men flocked to enlist. That same issue of the *Democrat* reported: "It is said that 90% of the rejections in the state guard is (sic) due to the deadly cigarette. Young men, if you want to serve your country in the field, give up cigarettes!" Does this 80 year old admonition sound vaguely familiar?

Among the first to enlist in West Bend were Adam Kuehlthau, George Ott, Fred Heipp and Will Groeschel. The latter two boys wrote letters to the press from their training tent in Camp Douglas and spoke of a typical mess (meal) of hardtack, pork and beans and coffee. "It takes some time to get used to the bill of fare." To alleviate their boredom, for training was not strenuous, the YMCA brought in writing paper and reading material.

Whenever a railroad train full of enlistees passed through West Bend on its way south, local citizens gathered at the depot, often with a band, to shout their approval. One tragic note for West Bend was the death of Peter P. Haan in Santigo de Cuba of malaria. Otherwise, the town celebrated the victory over Spain as heartily as the rest of the country and it flew the flag proudly over every flagstaff in the city.

CHAPTER 3

The 1900's

By the early 1900's West Bend joined the nation in mourning the death of President McKinley and shared the apprehension "about that cowboy" (Teddy Roosevelt) now in the White House. The nation was busy exterminating yellow fever in Cuba and reserving the right to intervene to maintain "law and order" (and where has THAT expression been heard?), while disclaiming all intention of ruling Cuba — to what future disaster.

Street Scene, 1903 — Fifth Avenue.

Panama was in revolt against its Columbian master and proponents of imperialism were gleefully ready to negotiate a treaty with the ill-prepared Panamanians. New fangled Eastern road asphalt — asphalt and cement — was beyond the ken of people used to dirt roads, and the Wright Brothers were tinkering with some crazy flying machine.

Immigrants were pouring into the nation by hitherto unheard of millions and some came to West Bend, while the former immigrants were busily demanding that this nation be preserved for the "natives," referring to those who so recently themselves had been deprecated as foreigners. Tariffs were at an all-time high and business was booming, but those in horse and wagon related industries were about to fold — although they did not know it just then.

Laborers throughout the country worked long hours for minimal wages while the powers in control liked the status quo and forced labor into a desperate struggle which they would eventually at least partially win.

Culturally, people were playing the rousing "Stars and Stripes Forever" on the great talking machine of Tom Edison's and were beginning to experiment with Kodaks. All were excited

Typical Living Room, 1913 (Heidner).

about the magic lantern shows, the forerunner of the modern movies, and readers were devouring Jack London, Bret Harte, James Whitcomb Riley and Hamlin Garland. West Bend citizens could hop one of the many daily trains in time to get to a celebrated play or one of the new musical comedies in Milwaukee and return yet that day, or they could travel to Chicago to marvel at Louis Sullivan's skyscrapers. Chiropractors were new and medical men were beginning to save lives on the operating table, especially with appendectomies, but the losses were still more numerous than the lives saved. Women were ecstatic about an electric stove or an electric flatiron to make their life easier in the kitchen.

A West Bend landmark that has long ceased to exist was Kuester's Island, formerly at the foot of Barton Hill. The five acre piece of land was a popular resort for swimming, boating and fishing when it was completely surrounded by water. Over the years the water was filled in, creating first a peninsula, and finally completely joining the island to the rest of the land in the city, so it is hard to visualize it as having been an island at one time.

Altogether it was a wonderful era, with nothing but progress — progress and more progress in the immediate horizon. Never mind the ills in the cities — or in Europe. This was America and the only way to go was up, and West Bend had caught that fervor, too.

SECTION XIV

WORLD WAR I

As we recall West Bend during the Civil War, let us see how the city fared during the first of the world wars. In addition to the sorrow over the departure of the boys for training camp and overseas, there was the agony of a caller from the Red Cross to report the injuries to or an illness of a loved one — or more tragically — a death. Otherwise West Bend settled in to help win the war. Business boomed. Those local factories that had had the time to convert to war production received profitable war orders. There were jobs for everyone.

Now people had their first taste of what it means to conserve essential materials, one of which was paper, and citizens were even admonished to use only one two-cent stamp instead of two one-cent stamps to save the precious commodity. Stores were urged to cut deliveries. "The woman who calls up to have a five cent spool of thread delivered is not being very thoughtful." But the biggest topic of conversation was food, with meat and white flour being particularly scarce as America was trying to feed her Allies, too. The thing that irritated most women was the lack of white flour, and numerous recipes were printed to show women how to make do with substitutes. One local recipe called for two parts of wheat flour, one part of rolled oats, 1/8 part bran flour, and 1½ parts cornmeal, to be augmented with whatever was at hand, such as cooked oatmeal, rice, etc.

Tin was valuable, and could not be allocated to canning vegetables, so all those who owned vacant lots were urged to plow them and then find someone to grow the vegetables. Carl Pick, Ray Flaherty, H. B. Kaempfer, and Robert Rolfs were in charge of this aspect of the war. Governor Phillips had declared, "The man with the hoe can be a hero, too." Women were urged to learn the new cold pack method of canning in glass jars and the Washington County Defense League bought a cold pack canner and taught women how to use it. Mrs. H. Wagner was in charge of food conservation generally.

Women were affected in other ways, too. When the men left for war the women filled their positions, and were even employed in heavy industry. While a few women had worked at paying jobs before the war, they now entered the market for good. The

Red Cross was active also, and its more than 100 local members made comfort bags, knitted sweaters, etc. Their headquarters were in an upstairs room of a department store, and women were encouraged to come to the room every afternoon or on Tuesday evenings. In addition, women took handwork home. Even the upper grade school girls were taught to knit simple things such as scarves. The boys at the front needed an endless supply of wool socks and local Red Cross leaders asked women to make them big enough, casting on 72 stitches with large needles in order that the foot would be at least 12 inches long.

Farmers in the area needed workers, so school boys were dismissed in April to work on the farms. However, the boys in town were chagrined to learn that farmers took a dim view of hiring "city boys," even though the lads volunteered to spend Saturdays in April at the farm learning how to cope with an unfamiliar world.

Finances

Unlike the days of the Civil War, West Bend citizens supported the Liberty Loan drives. All were over-subscribed, one of them by 146%. Another was subscribed in only three hours. Bonds were made available in amounts ranging from $50 to $1,000, paying 3½% interest in gold semiannually. Inasmuch as the bonds were tax free, the effective interest was 6½%, substantially more than that received in banks. A local photographer, Louis Schreiber, never seemed to buy any bonds, and the thought circulated that he was unpatriotic. So one night some boys took it upon themselves to demonstrate their own brand of patriotism by throwing egg shells containing yellow and orange paint at the front of his shop. Much later it was learned that the unfortunate gentleman had invested unwisely somewhere out west and indeed did not have any spare money for the bond drives.

Incidentally, no bonds were registered in World War I and consequently they were frequently stolen. Thieves roamed the area to purloin the precious paper. This sad situation was remedied in World War II when every bond was registered in the owner's name.

Another incident involved a local druggist who had an illegal extra 1,000 pounds of sugar to keep his ice cream and soda fountain customers well supplied for the duration, but he was

Recruits leaving for Camp Grant.

Liberty Loan Drive

accused of falsifying a report, forfeited the sugar, and was ordered to close his soda fountain.

By 1918 there was no oil available to sprinkle on city streets, so the citizens suffered from dust, for paving had not yet arrived. When the flu epidemic struck West Bend, many were

Armistice Celebration

Dedication of Soldiers Memorial.

Schloemer brothers — Herbert, Gerald, Oscar, Daniel (seated).

seriously ill and there were several deaths. Doctors were scarce and seriously overworked. One doctor, incidentally, a loyal German, left West Bend when hostilities began and served on the German battlefield, receiving a decoration from Germany for his valor. Understandably, he never returned to West Bend to practice medicine.

West Bend Sentiments

In spite of all this, West Bend made no secret as to where its sentiments really lay. This was still a German community. As late as 1895 E. Franckenberg had sent birthday greetings to Otto Von Bismarck. Before the United States declared war on Germany in 1918, the local paper was full of articles sympathetic to Germany. People collected money to help distressed Germans, especially their relatives and the children. But when we officially entered the war, the editor of the West Bend *News* wrote, "We have not made any secret of our sympathies with Germany . . . that is all past and we now stand behind our government with all the might we can muster. It is no use to assert that 90% of the American people are against being dragged into their fearful war. Our Congress has spoken and we must uphold its decision. Congressmen must not necessarily comply with the wishes of the constituency. They may vote at any time to suit their individual self. Our Senator LaFollette and our Congressman Edward Voight, we are glad to notice, stood on the side of the overwhelming majority of the people, albeit not that of Congress . . . We again will be ready to fight for our American institutions as our predecessors have done in the Civil War." It is easy for someone to assume that his private feelings represent the feelings of many in West Bend.

In spite of the brave words of backing America, the *News* printed advice on how to answer the draft questionnaire and suggested the proper answers for exemptions. But many boys volunteered for this war, the first reported ones being Herman Claus, Chester Wendleborn, and August Hefele, who left in September of 1917, five months after we entered the war. The first to enlist in the signal corps of the National Guard were Wareham Kuehlthau, Carl Kuehlthau and Walter Gumm. Others who soon followed were Waldemar Erler, Leroy Poull, Earl Kuehlthau, Donald Hansen, Eugene Gehl, Lawrence Huber, Emil Lehman, Milton Krueger, John Slavik, Ray Pahle, Jerome Schlegel, John Herdt and Otto Heldt, most of whom also chose the Signal Corps of the Guard. Harvey Bruhy volunteered for the Aviation Corps. Four Schloemer brothers, Oscar, Herbert, Daniel and Gerald, served in World War I, the only family quartette from West Bend.

An early letter from C. F. Leins expressed his sorrow that the world seemed to want to "pound" on industrious Germany, but he felt she was too tough to defeat. He accused England of jealousy, France of lust for land, and Russia of a desire to Russianize the globe, while he predicted that England would pay for her indiscretion in drawing the sword against her Teutonic cousins. It is still difficult for some people today to admit the depredations of the Germans, especially in the early years of the war.

Letters Home

Many of the boys had their letters home printed in the *West Bend News* so that all might know how they fared. Edward DeTuncq, for instance, wrote of being in the navy when it took over the German fleet in the Firth of Forth. The Allies had expected trouble from the German guns, but their Admiral sent a ship to the Allied side to negotiate, and the world learned that the German boys were half starved, and their navy was out of coal to such an extent that an Allied vessel had to give them enough coal to get them back to their own fleet. DeTuncq was also on the flagship New York when it was visited by the English King and Queen and so was proud to say he saw the Prince of Wales.

John Frank Lynch of the *West Bend News* staff spent Christmas of 1918 in Varennes, France, on the spot where 40,000 Frenchmen had died in 20 minutes in one of the worst battles of the war. There among the dugouts and the pillboxes and the trenches with their wire entanglements the Americans ate turkey, and all the boys washed their largest and best socks to hang on a tree cut from a nearby swamp in an attempt to relive an American Christmas.

Another local boy, Oswald Claus, was interned on the USS Scorpion in Turkish waters when the US entered the war, was put under close guard, and allowed to go ashore only once every ten weeks, speaking to no one except his guard and an interpreter. He and his buddies had a scare when the Allies bombed the area, but he survived to help raise the American flag over Constantinople.

Several boys were in the famed 32nd Division, and one of them, Corporal Walter Kuester, helped plant the American flag in Alsace. Captain Edward Gehl was cited by General Pershing. And one of the local heroes was a woman, Thecla Richter, who served as a nurse in a base hospital in France.

Thecla Richter's Story

Inasmuch as Miss Richter was the only nurse from West Bend in the armed forces, her story rates attention. She was a nurse in Evanston, Illinois, when she joined the Northwestern University Hospital Unit of U.S. Base Hospital No. 12 composed of doctors, nurses and students from four hospitals in the Chicago area. The Surgical team had one surgeon, one anesthetist, one

Thecla Richter

surgical nurse (Thecla), and three orderlies, one of whom was called a batman (or the one who shined the shoes, etc.). Altogether there were over 200 people in the unit.

They sailed from New York on the 14th of May, 1917, in dangerous waters. To forestall an attack there was daily target practice and the nurses and others were allowed up on deck to watch. One day the casing of a shell burst and killed several of the spectators, including our heroine's best friend. As an example of the unpreparedness of the American navy, the gun was from the Spanish-American War era. So they returned home to New York, and after a thorough search of the ship they left for Europe again, this time escorted by a British torpedo ship.

Because no American soldiers were in the war as yet, (war having been declared only about a month previously and the U.S. army was completely unprepared for duty) the surgical teams were assigned to work along with British, French, and Belgium units in northern France. They had three huts for very seriously injured patients. The rest of the wards were tents, four tents to a ward, fifty beds to a tent. The tents had wooden floors and a stove burning soft coal to heat the water used for sterilizing.

No surgery was performed at the front, just emergency measures, for the injured were taken by ambulance to the base hospital where the surgical team went into action. Miss Richter's team served nobly for the duration and for a time afterward.

Upon her return to West Bend in June of 1919, she was feted by the West Bend citizens at the Washington House, presented with a dozen American Beauty roses and a diamond ring which she still wears proudly.

There was tragedy for West Bend, too. The first West Bend boy to lose his life was Harvey Bruhy, who was killed in San Antonio, Texas, when an airplane exploded. The playing field on the Badger Middle School grounds is dedicated to his memory. William Ott's son Arthur was killed in France and Arthur J. Develice was severely wounded in France. No complete record of the local tragedies exists as yet.

Celebrations

When the war was over, West Bend went wild with joy. First there was the premature celebration when the country thought there had been an Armistice. The factory whistles blew on Thursday and young and old, rich and poor, male and female, reported the *News*, marched and danced in the streets in the atmosphere of a wild carousel. When the real Armistice came on November 11th, the factory whistles again screamed and everybody had enough steam left for a second celebration. Main Street was the meeting point for the thousands. Hundreds of cars came into town and more hundreds arrived from Hartford with celebrants and war trucks from the Kissel Company. There were bands, parades, bonfires in the middle of the streets, a victory speech by Judge O'Meara, dancing of the two step and foxtrot, and such general revelry as playing ring around the rosy. At long last West Bend thought it could get back to normal.

In the next months, West Bend citizens adopted 66 French orphans by paying $36.50 for each one. C. F. Leins had letters and pictures in his office and he spearheaded the drive. France had half a million orphaned by the war and the United States assumed responsibility for about half of them.

American Legion Organizes

The American Legion organized with 75 charter members in 1919, and chose D. J. Kenny as its first Commander. He later

AMERICAN·EXPEDITIONARY·FORCES

UNITED ★ STATES ★ ARMY

DISTINGUISHED SERVICE · CROSS

★ CITATION ★

First Lieutenant Ray F. Dickop (Deceased) 127th Infantry
DISTINGUISHED HIMSELF BY EXTRAORDINARY HEROISM IN CONNECTION WITH MILITARY OPERATIONS AGAINST AN ARMED ENEMY OF THE UNITED STATES AT Fismes, France ON 4 August 1918 AND IN RECOGNITION OF HIS GALLANT CONDUCT I HAVE AWARDED HIM IN THE NAME OF THE PRESIDENT THE DISTINGUISHED SERVICE CROSS

AWARDED ON 17 September 1918

John J. Pershing
COMMANDER-IN-CHIEF

No 499

Lt. Ray Dickop Citation

went on to become State Commander. Other officers were Harry Rolfs, Vice-Commander; E. J. Altendorf, Adjutant; R. Froelich, Finance Officer; and Henry Regner, Historian. The post was named after Lieutenant Ray Dickop, who had served in the National Guard in the 1916 Mexican border affair and died in France at the Battle of Chateau Thierry in August of 1918. "Though mortally wounded he continued to give orders to his men, and to lead them forward until he fell dead." Two posthumous awards were presented: the Croix de Guerre from French Commander Petain and the DSC from General Pershing, who named him one of the 100 heroes of the war. While Dickop was not a West Bend boy, his name was selected to avoid the local jealousies over choosing which local boy to honor in this fashion. One of the services of the first Legion Post was to establish a night school in West Bend to meet the needs of local industry in bookkeeping and mechanical drawing.

Senator LaFollette, one of the few United States Senators to vote against the entrance of America into the war, came to West Bend in 1922 and spoke at the Mermac Hotel. He told his wildly enthusiastic audience that it was indeed a black day in our history when the United States helped to starve out Germany. He felt that we had entered the war too hastily inasmuch as Germany had sunk only one or two of our ships, when in 1812 the British had sunk hundreds before we went to war. He recalled the American horror over the sinking of the Lusitania, but he reminded the audience that the ship was a floating arsenal and it was well within German rights to sink it during the war. He deplored the fact that 93 cents out of every tax dollar now went to pay for wars past and present, and the rich were getting richer while the poor became poorer. While America boasted of 22,000 new millionaires because of war profits, the world had 70,000,000 homeless people because of that same war. He ended by suggesting that in the future the American people be asked to vote on whether or not the country should go to war.

Gradually the city assumed its normal pattern. One lonesome soldier, Leo Bratz, wrote home that he would not trade all of Central Europe for Washington County. He had met a lady who had had no soap for three years and he realized that his homeland was a paradise.

Soldier's Memorial Dedicated

One more celebration was in order. On November 16, 1927, the Soldier's Memorial was dedicated. The largest crowd to ever attend a ceremony here, at least 10,000 people, witnessed a parade of 6 bands, 2 drum corps, and three to four thousand marchers. On the reviewing stand at the Court House Square were three Civil War veterans from West Bend, Martin G. Blackman, Peter Dricken and John Rilling, along with three others from the county.

It might be interesting to note in detail the facts about the dedication of the Soldiers' Memorial on Sunday, November 13, 1927. At 1:30 P.M. there was a parade with the following units:

Section I

Police
Color Guards
Colors
Milwaukee Legion Band
Hartford National Guard
Fond du Lac Drum Corps as official escort for
National Commander of the American Legion

Civil War Veterans — in cars
Disabled Veterans — in cars
Spanish-American War Veterans

Section 2

Beaver Dam American Legion Band
Washington County Veterans of World War
Hartford Legion Band
Visiting Legionnaires

Section 3

Oshkosh American Legion Drum Corps
American Legion Auxiliary
Mothers, Wives, Daughters, Sisters of Veterans

Section 4

West Bend Moose Band
County, City, Village and Town Officials
First Section of School Children

Section 5

West Bend High School Band
High School Students
Second Section of School Children

Section 6

Watertown American Legion Band
Firemen from all Cities and Villages
of Washington County

Section 7

Fort Atkinson American Legion Drum Corps
Camp Fire Girls
Girl Scouts
Boy Scouts

At the 2:30 Dedication Program on the grounds of the Court House, Fred Stork, who was the motivator for the monument, gave the presentation address and the American Legion Auxiliary unveiled the monument, with Mrs. D. J. Kenny, Pres-

Soldiers Memorial

ident, Mrs. J. F. Baumgartner, President-Elect, Marion Peters, and Olga Bezold pulling the strings, revealing a life-size doughboy posed as though going over the top, a grenade in one hand and a bayonet in the other. At least five other gentlemen made addresses, the major one by the National Commander from New York City. At five o'clock there was a banquet at the High School gymnasium for all service men and their friends.

The monument was erected in honor of the soldiers, sailors, marines, and nurses of Washington County who served in the Civil, Spanish-American, and World War, and the dedication day was a memorable one in West Bend history.

Back to Normal

By 1922 industry was back to normal in the city and factory whistles were blowing four times a day. Nearby farmers began to return to better times, and Gehls was selling machinery. The West Bend Equipment Company was selling stanchions for the cattle again. Amity and Enger Kress and the Woolen Company returned to normal, and the West Bend Lithia Company began to ship out 500-1000 cases of its malt beverage to Milwaukee daily. The youngest company, Picks, had been in trouble, but as more prosperity returned, such companies as Kissel and Yellow Cab Company sent in orders for hub caps and brake shoes. Both the West Bend Aluminum Company and Cooleys had felt the slack times the least of all in West Bend. So West Bend returned to its former state, and the war receded in memory as prosperity in the Twenties replaced the war years.

SECTION XV

THE ROARING TWENTIES AND THE DEPRESSED THIRTIES

CHAPTER 1

The 1920's

And now the war was over and words like Versailles and the numerous naval conferences seemed so far away. Historians love to call the decade the "Roaring Twenties." Women began to vote and to cut their hair; smoking came out into the open and skirts crept up to the knees. Everybody wanted to own an automobile and the Charleston was the dance craze. On the more cultural side people read Hemingway and Sinclair Lewis and were becoming acquainted with names like Horowitz and Toscanini; they enjoyed the popular art of Rockwell Kent while they shook their heads over the new art form called cubism. First talking pictures and then technicolor revolutionized Saturday night entertainment habits, and a young idealist whose name was Disney drew his first cartoon.

Locally, West Bend held a slogan contest in 1923 and Erwin Kannenberg won $20 with "Famous for Varied Industries," while the second place slogan was "Large enough to protect you, Industries enough to employ you, and Small enough to know you."

On the lighter side the Aluminum Company closed its park nights because people were "engaging in aphrodisical adventures," and when the county was putting in a road in 1923 the road crew broke 600 windows in a city neighborhood when they placed the nine charges of dynamite on *top* of the concrete to be broken up instead of under it. (This was, of course, not one bit funny to the unfortunate householders.) At another time a

1924 flood when 7.9 inches of rain fell in August. Fifty Legion members filled 2,000 sandbags and stood watch. West Bend Company employees served coffee and sandwiches.

miscalculation on the part of some road builders resulted in Cherry Street being laid 15 inches lower than Highway M (now 18th Avenue), the road it was to meet, and drivers contemplated the leap needed to continue their journey, while the fur flew as each construction engineer blamed the other for the fiasco. One era's tragedy is another era's smile.

One way to summarize the decade would be to list the impressive achievements of the administration of Henry Regner, Mayor from 1926 to 1930. During this time gas mains were laid in the city for both cooking and heating purposes, traffic lights made their appearance, and unsightly poles in some down town areas disappeared. There were curb and gutter extensions, the long delayed cement sidewalk was built to Barton, automated railroad crossing signals were installed, a band stand was built with benches for people to sit on, hundreds of trees were planted and other city trees trimmed. Several miles of water mains and sewer pipes were laid and also extended into Barton. Sleigh-rides and a community Christmas tree for kids were new on the scene and mounted policemen kept order in the city. The city bought a fine park site and purchased a new well and pumping

Kohlsdorf house, corner of Main and Decorah.

station and for the first time it began to collect interest from banks on city funds deposited there. The first tentative steps to a revised river project were taken when 28 owners agreed to give up 30 feet of their property to construct a street and put in a concrete wall along the river.

Perhaps City Attorney Thomas O'Meara stated it well when he reported that in the 1920's West Bend made more pocketbooks than any city in the world; it could furnish every household in the country with aluminum ware and its express company had more business than any city twice its size in Wisconsin while its post office receipts were equal to a city of 10,000 (the population was less than four thousand). Its freight business was greater than any other city in the state due to its thriving industries which included ten carloads of condensed milk daily.

But all of this was subservient in local interest to the tragedy involving Snowball.

CHAPTER 2

"Snowball"

If there is any one character that everyone hears about sooner or later in connection with West Bend it is "Snowball." He was Elmer Lynden, a young Negro about 25 years old who lived and worked in the area. On the Saturday night of July 19, 1924, he had attended a dance at Nenno and was walking home toward Barton when a local police officer, Henry J. Lemke, tried to arrest him after receiving a call about a disturbance. He was alleged to be intoxicated. According to later testimony the young man resisted arrest and in the melee drew a pair of pliers and struck Lemke. When Chief of Police Berend arrived he tried to reason with "Snowball," who fled, after allegedly "using abusive language" and "refusing to listen to reason." Two warning shots were fired, but the third shot fired by Lemke hit Snowball squarely in the abdomen while he was backed up to the brewery wall. He fell.

He approached death on the evening after the shooting, so three doctors worked over him at the hospital in a desperate attempt to save his life, but he died that evening. The official cause of death on the death certificate is listed as "Shock."

In the investigation which followed, testimony was drawn from attending physicians, police officers, and bystanders who claimed to have witnessed the event, but the official report concluded that the evidence against Henry Lemke was "not conclusive." The furor over the shooting continued, however, and many were not satisfied with either the testimony or the resultant freeing of the police officer. Especially incensed were the members of the Washington County Humane Society, so Charles Leins, president of the organization, brought charges of manslaughter against Lemke, who was released on a $10,000 bond.

In the interim District Attorney Hy Schmidt received the following communication through the Post Office: "You better do justice in this Lemke case if you care to live long and save your dome." Signed: KKK. To which the D.A. replied through the pages of the *West Bend News*: "The District Attorney wishes to say to the writer that he is not interested in the length of his life, but while he does live he would like to save his dome." Someone can do a service some day by thoroughly investigating the Ku Klux Klan in West Bend.

On the 19th and 20th of January, 1925, the case of the State of Wisconsin versus Henry J. Lemke was tried in West Bend, six months after the incident. The first difficulty arose when it became almost impossible to draw a jury, for everyone seemed to have an opinion on the case, on one side or the other. When the jury was finally selected, District Attorney Henry Sloan, Lemke's lawyer, called a total of 18 witnesses, but, of course, the chief witness for the defense was dead. The jury deliberated for 2 hours and 45 minutes before returning a verdict of "Not Guilty." End of case.

Not quite. First of all, just who was this "Snowball"? Born to a Negro father and a white mother, he was sent to St. Amelia's Orphanage in St. Francis at the age of two, for his father had died of gunshot wounds in Milwaukee. As was customary, when he became big enough he was farmed out to work and spent some time in Hartford working for Mathew Gehl when he was 15, but at 17 he was back in the orphanage. Then Fred Riesch took him to work for him in West Bend; at the time of his death, he was driving a team for Ciriacks and Groth.

Probably few people were as well liked as he; it became difficult to find anyone who would speak ill of him. He had always appeared happy and cheerful; his beautiful singing voice and his skill on the banjo made him a popular entertainer. The press reported that "lately he had become addicted to drink and became unsteady and unruly," an issue hotly debated by his hundreds of admirers. No one knows the inner turmoil he might have suffered as the only dark-skinned person in the community. In his obituary we find these words: "His sad and untimely death is regretted exceedingly by his many acquaintances. He was so well known in this section that fully 1000 persons came to the undertaking parlor Monday and early Tuesday morning to view the remains . . . Snowball was held in high regard at the orphanage . . ."

And in equally high regard by most of West Bend. But the one man who did *not* so hold him, Henry Lemke, after an outgoing life of which much was spent in service to the community, became a virtual recluse and brooded his life away, the victim of his own intolerance.

Today all the tangible evidence that remains is the marker in Barton Cemetery, but the unkind hand of time and bigots have eradicated the dates on his tombstone. But he has never really "died" for each generation hears the story and seeks anew the facts. Whatever they are, the shooting left a blot that is as yet ineradicable.

The only other story involving a negro in the area concerns Raif Adams, who had been a slave for 40 years and sold three times before Dr. Hayes brought him as a free man to Barton in the 1860's. In 1883 he joined the Methodist Church in West Bend. Older residents recall that his wife (he was married three times) made the best cookies and they were available for youngsters. He won his way to the hearts of his neighbors and made numerous friends, so that when he became infirm his neighbors cared for him. He died in 1899 at the age of 85 and was buried in Young America in Barton from the Presbyterian church after a large funeral.

CHAPTER 3

The City in the '30's

The city continued to enjoy its low tax reputation, it being only $20/$1000, which it had held for years. It started the Community Chest drives and built a sewage plant off Forest Avenue with $70,000 in city bonds and a WPA grant. When the Water Street bridge was completed at long last there was a big community celebration with three bands to entertain the large crowd.

City zoning and intelligent planning for the future became an issue. The right of an individual to build where he wants to versus the public good is an age-old problem. One speaker reminded an audience that even the Israelites planned for zonings in 3000 B.C. Most early houses in West Bend had been built as close to the street as possible so that they might better see who was passing by. One of the finer plans in 1938 was to build a civic center and garage with government help. By using government labor West Bend could have a library, a pool, a gym, and relieve the overcrowded fire department. When the topic had been thoroughly threshed out, the city decided that the costs were too great and withheld the application. Disgruntled citizens succeeded in getting a citizen committee appointed, some of which did not want to use government red tape, but wanted the structure, while others felt that "We have the money coming. If we don't use it, someone else will." The long procrastination delayed the issue, and when World War II broke out, the issue was dropped.

The morals of the city became a public issue again, instead of leaving morals to the realm of the home, church and school. The issue was over some people's opinion that literature on the newsstands was objectionable and obscene. Many popular magazines were under attack, for some of them seemed to the objectors to glorify crime and criminals, while others contained what they thought were filthy pictures and objectionable advertising. Books and greeting cards were guilty, too.. A committee was appointed consisting of Judge Bucklin, Baltus Rolfs, H. A. Arnfield, Mrs. B. C. Ziegler and Miss Gertrude Forester who were to appear before every church and civic organization with their story. If Milwaukee could eliminate its "filthy" literature, why not do it here? Little happened in spite of the to-do by a few people.

Avid readers devoured *Gone With the Wind* and advertising touted the wonders of that new invention — nylon. Whistlers reveled in "Easter Parade" and "God Bless America" while a new radio form — FM — made its welcome appearance.

West Bend now had 15 factories and 738 single dwelling houses along with 124 mercantile buildings which contained 140 establishments and 71 apartments. There were still four farms inside the city limits and 434 vacant lots.

It seemed sort of a joke that a feisty fellow with a crazy mustache was becoming a hero in Germany, while all around the world one word took precedence — DEPRESSION.

CHAPTER 4

The Depression

Hardly anyone who lived in the United States during the 1930's can forget the Great Depression, yet Robert Ripley's *Believe it or Not* listed West Bend as the city that never knew depression. It all began officially on Thursday, October 24, 1929, when the stock market finally collapsed. Signs of impending doom had been obvious for some time in the otherwise Roaring Twenties. Some banks had loaned money without proper security, wages had not kept pace with profits, and consumers were tempted by the pleasing array of goods on the market to over-use their new credit cards. Every home either had or wanted to have a radio, and those big console types were expensive. Nearby farmers had never shared in the prosperity either, for they had purchased more land during the prosperous World War I years, built silos, bought machinery, and then had seen their market collapse when Europeans laid down their guns and took up their plows again. How, then, was it possible that West Bend could escape a depression?

From its very inception West Bend had been known for its conservatism. The city was now an important manufacturing center and the businesses were run by true conservatives who generally delayed expansion until they had the cash, or most of it. B. C. Ziegler had unusual financial foresight and when he noted that the farmers in Kansas were in trouble, he knew it was just a matter of time before the malady spread, so he ordered retrenchment, and halted the building expansion at the Aluminum Company. The money saved helped to keep the factory afloat after the crash. Then, too, most of the local bankers were conservative enough to loan money on the real value of the land, and not on the inflated price.

When the depression struck, local factories did receive smaller or fewer orders, but when it was necessary to lay off men they chose to do so to those living outside the city or those who had other occupations such as farming. Then, too, if one company laid off a workman, a mutual arrangement with the other locally-owned companies resulted in another factory hiring that person, with the implicit understanding that as soon as conditions warranted, he would return to his prior job. The advantage West Bend had then was that all businesses were locally owned. The owners were neighbors and/or relatives of their employees, attended the same church, and had common interests, a condition that no longer exists. Besides, most companies had some cash reserves to tide them over.

In 1932 the West Bend *News* proclaimed, "The worst is over," and when their hero Herbert Hoover was roundly defeated by Franklin D. Roosevelt, they had no time for FDR's efforts to rescue the United States from its worst tragedy, so little felt here. In 1933 Washington County had an official 2.3% unemployment.

West Bend Collects Federal Money

Little is recorded of West Bend in those early years of the world-wide depression, but when the PWA began to offer money for projects, the city fathers began to think of collecting. When funds were made available through the PWA, West Bend decided to take advantage of it. "We might as well avail ourselves of the money. If we don't someone else will," was a commonly echoed phrase.

So they appealed to the government for help in building their sewage plant in 1933, and received 30% of the $120,000. Regner Park was largely built with PWA labor, men who worked with shovels and wheelbarrows to create one of the city's treasures. Water and Mill Street bridges were built, as was the Kuester Island Water Plant. Concrete work along the river downtown, the airport, McLane School and the vocational wing of the High School were built with government funds and workers. During Christmas vacation of 1934 twenty-five experienced men were hired with Federal funds to paint and repair the local schools. In 1935 rotting timber in the City Hall was replaced.

Bank Troubles

One government decree was felt by everyone in the city when Governor A. G. Schmedemann ordered all the banks of the state closed. When the order was lifted, West Bend banks did not open immediately for withdrawals, although they were open for deposits. They were "awaiting further orders from Washington." When it was over, two banks, the First State Bank and the First National Bank, were as sound as ever, but the Bank of West Bend was in trouble. They had loaned money to farmers who could not repay it, and in 1934 it was taken over by the First National Bank. Previously their depositors had received 10% of their money and with the takeover they received an additional 25%, but by 1942 trustees Paul Morlanus, Robert Kraemer, and E. G. Franckenberg had paid off the full amount to their former depositors. About this time, the First National Bank pioneered in permitting people to pay their mortgages on a monthly basis instead of over a longer term, and this action saved many a person's property.

Farmers' and Teachers' Woes

Among the most vivid memories of the depression is that of the milk strike of 1933 when disgruntled farmers of the Washington County Cooperative Milk Products started a drive for a living wage. At first no milk factories hauled milk, then one by one they resumed business. The crack of baseball bats used by county deputies on the heads of the strikers was a sorry sound. Some milk was dumped along nearby roadsides. A few rocks were thrown through windows of those who had capitulated. One hundred pickets met a condensed milk truck on highway 33 near Allenton and opened the valves, releasing 10,000 pounds of milk. Fear of widespread violence gripped the area, but West Bend escaped relatively unscathed as farmers in the area nearby proved unwilling to withhold milk for very long.

One group that did feel the depression was the teachers. Those who were here at the time recall the day that D. J. Kenney called the teachers together and gave them a graphic picture of the bread lines in Milwaukee — and ordered an immediate 7% wage cut in West Bend, followed shortly by another one of 3%. After that, raises were unheard of for years, although the cuts were gradually restored. County Superintendent of Schools M. T. Buckley said in 1935 that teachers bore the brunt of the cuts and that it was time to remedy it.

Socially, hard-time parties were fashionable and the jigsaw puzzle, the latest craze, kept families happily at home. Movies and hamburgers were a dime each, and a coke was a nickel, so one could have an evening out for a quarter.

But all this came to an end with the onset of World War II when West Bend business really came into its own and the city prospered mightily. The word "depression" vanished from people's vocabulary.

SECTION XVI

THE FORTIES AND WORLD WAR II

CHAPTER 1

West Bend in the 1940's

In the 1940 census the city had a population of 5452. Antibiotics, penicillin and Polaroid were entering the vocabulary. During the decade Americans would whistle "White Christmas" and read Ernie Pyle and Lloyd Douglas while *Forever Amber* would keep the reader awake until the book was finished and *The Egg and I* would be chuckled over for days. If one went to the theater it was popular to prefer Tennessee Williams or Arthur Miller. After the shock of the war was over, an invention such as the A-Bomb would be debated and re-debated: ought the United States to have dropped it in the first place? And then Americans were caught up in the intricasies of the Chamber-Hiss case, and just beginning to learn about Korea.

But there were issues close to home, too. Starlings had plagued the city and no one seemed to know how to eradicate them until E. W. Dewey and a like-minded group stationed themselves under the afflicted trees and fired their guns on signal. Some left.

The decade opened with another drive to clean up the reading habits of the city. Fifty voters appeared at a public meeting to discuss ways to remove the offensive material. They decided to get a list of all offensive material and distribute it to all civic, religious, and service organizations. The only problem was, where would they get a list and what material should be excluded? The answer was that Milwaukee had such a list and they had had success in eliminating pornography!

Another moral issue involved pin ball machines. Should they be removed? Were they contributing to the disintegration of the morals of the youth? While the debate raged, the City Council vacillated, finally tabling the ordinance. Mayor Schloemer stepped in and banned the offenders.

Parking meters were a big issue, especially after the war. Store owners and their employees were accused of usurping all the available spaces in front of their stores, but no one really wanted to pay to park a car, either. Some were installed in 1946 on a six months' trial basis, but a public outcry (810 signed a petition to remove them) caused them to be yanked out. Then an advisory referendum was held, with only 969 votes for it and 1367 against it, while the complaints continued over the unavailability of suitable parking space! Four years later a second referendum reversed the first one, 1129 to 860, and yet the City Council postponed their installation.

When the war was over there was a concerted demand for over-all city planning. The river was a particular sore spot, with rubbish everywhere along it. Mayor Schloemer tried to get the Council to ask for federal help in long-term planning. If their plan were adopted the city could borrow money at no interest; if the plan were never used there would be no fee. The city had experienced government largess on several other occasions, one of them being at the beginning of the decade, $85,000 in 1940 for curb and gutter, storm cellars, sidewalks and resurfacing of the streets. This time, though, nothing happened.

But the news that dominated the decade was war — World War II.

CHAPTER 2

World War II

When one remembers the anti-war feelings of West Bend in the Civil War, and the reluctance of some people to fight Germany in World War I, it is well to know that World War II changed all that, although the city still had a strong pro-German minority and was bedeviled by German propaganda in the later years of the 1930's. Parades of speakers came to West Bend to influence their audiences in favor of Hitler and his Nazis. One of the more influential was Dr. Richard Hertz from Hamburg, Germany, and it is worthwhile to cite from his lecture to show how the feelings of pro-Germans were bolstered.

He began by reminding his audience that "it is not always possible to obtain satisfactory living standards by allowing economics to run its course." Sometimes mass action is needed, and Nazism served as a tonic to Germany. If that action seems immoral (such as the persecution of the Jews), he continued, in the long run Germany would become an economic power and then it would assume "a moral aspect" because of the benefit it could produce for its people. (If something succeeds economically, men justify it morally.)

He reminded Americans that Nazism was a "defiance of the business minded democratic concept of the world," and a "reasserting of German right to see things in their own way," regardless of whether the victors in World War I liked it or not. He felt that America always tended to overrate the commercial and technical aspects of nations, and to underrate the more important psychological factors. Germany was not only defeated in World War I but forced to convert its government to democracy, and the result had been two decades of tragedy — hunger, unemployment, and restlessness. There was no need to fear a war, he concluded; Germany did not want war. In fact, the "German people will not countenance" a war; they merely seek "territorial expansion."

This sort of thinking helped to support the position of the dwindling but still vocal pro-German element in West Bend. When glowing word of the employment possibilities in Germany reached West Bend (Hitler boasted that there was no unemployment in Germany) at least one local family went there to find work. Otto Friebrantz had been unemployed for three years, so he took his wife and seven children to Hamburg where he reportedly found work. The family had come to West Bend in 1923 and had cost the city $10,000, so people breathed a collective sigh of relief at their departure.

The Bund

In 1940 two German-American camps were opened south of Grafton — the work of the German-American Bund. Every boy of German descent was eligible up to the age of 20, and when he had completed the requirements to become a full-fledged Bundsman, he was entitled to wear the uniform. Inasmuch as they advertised in West Bend, there might have been an appeal to some local people, but their records were all secret so there is no evidence to show that anyone from West Bend attended the camps. Thus we see that the German viewpoint of the impending war was well represented.

Before the actual explosion at Pearl Harbor there had been warning signs. In a *West Bend News* article, Mrs. Minnie Salter's son Wayne wrote from Pearl Harbor that "something is breezing up," for all the soldiers were issued steel helmets, and all trucks were armed with heavy guns. When war appeared imminent, a county defense system was organized which included the leadership of D. J. Kenny, Guido Schroeder, Bob Hackbarth, Robert Rolfs and Mayor C. J. Schloemer from West Bend; B. C. Ziegler served as chairman and Miss Edna Schloemer* became Executive Secretary of the Washington County Council of Defense. Fear of sabotage, air raids, and germ warfare spread, and after the war began, the fear of suicide raids was added to the apprehension, so air raid protection practices were held. The City Council gave Mayor Schloemer broad powers to "enforce any rules necessary for the public safety and welfare." He divided the city into 8 units for disaster aid, and a bomb squad of husky volunteers was organized. By 1942 regular practice blackouts were held at 10 P.M. for periods of fifteen minutes, with block wardens checking to see that not one ray of light would betray the presence of a city.

All Germans, Italians and Japanese had to register after we went to war. Women organized almost immediately under the Presidency of Mrs. Austin Hancock, with Miss Edna Schloemer as Vice President and Mrs. Eberhardt as Secretary. Their concerns were with air raids, canteens, first aid, housing, sewing, conservation of scarce materials and jobs for all. Mrs. George Martin and her committee organized canteens, housing facilities, emergency stations and motor corps. First aid classes were taught.

---

*All fund drives, clothing drives, air raid wardens, victory gardens, block chairmen, rationing, etc., for the county (including West Bend) were handled through the Council of Defense office. The Red Cross trained several classes of Nurse's Aides who spent many hours doing volunteer work at St. Joseph's Hospital.

128th Infantry Band. First row, left to right: Capt. William Burton, Warrant Officer Joseph Clauder, Charles Woerpel. Second row: Fred Zimmel, Walter Feutz, George Butzler, Herbert Boomer, Frank Nilschke, Merton Wolcott, Erle Kissel. Third row: Donald Kolb, Howard Werner, Robert Collins, Robert Steinbach, Elroy Gessert, Walter Degner, Wayne Snyder, Paul Hrom. Fourth row: William Knoll, Leonard Kitowski, Lester Loehrke, Donald Peters, Max Moser, Felix Orthell, Robert Kuester. Fifth row: Elton Beck, John Schoeneman, Hugh McConaghy.

First Enlistments

Even before Pearl Harbor enlistments had begun. As early as 1940, the West Bend Infantry Band had left for intensive training in Louisiana under Band Master Joseph Clanden of the West Bend Florist Shop. Band members included Paul Hron, Max Moser, Walter Degner, Leroy Gessert and Robert Kuester. Under the 1940 Selective Service Act 680 young men were registered in the West Bend area. William Maaske and Charles Klumb left to work on the Alaskan Highway. One record lists Herbert Michaels, Melvin Riesch and Raymond Maaske in the first county quota of thirteen men in January 1941 to be drafted. Another says that Harold Warnkey and Charles Mueller were the first peacetime draftees. At any rate, the county held a ceremony at the Court House for the first named three, with a band and a benediction. In March of 1941 hundreds of people gathered at the depot to bid farewell to Ernst Guse, Alois Bremser, Edward Wenzlaff, Joseph Justinger, Franklin Butts, James Barber, Robert Cannon, Vincent Averill, Henry Leischinger, Jr., and Reuben Ramel. Each month more draftees left the city. Grannies who had already knitted for two wars were glad to serve again, and Clara Jaehnig and her Red Cross ladies were busy. They promised to see to the dependents of those who were drafted or enlisted.

Many airports in the state were closed for the duration, but West Bend was one of 17 allowed to remain open, and airport manager Ben Stanislau and his crew kept the area under tight surveillance 24 hours a day to report all planes. One amusing note concerns the "Neutral Hotel," which took a new name — the "Wischkerchen Hotel" — for "no one was neutral any more unless he was a blockhead." (*West Bend News,* May 31, 1941.)

West Bend Collects

While the most telling immediate effect of the war was the departure of the men for service, the city was immediately caught up in both collecting and rationing. And how West Bend did collect! At first it was primarily scrap metal, rags, rubber and tin cans. By 1942 collecting became a way of life, partly because the country needed the resources, but also because it was important to keep people busy feeling they were all contributing positively to the war effort. By 1942 West Bend had collected 18 tons of old rubber of which 25,000 pounds was contributed by children who had been promised a free ticket to the West Bend theater for their contributions. D. J. Kenny was County Salvage Committee Chairman and Mrs. Fred Baxter served as the local chairman.

Other drives were common. Boy Scouts collected paper. Women took their household fats to the meat markets to exchange for money and saved their old silk and nylon hose, for which Mrs. Emma O'Meara served as collection chairman. Veterans' hospitals asked for and received used radio tubes and musical instruments to entertain the wounded, and West Bend collected 1200 old phonograph records which were melted down and remade into new records for the men in service. When the "Save-a-Life with a Knife" campaign opened, Bill Jaeckel was one who sent his "sharp as a razor" hunting knife to the South Pacific jungles to kill the Japanese.

Scrap Aluminum Drive

Turning in Old Tires

Milk bottles appeared in the stores around town, courtesy of the American Legion, collecting "Smokes for Yanks" and in the fall of 1944 West Bend collected 310,000 cigarettes. All in all, the collecting spirit was high in West Bend as people cooperated whenever they were asked. They also adapted quickly to V-mail, a light weight paper, the message being filmed to save vital overseas shipping space.

Rationing

Rationing began in earnest even before Pearl Harbor. By March of 1941 there was a scarcity of sugar, for the Japs had conquered many of the sources of our usual supply, and citizens went to the public schools to register for rationing coupons. By 1942 one could have an additional allotment for canning purposes, and by 1943 the allotment was 20 pounds for a family for canning with an additional 5 pounds if they wished to make jam or jelly.* Most ration book holders declared they were going to can. Coffee was rationed to a cup a day or one pound for every five weeks and this worked a hardship on the confirmed caffeine addict, who resorted to all sorts of ways to stretch the allotment. The chocolate candy bar virtually disappeared.

Next on the list of materials to be rationed were leather shoes and by 1943 all shoes with rubber soles were also rationed. Canned goods were nearly impossible to obtain because the Japanese had conquered our source of tin, too, so they were added to the rationing list. People were encouraged to grow victory gardens, and the library became the center for books and classes on gardening. In addition to the many backyard gardens that sprang up, 135 plots in vacant lots were worked by those who had no land of their own. Ida Wiebe was the Victory Garden chairman for the county. The West Bend Company bought seeds, and the county home inmates raised the plants which were then distributed free to those planting gardens. The Old Settlers joined other groups in cancelling their annual banquet because of rationing. When the area received no new cars, strictly rationed also, Sampson Chevrolet closed its doors for it had nothing to sell. A huge demand for used cars rose, and a ceiling was placed on the prices to keep them in some sort of rational bounds.

---

*One amusing story concerns the man who returned to the rationing board to request an additional allotment of sugar. Unbeknownst to his wife he had used the entire 25 pound canning allotment to make wine! Request denied.

New tires had been impossible to obtain for years, for here again the Japanese controlled the southeast Asian source of supply. Each car owner was to keep only five tires and turn in the rest, but a huge and profitable black market kept those who could afford it in good rubber. Many people just put their cars up on blocks for the duration. And there was no more Kleenex; nylons were a rarity and not a yard of elastic could be bought anywhere. Other shortages were in housing and substitute teachers.

The worst of all rationing for West Bend to accept in 1942 was that of gas, and West Bend accepted it in less than a gracious spirit. When cars were supposed to be stopped on the highway in July, 1943, to test the validity of the trip, West Bend did not comply and was accused by the OPA of restricting the war effort. But Mayor Schloemer declared that he was following the rules, and would not stop cars indiscriminately when inspection stations were set up at the city outskirts, while local businessmen declared this interferred with the tourist trade and their natural rights. The *Milwaukee Journal,* among other papers, aired the negative publicity, and reported that the mood in West Bend was one of disdain in regard to the entire affair and as a result the local Rotary Club censored the *Milwaukee Journal* and the OPA for the bad publicity. By 1944 there were only two gallons of gas per week per car.

Even before Pearl Harbor, the CAP was organized and performed many valuable services during the war. One service occurred in 1943 when a local factory needed a vital tool repaired in order to keep the war orders rolling off the line, so the CAP flew the tool to Freeport, Illinois, for repair and returned it immediately.

Financial Contributions

When it came to contributing money, West Bend was not to be denied, either. At one time it led the state of Wisconsin in the per capita buying of E bonds. The Red Cross drives were all successful, USO drives went over the top, and war bond drives exceeded expectations. Numerous devices were used to bring money into the fund. In 1942 the American Legion made the 4th of July a "buy a bond day" and sold $65,000 worth. Minutemen went from house to house to solicit pledges, and when interest flagged, the government resorted to such ruses as bringing in a captured Jap submarine to the city, and if one wanted to see it he had to buy a bond.

As the war dragged on, it was necessary to have even more money, so the county was promised that a flying fortress would be called "The Spirit of Washington County" if citizens would raise $300,000. This proved slow work, but eventually the money was raised with West Bend contributing its share. Early in the war Mr. Robert Rolfs had volunteered his services to the United States Treasury Department to promote the sale of bonds, and when the rural area around West Bend turned in the highest per capita sum for any rural area in the United States, the U. S. Treasury adopted his proposals.

Laborers began to receive defense savings stamps and albums even before Pearl Harbor, and local plants continued to make it easy to buy stamps and bonds. When the Pick Company gave a 12½% pay raise in 1942, it set aside 30% of that for the day when the war would be over, and production might cease, idling the workers. There was, fortunately, no lack of employment for the men after the war.

White collar workers contributed their share, too. Office stenographers of both the West Bend Aluminum Company and Amity Leather Company worked as stenographers for war relief groups; employees of the First National Bank, the First State Bank and the B. C. Ziegler Company took at least ten percent of their salaries in stamps and bonds. In all, the working force of the city was extremely proud of its efforts and when local companies received coveted national honors such as the Navy E, they were a happy part of the celebrations.

Young people had their role also. When the teenagers in high school volunteered to go to work on farms, the farmers were as skeptical of their efforts as they had been in 1916, but many youths were used to harvest the crops. Others went to Door County to pick cherries.

POW Workers

Eventually the area ran out of workers, and then they were brought in from the POW camp at Rockfield; the Pick Company used more of these German workers than any other local company. They were housed in surroundings equal to those of American servicemen in camps, the food was of the same caliber, and they were paid 80 cents a day for their labor to buy personal needs at the canteen. The firms which employed them paid the government the difference between the prisoner's wages and the pay given to other workers. Many of them tried to learn English, and in their free time they had an orchestra; there were church services for both Protestants and Catholics and some of the prisoners taught others the art of water coloring, oil painting, and such. Others were cooks and helped out in the kitchen. All were expected to work and if they refused, they were not allowed to eat.

Industry's Role

The role of industry in West Bend and surrounding area cannot be underrated. Sgt. Robert Rayome wrote from Italy that their tent poles came from Picks, the corn from the West Bend Cannery, beets from the nearby Rockfield cannery, the canned milk from the White House Milk Company, their carrots from Plymouth; Kieckhafer's saws sawed their wood, and the water was pumped with Cedarburg motors. The West Bend Company produced a steady stream of 20 millimeter cartridge cases for 20 MM anti-aircraft guns that could throw 400 rounds a minute. When one of the U. S. battleships bagged 32 Jap planes in one action of 52 minutes with these guns, the United States Army sent an AA gun to the company to show the employes how it worked, for in action the worker was strapped to the gun so he could keep his eye on the sights at all times.

Enger-Kress made 20 war-time products, including pistol holders, nurse utility bags, spare parts cases for machine guns, chin straps, head bands for combat helmets, etc.

Picks was just as proud of its achievements. One particularly trying time occurred when the army immediately needed some supports for equipment and target stakes. After putting in a full day's work at the plant, four men pored over the blueprints from five until ten o'clock without being able to figure out how they could do it. Just as they reached the point when they were sure it could not be done, they decided to give it one more try, and the plan came to them before 10:30. Eagerly they rushed their bid to the Rock Island Arsenal the next day to beat the deadline, only to find that they were the only company which had been able to decode the blueprints and submit a bid. They also made 3000 folding cots and 65,000 folding chairs. In order to do all this they had to take over a lumber mill in northern Michigan, build a dry kiln, and run a spur from a nearby railroad. They subcontracted for Heil brake bands, aircraft winches, brake shoes, etc., and made parts for pontoons. At first when they went into production of tent poles they made 6,000 a day, gradually increasing this until one proud day they manufactured 57,000. In order to do this they built their own machinery, had conveyors synthesizing everything, and shipped out the equivalent of five carloads of material every day. All this while 84 of their regular employees were in the armed forces and prisoners of war replaced them.

The Armed Forces

But, of course, the real stories of the war belong to the men and women who served in the armed forces of the United States. Surely the most famous soldier who served in World War II was Colonel Herbert P. Schowalter. A graduate of the West Bend High School, he entered World War I as an enlisted man and became a 2nd Lieutenant in 1925. During World War II he served under General Mark Clark in North Africa as a Battalion Commander with the famed Fifth Army and as General Supply and Maintenance Officer under Generals George Patton and Alexander Patch, Jr., in North Africa, Italy, Germany, France and Austria. Among his many honors were the Legion of Merit, the Bronze Star with Cluster, the Croix de Guerre from General Charles de Gaulle personally, the Divisional Lorraine Cross from General Le Clerk's 2nd Armored Division, 5 battle stars, 7 theatre ribbons and an invasion arrowhead, the most honored of West Bend fighting men. After the war he returned to West Bend and served as Export Sales Manager of the West Bend Company and accepted many civic responsibilities in the American Legion, Veterans of Foreign Wars, West Bend Chamber of Commerce, Kiwanis Club, Knights of Columbus, etc. He traveled widely and entertained with his slide lectures. He died in 1972 at the age of 79, a most successful citizen.

Brunetta Kuehlthau Story

One of the most interesting stories from the war concerns Miss Brunetta Kuehlthau, one of the 68 "Angels of Bataan." She was among those who fled with MacArthur to Bataan and then to Corregidor to hold out until their supplies ran out. When she was captured, the Japanese were not sure what to do with the women, so they put them in a civilian camp in May of 1942 on slim rations with 3,000 to 4,000 other prisoners. At first, ma-

Lt. Brunetta Kuehlthau

Lt. Col. Beulah Schloemer

terial was allowed to be sent in from the outside, but later no goods could be received from anybody. They were permitted a garden and grew rice and corn, but just before they were rescued they were cut to 700 calories a day and had been promised further cuts. Their medical supplies were fair, and there were doctors in the camp, who also treated some of the Jap soldiers.

She was interned at the notorious Santo Thomas Internment Camp located at the University of Manila, a camp controlled by Japanese committees, and if the Americans obeyed the rules, they were left rather much to themselves. They lived in classrooms, and after her duty stint from eight to four daily, she and other captives played bridge, knitted, and read to pass the time, but they were not allowed access to any radio or newspapers and had to rely on rumors. There was no sports equipment and they were denied all Red Cross parcels. They had to make the clothes they wore last for the duration, too, for after the first few months they were issued nothing else. After her release, she returned to a hero's welcome, but after a brief stay with her parents she returned to duty and remained until 1958 when she retired as a Major and Chief of Army Specialist Corps, having earned a bronze star.

Beulah Schloemer's Service

Another woman of high rank was Lt. Col. Beulah Schloemer, who joined the Army Nurse Corps in 1937. She was on duty stateside until December of 1941 at which time she was assigned to the 156th Station Hospital-Mid Pacific. Later her assignment was to the 204th General Hospital which served in Hawaii, Oahu, and Guam. After the war she returned to the states and served stateside until 1950 when she was sent to the 97th General Hospital at Frankfurt-au-Main in Germany as Principal Chief Nurse. Four years later she returned to the states for additional advanced training and then became Principal Chief Nurse at Valley Forge Army Hospital. She retired in 1957 and returned to West Bend.

Several other stories had happy endings. In 1942 Walter "Red" Schaller survived the sinking of the Yorktown in the Coral Sea and was the first war hero to return home unscathed. "War is hell — you can say that again," he reported while recounting the story of the bombardment of his ship for two or three days by Japanese bombers and torpedo planes until the order to abandon ship was given and he dived into the ocean, swam for an hour and was rescued by a destroyer. Although he lost all his belongings, he was safe and could admire the skill of the Japanese pilots.

Captain Walter Gonring earned a Silver Star for gallantry as a P-38 pilot in France when he brought back a plane on only one engine, at great danger to himself. Later he was chosen to help escort the Big Three to their famed Yalta meeting. Lt. Wells Grogan had been a prisoner of war and reported that his interrogators knew all about him, dating back to his high school days, and they knew more about West Bend than most of the people living here. Another happy prisoner upon his release from the German Stalag #7 was Sgt. Walter Bruesch, who had been wounded in battle and recovered. Air Force 1st Lt. Henry Renard had been forced down over Czechoslovakia but he had had a radio and listened to the BBC's reports of the war during his internment. Julius Kuhn had also suffered as a POW.

Clara Jaehnig was cited for her Red Cross war service, and the *West Bend News* received a citation for meritorious war service, having printed a record 36,000,000 words or 570 miles of war news.

On the lighter side, S/Sgt. Ralph Boettcher gave up his bed

for Marlene Dietrich and drove her to a performance, having had the dubious distinction of having seen her just as she climbed out of bed.

But the real heroes never returned and the honor roll of those who paid the supreme price is a lengthy one.

The roll of the dead:

Lt. Lynn Moths—Panama Canal Zone Air Corps—March 6, 1943
Sgt. Vernon Lehrman—Camp Stewart, Georgia—August 7, 1943
Lt. Adrian Frankow—Rochester, Minnesota, Medical Corps—August 10, 1943
T/Sgt. Walter Kellbach—Elverson, Pennsylvania, Air Corps—December 4, 1943
PFC Gordon L. Wendelborn—Army in France—August 6, 1944
PFC Curtis W. Schmidt—Army in France—August 7, 1944
PFC Lester Weasler—Army in France—August 10, 1944
Sgt. Charles V. Cooke, Air Corps in Germany—August 14, 1944
Capt. Melvin L. Riesch, Army in Germany—October 3, 1944
Sgt. Michael Kratzer, Army in Luxemburg—January 2, 1945 (posthumous bronze star)
T/5 Raymond Hinsenkamp—Army in Belgium—January 3, 1945
Capt. Robert Cannon—Army in Straussburg—January 17, 1945
Capt. M. O. O'Melia—Marine Corps in Iwo Jima—March 5, 1945
Robert Burckhardt—Guadalcanal (silver star)
PFC Stanley Schneider—Army in the Philippines—April 4, 1945 (posthumous DSC for indomitable fighting spirit in Manila Bay)
PFC Alfred Wienke—Army in Germany—April 8, 1945
Pvt. Fred Backus—Army in Germany—April 26, 1945
PFC Edward Klumb
Pvt. Henry Schalles—Marine Corps in Okinawa—May 15, 1945
Phm 2/C Kenneth Fassbinder—Navy in the Pacific—June 1945
Charles Caske—Killed in Germany—1945

In addition to the above, the following alumni of West Bend High School died in the war: Gerald Bell, Harvey Kohl, S/Sgt. Henry Gumm (paratrooper Luzon '45), Russel Petri, Stewart Vincent, and Raymond Wiedmeyer. The list may be incomplete for lack of adequate records.

V-E day was treated surprisingly calmly in West Bend. The school had special programs and people stayed home and listened to their radio or went to church services of Thanksgiving.

Most stores were open as usual for business, while the taverns and the brewery were closed for the day. But V-J day was another story entirely.

Victory was ours at long last, so when the bells and whistles began at 6:01 on Tuesday night, August 6, 1945, the town went wild. Milling masses of humanity danced and sang in the streets for hours, cheering lustily. At 8:30 a parade was organized and confetti, caps, horns, and noisemakers appeared from everywhere, as though awaiting this glorious moment. The local civic band gave a band concert in downtown West Bend. The cavorting was orderly, however, and everyone dreamed of the end of gas rationing and price ceilings on luxury items.

But it was still necessary to ration gas for a little while longer, and when the rationing was removed, the papers told of a rash of accidents on the highways again. It was necessary to save fat into 1946 and sugar was still difficult to obtain. In 1947 the Draft Board was still meeting and the three West Bend men on the county Draft Board, B. Rolfs, A. C. Berkholtz and Thom. J. Weinand reported that they had met 374 times in 6½ years, and had spent from 35-50 hours a week for the first three years of the board's existence. Yes, West Bend's citizens served admirably in World War II.

SECTION XVII

THE 1950'S AND KOREA

CHAPTER 1

Life in the 1950's

Many major changes occurred in the city in the 1950's for its nearly seven thousand inhabitants. The most noticeable was a home building boom, to counteract the necessary neglect in the city over the war years. The City Council finally approved parking meters, experienced Civil Defense alerts, and caught Milwaukee Braves fever. It banned the keeping of all fowl in the city, the last vestige of the "good old days."

One of the big topics was — have you heard this before? — river improvement! Whose project was it? Was it the cost that was delaying any action? Those and countless other questions kept the talk lively, but it was just that — talk. A Memorial Fund existed in honor of the dead of World War II, and many thought it ought to be used to beautify the river. By this time, the West Bend Company had improved the portion of the river running through its property and the Woman's Club had beautified 14 spots in the city, donations coming from public spirited citizens.

The worrisome topic that continued throughout the decade concerned the relocation of Highway 45. WHY was it not accomplished? Senator Frank Panzer reminded an interested audience that it's the squeaky wheel that gets the grease, and if the road were to be improved and relocated, the people would have to get involved. This happened in the 1950's and the topic is still being discussed nearly thirty years later.

Direct dialing became a reality and the water was flouridated. The city fathers tried to convince the merchants to pay for garbage and rubbish collection, but there was no force behind it, so the merchants ignored the "suggestion." Gypsies might still be seen on the down town streets occasionally. There was one scandal — District Attorney Dean Bascomb withheld the fines for which he was responsible — several thousands of dollars' worth — and he resigned and paid the penalty.

But most people were interested in the newest media — television. Antennaes sprouted from nearly every roof, and some who owned no TV set installed an antennae anyway so that their neighbors would not know they were without the tube. There was Milton Berle and Imogene Coca on Saturday nights to keep people home. Westerns and "I Love Lucy" competed with Jackie Gleason and Mr. Peepers for audiences. Men loved the fakery of TV wrestling and whole families agonized with Charles Van Doren until they learned that he, too, was a fake. And then there was TV's finest hour — the Army-McCarthy hearings. Housewives made the beds and washed the dishes and then sat glued to their sets to watch the disintegration of Wisconsin's junior senator.

Politically West Bend loved Ike, and musically the young danced to rock n' roll. They had one hero — Elvis. Suburbs developed and the new home owners bought outdoor grills to capture the good life, but they did not necessarily find it and began to pop pills and consume unbelievable quantities of aspirin, according to a local druggist.

When they tired of TV, there was always the movies, and James Dean or Marilyn Monroe could bring in a crowd any night. Men bought pink shirts, the manufacturers who could add chlorophyll to a product made a fortune, and if you had the creative urge without being artistically endowed, there was the paint-by-number kit.

Altogether, it was an unusual decade with an unwarranted fear of Communism followed by the horror of another war — this time in Korea.

CHAPTER 2

The Korean Conflict

Few local facts are readily available about this war. It is known that the city organized a local civil defense unit under the leadership of Harold Schatz, and local doctors and dentists were registered for possible service. In 1950 coal was rationed, as much due to strikes as the war, and all public buildings including the schools were closed briefly.

The city did produce its heroes, though; the highest ranking officer from West Bend was Brigadier General Andrew P. O'Meara who earned a silver star for gallantry in action in Korea. He had participated in the Normandy Invasion in World War II and had been artillery commander of the 7th Division. He became General O'Meara later and in 1964 commanded the armed forces in Panama. In his years of service he earned the D.S.M., Legion of Merit (Oak Leaf Cluster), Bronze Star (Oak Leaf Cluster), Air Medal, Army Commendation Medal (Oak Cluster), a Distinguished Military Service Medal (Gold Star) from the Republic of Korea. In 1965 he was promoted to Commander-in-Chief of the 250,000 troops in NATO and Group Commanding General of NATO's Central Army Group.

Captain Walter Ottmer received two gold stars for meritorius service in the Marines and was promoted to Major. Lt. Richard Larson became an air force base squadron leader in Massachusetts, and Major Reuben Ciriacks received the bronze star. Sgt. John Schlosser was decorated with the air medal and Cpl. James Kalmer, Jr., was awarded the silver star for gallantry. Frank Uttech came home to meet his seven month old twins.

As in every war, some must pay the supreme price — their lives. Korea had its victims, too: Pvt. Melvin Klein had served four years in World War II and was recalled, only to lose his life in 1950. PFC Raymond Backhaus and Pvt. Richard Schoot both gave their lives, too. When it comes the subject of war, man is an inept learner. How many more West Bend youths must so die?

SECTION XVIII

THE 1960'S

Surely the biggest event and the most important one to the future of West Bend in the 1960's was its consolidation with its sister city to the north — Barton. In their founding years there was a great deal of rivalry between the two communities, and for a time Barton had the better of it. But the two cities developed quite differently over the years. Their close proximity and the sharing of the same problems prompted the wise among both towns to advocate one city government for both of them. Ample time was allowed for the debates that inevitably accompany a project of this magnitude and after the 1961 voting people eagerly awaited the results. In West Bend, the vote was 1147-643 with 33% of the eligible voters voting, a not quite 2 to 1 margin. In Barton 60% of the eligible voters said YES by a 384-187 margin, a little more than 2 to 1.

Several adjustments had to be made in both areas. West Bend ordinances would govern both places if those in Barton were inconsistent with those of West Bend, except for zoning, streets, traffic violations, current water bill collections, the official map, permits, and licenses, until they all expired. If there were any street name duplicates, one set had to be changed. The new municipality would hold all the assets. Only two big problems arose: the number of aldermen from Barton and the coordination of the fire departments, both of which were solvable when the area was redistricted into seven wards. Barton Village President Earl Steiner became the new 7th Ward alderman, Mrs. Helen Bunke became a supervisor on the county board, Mrs. Verna Schmid was appointed to the Library Board, and a few streets were renamed. It had been — and continues to be — a peaceful marriage.

New subdivisions were added. The fancy name of Maplewynde was given to one along Highway 45 south, it being an old English word for a road or lane that is bordered with maples; the street names there are reminiscent of a rural nature: Sylvan Way, Eder Lane, Heather, Bittersweet, etc.

Still plagued by the dilemma of the river project, the city hired a consultant who recommended that the river be paved over! Luckily, wisdom rejected the proposal.

These were the troubled years — the 1960's. America moved from the promise of Camelot to the tragedy of Vietnam, and in between she suffered through the murder of a beloved President, that of his brother, and of the man who made "I have a Dream" famous — Dr. Martin Luther King. There were Civil Rights marches, and fires in places such as Watts burned into our souls. Marijuana. Goldwater. Appollo 8. Astronauts and a man on the moon instead of in it.

On the lighter side there were Joe Namath, Jack Nicklaus, A. J. Foyt and Cassius Clay. Music from Bobby Dylan and Paul Simon and Arlo Guthrie inundated the air waves and people talked of DNA and began to fear the eventual domination of computers over their lives as they became mere statistics. It was quite a decade, but through it all seared the fire of America's conscience — Vietnam.

Vietnam

The Vietnam story remains to be written. Once again West Bend sent some of its finest to feed the fires of the war god — and some did not come back, the first being a promising young cornetist, Glen Dean, who had been sent to Vietnam as an Advisor. Those who watched the evening news in their living rooms drank in death as casually as one sips a cocktail. Gradually the talk in the taverns and over the bridge tables in West Bend changed from defense of the position of the United States to doubt to wide-spread opposition as the facts were made available. And, sadly, never again would West Bend be accepting of the words of its politicians.

SECTION XIX

THE 1970'S

And now we arrive at the present decade — the 1970's. It is given to none to accurately and adequately judge the time in which one lives; all that can be done is to report what actually exists, list the controversies and problems, and let the reader draw his or her own conclusion.

On the national and international scene, we survived Watergate, saw the election of three Popes in a decade, and witnessed the end of the Vietnam travesty, but not before at least one other young man, Gerald Schaeffer, had lost his life. News of the impending tax revolt vied with Mid-East peace and the Equal Rights Amendment for space on the evening news, but the biggest topic of all continued to be — INFLATION.

Locally, there have been changes, too. The city completed its sidewalk extension, to the satisfaction of some and the dismay of others. Richard Maslowski was hired by the city to help with city planning, reorganize the several city departments, and spell out job descriptions. The popular summer Farmers' Market continued to draw buyers desirous of purchasing fresh garden produce on Saturday mornings. On the negative side, the backers of the Metro Plan met with continued defeat, while the Chamber of Commerce continued to lobby for an extension of Highway G (partially successful) and the Highway 45 Bypass, which has plagued the city for decades and shows no sign of completion.

The city's retail business continued to grow with the addition of The Frontier Shopping Center on East Washington Street and Kohl's Department Store and Mall on South Highway 45, while an amazing proliferation of fast food restaurants included the latest on south 45, Arby's.

As the decade draws to a close, a few statistics might prove interesting. West Bend has become one of the highest car-owning areas in the nation, which may or may not be a blessing. It is a young city, with half of the residents under the age of 40 and only 10% over the age of 65. Three-fourths of the people have lived here over five years, making it a relatively stable community, and well over 40% of the adults have had at least some education beyond high school, a proportionately high figure. About half of the employed are either skilled laborers, in the

St. Joseph's Community Hospital

West Bend Gallery of Fine Arts

West Bend Community Memorial Library

professions or in managerial positions. There is work in the city for over half of the city's fathers and over three-fourths of the mothers, a school survey revealed, with an additional 10% and 17% respectively employed in the county. Others commute greater distances.

West Bend is proud of its radio station, airport, relatively low crime rate, its proximity to Milwaukee (51 kilometers) enabling one to attend cultural events and conduct business there easily, its excellent medical care, and a superior school system with facilities for all those from pre-school through a two-year post-graduate program. It takes pride in its churches, art gallery, hospital, public library, and facilities for the underprivileged and handicapped. While it is an industrial city, it has few of the handicaps of such a city, for most of the work is classified as light industry, while the home offices of numerous insurance and financial institutions provide work for women that enables West Bend to enjoy a relatively high family income, the way it prefers to report local income statistics. The AAA has commended the city for its safe pedestrian record, and if a citizen has a complaint the city officials remain open to listening.

The city has grown dramatically, too. In 1960 the census showed a population of 9900, while in 1970 the figure had grown

Kettle Moraine YMCA

to 16,500; the estimation for today is at least 23,000. Altogether it pays over five million dollars in income taxes, more than a million in corporate taxes, an additional three million in sales taxes and approximately a half million in excise taxes on beer, liquor, cigarettes, etc. The last available figure shows that in 1976 $86,000,000 was spent in retail establishments in the city, with grocery stores accounting for the largest category, followed closely by automotive businesses, and then general merchandise. The fastest dollar growth is in the serving of food and drink.

The 1978 assessed evaluation of the city was $293,177,316, or a full evaluation of $392,476,320, but it has grown since. Its 7250 acres include 350 acres of parkland and 500 as yet undeveloped acres. There are more than 7000 buildings in the city, of which over 4000 are single family dwellings, 46 are industrial, 256 commercial, 50 churches and schools, and the rest multiple dwellings or government property.

During the decade West Bend built the nearly two million dollar YMCA building that serves about 4000 members (or over a thousand more than anticipated). In addition the Threshold conducted two separate campaign efforts throughout the county, the first one in 1972-1973 and the second one in 1978. These drives netted $450,000 and $250,000 respectively. Hundreds of

Washington County Court House Built 1961-1962

Washington County Court House Addition and Jail Built in 1979 at a cost of $6,500,000.

University of Wisconsin–Washington County Center
Left—Auditorium and Student Union; Right—Classrooms and Offices

University of Wisconsin–Washington County Center Library

Samaritan Home
Washington County home for disabled and aged

The Threshold, Inc. — 22,000 square feet production area, sheltered workshop for approximately 150 handicapped workers. Also operates a Developmental Learning Center for handicapped children under age 3.

workers canvassed the area with the motto "Share Your Life — Help the Handicapped." Total cost of the two buildings was approximately $900,000.

West Bend continues to go over the top in such financial drives as the United Fund, for example. In a January 31, 1973, editorial, the *West Bend News* editorialized: "We'd like to see the IRS computer when it comes to charitable deductions of people in Washington County. These computers monitor tax returns and send up a red flag when any section of a person's statement is out of profile with national averages. Our guess is that these days they are regularly popping up when it comes to deductions of people in this area. The Threshold had a goal of $300,000 and took in $450,000." This had been the work of co-chairmen Bob Steiner and Norman A. Schowalter, together with 8000 individuals, clubs, businesses, industrial firms and organizations contributing.

One of the more unusual examples of the Spirit of West Bend is exemplified in the scholarships it awards to local high school seniors each year. In 1979 the awards totaled over $100,000. One of the larger donors is an organization originated by Mr. B. C. Ziegler as a scholarship foundation and later incorporated into West Bend Community Alumni Foundation, Inc. (Columns), with

Norman A. Schowalter as the first president. Columns is funded by private donations and memorials in memory of loved ones and friends, and provides a substantial amount to deserving high school graduates.

On the lighter side we read of hiker Bob Lauson, who is the city's chief proponent of physical fitness through hiking. His record hike is 64 miles in 18 hours. Lean and agile, he finds walking a challenge. Nonagenarian Walter Sinclair contributed salty poetry to the pages of the *West Bend News* into his 96th year, after a long career working for large city newspapers, Paramount Studios and directing publicity for the American Red Cross.

During the decade citizens became aware of the impact of our folly on the precious environment and pinpointed the chief sources of pollution in both the Milwaukee River and in the air we breathe. An environmental Teach-In sponsored by Senator Nelson, and the clearing of the Milwaukee River by adults, Boy Scouts and Cub Scouts highlighted the effort.

West Bend's biggest trial appeared in February of 1976 when an unprecedented ice storm deposited more than an inch and a half of ice on wires built to hold a maximum of a half inch. This resulted in the collapse of the electric wires, although the telephones generally continued to operate. As residents experienced their first mass disaster with heatless homes, and tried living without the amenities of electric lights, radio, and television, they understood the nearly totally dependent world in which we live. Families learned the joy — or in some cases the terror — of isolation, and were heartened over the many examples of sharing and compassion that the tragedy brought forth. Schools and factories were closed for up to five days, although many of the surrounding areas were without electricity for several more days.

Bridge playing continues, and baseball fans support their local Lithia team. The professional Brewers baseball team and the Bucks basketball team have hundreds of followers, but it is the Green Bay Packers that steal their hearts, win or lose. Nearby hunting grounds, swimming, snowmobile trails, golf courses, hiking trails, campgrounds, and fishing occupy the outdoor lover. People travel widely and often, a change from 1880, for instance, when a trip west meant to venture to LaCrosse.

But the city has had its problems, too. As always it is struggling with the concept of progress — is "bigger" and "more" necessarily "better"? Increasingly, the answer is that the quality of life is more important. The traffic problem in downtown West Bend is deteriorating, while travellers trying to go through the city on a Friday night find it an exercise in frustration, and local shoppers prefer the convenience of the outlying shopping centers or nearby Milwaukee.

Recently the city wrestled with the prospect of a huge shopping mall west of the city off Paradise Drive, and so far there has been no solution. The inadequate sewage problem is nearing solution, but street care and snow removal remain pockets of acute discontent.

Mixed feelings accompany the topic of increasing the number of manufacturing plants in the city; some employers fear that an industrial plant of significant size would upset the wage scale and hurt the established employers, while other businessmen see the growth of industrial parks and the entrance of new industry as a boon. This brings up the question of inadequate reasonably-priced housing, a factor in deterring new industries.

So now we face a new decade. An allotment of $1.5 million has just been approved for the University of Wisconsin-Washington County Campus to relieve the most serious overcrowding. The city's social conscience continues to improve with such organizations as Friends for Battered Women (more than 300 such cases occur annually in the county). The Open Door Hot Line continues its 24 hour telephone counseling, and the Moraine Park Technical Institute offers courses for women in legal rights, assertive training, and job finding skills. Comprehensive Community Services Agency (CCSA) provides telephone counseling as well as marriage and personal counseling, the Department of Social Services increases its counseling and aid, and the Washington County Council on Alcoholism aids victims of drink. Big Brothers and Sisters provide a useful service to youngsters who need an interested adult to help guide them. All these in addition to the other city and county agencies previously mentioned.

The Chamber of Commerce continues to list superb health services, a full time fire department, a full time rescue squad, a modern police department, all of the major denominational churches, fine recreational programs under both city and YMCA direction, an extensive park system, a city owned airport, good schools, a daily newspaper and AM/FM radio station, fine residential and commercial areas, and an ample labor source among the reasons for choosing West Bend, claiming it is Wisconsin's fastest growing city.

But the most exciting advance of all is that of TIF funding, courtesy of the Wisconsin State Legislature, to provide funds for relief from downtown congestion and a beginning to the beautification of the city. Inasmuch as a city is always judged by its downtown area, the deterioration has been a source of concern to many. A traffic loop around West Bend is planned, the addition of ornamental and more powerful lighting together with benches, trees, and other amenities of civilization is on the agenda, and it is to be hoped that the river may become a source of pride instead of being a historical eyesore. In addition, the more progressive businessmen plan to contribute to the renovation in various ways.

The City Council's recent decision, then, may provide the impetus that will enable our generation and those who succeed us to live with pride in a city with an unusual spirit—the Spirit of West Bend.

BIBLIOGRAPHY

NEWSPAPERS

Washington County Democrat, June 27, 1859-December 31, 1860.

Washington County Pilot, February 24, 1892-June 30, 1954.

West Bend Democrat, September 15, 1875-December 31, 1902.

West Bend News, January 7, 1903-December 30, 1970.

West Bend Post, January 14, 1861-June 8, 1867.

West Bend Times, June 3, 1880-October 27, 1887.

GOVERNMENT PUBLICATIONS

United States, Department of the Interior: Census Office, *Report on Population of the United States at the 11th Census—1890, Part I,* Washington, D.C., Government Printing Office, 1893.

United States, Department of the Interior: Census Office, *Statistics of the Population of the United States at the 10th Census,* 1 June, 1880, Washington, D.C., Government Printing Office, 1864.

United States, Department of the Interior, Joseph C. G. Kennedy, Superintendent of Census, *Population of the United States in 1860,* Washington, D.C., Government Printing Office, 1864.

United States, Department of the Interior, Census Division, *Abstract of the 11th Census, 1890,* Washington Government Printing Office, 1896.

West Bend, Wisconsin, *Clerk Ordinance Book, 1885-1906.*

West Bend, Wisconsin, *Council Proceedings Record Book, 1869-1871.*

West Bend, Wisconsin, *Council Proceedings Record Book, 1879-1888.*

West Bend, Wisconsin, School District No. 1, *The Public Schools of West Bend, Wisconsin, 1892-1893,* West Bend, *West Bend Democrat,* 1893.

West Bend, Wisconsin, School District No. 1, *Minutes,* 1880-1910; 1915-1925.

Washington County, Wisconsin, Washington County Fair Centennial, *1858-1958: A Hundred Fair Years,* West Bend, Washington County Publishing Company, 1958.

Washington County, Sheriff's Department, *Ten-Four,* West Bend, 1875.

BOOKS

Austin, H. Russell, *The Wisconsin Story.* Milwaukee: Wisconsin Journal Company, 1948.

Austin, H. Russell, *The Wisconsin Story.* Milwaukee: Wisconsin Journal Company, 1964.

Bicentennial Committee, *West Bend Historical Album.* West Bend, Wisconsin: Serigraph Sales and Manufacturing Company, 1976.

Brinker, Marie Mathilde, *Backwards From Ninety: An Autobiography.* West Bend, Wisconsin Serigraph Sales and Manufacturing Company, 1967.

Callahan, John, "The Department of Public Instruction," *The Wisconsin Blue Book.* Madison: Democrat Printing Company, 1927.

Chamberlain, T. C., *Geology of Wisconsin: Survey of 1873-1879.* Madison: Commissioners of Public Printing, 1882.

Current, Richard N., *Wisconsin: A Bicentennial History.* New York: Norton, 1977.

Drake, Francis, *Indian History for Young Folks.* New York: Harper and Broh, 1884.

Draper, Lyman, *Collections of the State Historical Society of Wisconsin.* Madison: State Historical Society of Wisconsin, 1906.

Doudna, Edgar, *The 30th Star—1848-1948.* Madison: State Centennial Commission, n.d.

Draper, Lyman, *Collections of the State Historical Society of Wisconsin.* Madison: State Historical Society of Wisconsin, 1903. Vol. 1-10.

Gregory, John B., ed., *Southeastern Wisconsin: A History of Old Milwaukee County.* Chicago: S. J. Clarke Publishing Company, 1932.

Durand, L. and Bradbury, L. M., *Home Regions of Wisconsin—A Geography of the State.* n.p.: Macmillan, 1946.

Gregory, John G., *Old Milwaukee County.* Chicago: S. J. Clarke Publishing Company, 1932. Vol. I, III, IV.

Hinsdale, B. A., *The Old Northwest.* New York: Macmillan, 1888.

History of School District No. 1, City of West Bend, 1846-1919. n.p., n.d.

History of Washington and Ozaukee County, Wisconsin. Chicago: Western Historical Company, 1881.

Hulton, A. J., *Wisconsin, Its State and Local Government with the Constitution as Amended.* New York: Maynard, Merrill and Co., 1896.

Kellogg, Louise, *British Regime in Wisconsin and the Northwest, The.* Madison: State Historical Society of Wisconsin, 1935.

Kouba, Theodore, *Wisconsin's Amazing Woods, Then and Now.* Madison: Wisconsin House, Ltd., 1973.

Kuhn, Rev. E. A., *History of Washington County Humane Society, 1913-1923.* Hartford; n.p., 1923.

Magdeburg, Capt. F. H., comp., *Wisconsin at Shiloh.* Madison: Wisconsin Shiloh Monument Commission, 1901.

Mark, Frederick, *Economic Conditions in Wisconsin During the Civil War Decade.* Madison: State Historical Society of Wisconsin, 1916.

Merk, Frederick, *Economic Conditions in Wisconsin During the Civil War Decade,* Wisconsin Historical Publication Studies, Vol. I. Madison: State Historical Society of Wisconsin, 1916.

McDonald, Forrest, *Let There be Light: Electrical Utility Industry of Wisconsin, 1881-1955.* Madison: American Historical Research Center, 1957.

McKnight, Charles, *Our Western Frontier 100 Years Ago.* Philadelphia: J. C. McCurdy and Company, 1879.

Moraine Park Technical Institute, *Washington County: Economic Development—a Statistical Profile.* West Bend, Wisconsin: Moraine Park, April, 1979.

Naber, Sister M. Vera, C.S.A., *With All Devotedness: Chronicles of the Sister of Saint Agnes.* New York: P. J. Kennedy and Sons, 1959.

Nesbit, Robert C., *Wisconsin A History.* Madison: University of Wisconsin Press, 1973.

Paxon, Frederic, *Last American Frontier.* n.p.; Macmillan, 1924.

Polem, Sister Imogene, *Fieldstones—the Story of Caspar Rehrl.* Fond du Lac, Wisconsin: Badger-Freund Printers, 1969.

Quaiffe, Milo, *Attainment of Statehood.* Milwaukee: n.p., 1928.

Quaiffe, Milo, *Struggle over Ratification, 1846-1847.* Madison: State Historical Society of Wisconsin, 1920.

Quaiffe, Milo, *Movement for Statehood, 1845-1846.* Madison: State Historical Society of Wisconsin, 1918.

Quaiffe, Milo, *Wisconsin—Its History and Its People—1634-1924.* Volume I, II, III, IV. Chicago: S. J. Clarke Publishing Company, 1924.

Quickert, Carl, *The Story of Washington County.* Menasha: The Collegiate Press, 1923.

Quickert, Carl, ed., *Washington County, Past and Present.* Chicago: S. J. Clarke Publishing Company, 1912. Vol. and Vol. II.

Quimby, George, *Indian Life in the Upper Great Lakes.* Chicago: University of Chicago Press, 1960.

Raney, William F., *Wisconsin: A Story of Progress.* New York: Prentice Hall, 1940.

Roemer, Theodore, O. F. M. Cap. PhD., "In the Spirit of Fortitude," *The Cowl,* Vol. 5, No. 9, n.p., 1941.

Schafer, Joseph, *A History of Agriculture in Wisconsin.* Madison: State Historical Society of Wisconsin, 1922.

Schafer, Joseph, *Four Wisconsin Counties.* Madison: State Historical Society of Wisconsin, 1927.

Strong, Moses, *History of the Territory of Wisconsin From 1836-1848.* Madison: Democrat State Printers, 1885.

Smith, Alice E., *History of Wisconsin.* Madison: State Historical Society of Wisconsin, 1973.

Sullivan, Mark, *American Finding Herself,* Vol. II. New York: Charles Scribner's Sons, 1927.

Tuttle, Charles, *Illustrated History of the State of Wisconsin.* Boston: B. B. Russell, 1875.

Zimmermann, H. Russell, *Heritage Guidebook—Landmarks and Historical Sites in Southeastern Wisconsin.* Milwaukee: Inland Heritage Corporation, 1976.

Williams, Dorothy E., *A History of Secondary Education in the City of West Bend, Wisconsin.* 1966.

In addition to the above, there were various dedicatory and anniversary bulletins from many local churches, the West Bend Community Memorial Library, St. Joseph's Hospital, the Ziegler Company, the West Bend Company, West Bend Lodge No. 138 F & A M, Washington County Court House and Jail, West Bend Homecomings, Badger Fireman's Association, Wisconsin State Historical Society Bulletins, and many from the State Planning Board.

About the Author

Mrs. Williams teaches history in East High School in West Bend, Wisconsin. She is a graduate of Whitewater State Teachers' College and earned a Master's degree in History from the University of Wisconsin-Milwaukee, and has 30 additional graduate credits. She has two children, Robert (Jeri) of Waukesha, and Merrie Lee (Michael) of Calgary, Alberta, and a grandson Brian.

She is listed in *Leaders of American Secondary Education,* and helped to found and served as President of, the Washington County chapter of Delta Kappa Gamma, an international honorary woman teachers' society. At one time she edited the state newspaper for that organization. She was active in the founding of the League of Women Voters in the county and wrote its newspaper. In June of 1979 she received the Robert H. Rolfs Foundation Award for Exceptional Teaching Ability.

Dorothy E. Williams